EZEKIEL AND
THE LEADERS OF ISRAEL

SUPPLEMENTS

TO

VETUS TESTAMENTUM

EDITED BY
THE BOARD OF THE QUARTERLY

J.A. EMERTON – PHYLLIS A. BIRD – W.L. HOLLADAY
A. van der KOOIJ – A. LEMAIRE – R.E. MURPHY – B. OTZEN
R. SMEND – J.A. SOGGIN – J.C. VANDERKAM – M. WEINFELD
H.G.M. WILLIAMSON

VOLUME LVI

EZEKIEL AND
THE LEADERS OF ISRAEL

BY

IAIN M. DUGUID

E.J. BRILL
LEIDEN · NEW YORK · KÖLN
1994

The paper in this book meets the guidelines for permanence and durability of the Committee on Production Guidelines for Book Longevity of the Council on Library Resources.

Library of Congress Cataloging-in-Publication Data
Duguid, Iain M.
      Ezekiel and the leaders of Israel / by Iain M. Duguid
            p. cm. — (Supplements to Vetus testamentum, ISSN 0083-5889 ;
      v. 56)
      Includes bibliographical reference and indexes.
      ISBN 9004100741 (alk. paper)
      1. Bible. O.T.   Ezekiel—Criticism, interpretation, etc.
I. Title. II. Series.
BS1545.2.D84   1994
224'.406—dc20
                                                    94–14022
                                                        CIP

Die Deutsche Bibliothek – CIP-Einheitsaufnahme
Duguid, Iain M.:
Ezekiel and the leaders of Israel / by Iain M. Duguid. – Leiden
; New York ; Köln : Brill, 1994
   (Supplements to Vetus testamentum ; Vol. 56)
   ISBN 90-04-10074-1
NE: Vetus testamentum / Supplements

                        ISSN   0083-5889
                        ISBN   90 04 10074 1

PRINTED IN THE NETHERLANDS

CONTENTS

ACKNOWLEDGEMENTS

This volume is a revision of a Ph.D. dissertation completed in 1992 at the University of Cambridge, under the supervision of Dr. H.G.M. Williamson. Through a combination of warm encouragement, penetrating criticism, wide knowledge of the subject and ready accessibility he has contributed much towards whatever is good in this volume. I would like to thank Dr. André Lemaire for accepting this work for publication and offering helpful suggestions to improve the study.

I also owe a significant debt of gratitude to my teachers and mentors at Westminster Theological Seminary, where I spent my formative theological years. The model of academic excellence combined with devotional warmth which I saw lived out by, among others, Dr. Ray Dillard, Dr. Tremper Longman III, Dr. Bruce Waltke and Dr. Richard Gaffin Jr. first inspired me to consider further academic study.

I am indebted to the staff of Tyndale House, Cambridge, especially the Warden, Dr. Bruce Winter, the Librarian, Dr. Andrew Clarke, and the Bursar, Rev. Iain Hodgins, for allowing me to make use of the wonderful facilities of the library there, both in the course of my post-graduate studies and in making the revisions for publication. My thanks also go to Mr. & Mrs. Alan Thornton, who allowed me to use their laser printer to produce the camera ready copy. I have also greatly appreciated the support and encouragement of the congregation which I serve, Redeemer Presbyterian Church.

My greatest debt, however, is to my immediate family; to my wife, Barbara, and our four children Jamie, Sam, Hannah and Robbie. They have ungrudgingly shared my time and energies with my studies, in spite of our other heavy commitments. Barb has been my greatest supporter and encourager, along with always keeping my feet on the ground and my work in proper perspective. This work is therefore dedicated to her:

rabbôt bānôt 'āśû hayil wᵉ'at 'ālît 'al-kullānâ (Prov. 31:29).
"Many a woman shows how gifted she is; but you excel them all"
(Revised English Bible)

IAIN DUGUID
Redeemer Presbyterian Church
Oxford
February 1994

ABBREVIATIONS

Abbreviations used in this work follow Siegfried Schwertner, *Internationales Abkürzungsverzeichnis für Theologie und Grenzgebiete* (Berlin 1974) except as noted below. Except where indicated otherwise, all quotations of the Bible are from the Revised Standard Version.

AB	The Anchor Bible
AV	*The Authorised Version of the Bible* (1611)
BKAT	Biblischer Kommentar, Altes Testament
B.Shabb.	Babylonian Talmud, tractate Shabbat
FOTL	The Forms of Old Testament Literature
FzB	Forschung zur Bibel
GKC	*Gesenius' Hebrew Grammar*, E. Kautzsch, ed., revised by A.E. Cowley (Oxford 1910)
JNSL	*Journal of Northwest Semitic Languages*
JPS	Jewish Publication Society
JSOT	*Journal for the Study of the Old Testament*
JSOTS	Journal for the Study of the Old Testament Supplement Series
JSS	*Journal of Semitic Studies*
JTS	*Journal of Theological Studies*
KTU	*Die keilalphabetischen Texte außerhalb Ugarits*, M. Dietrich, O. Loretz, J. Sanmartín, eds. (Neukirchen-Vluyn 1976)
LXX	Septuagint
MT	Massoretic Text
NIV	*The Holy Bible; New International Version* (London 1979)
NKJV	*The Holy Bible; New King James Version* (Nashville 1984)
n.s.	new series
o.s.	old series
REB	*The Revised English Bible* (Cambridge 1989)
RSV	*The Holy Bible; Revised Standard Version* (New York 1962)
RV	*The Holy Bible; Revised Version* (1885)
SBLDS	Society of Biblical Literature Dissertation Series
SBLMS	Society of Biblical Literature Monograph Series
SCS	Septuagint and Cognate Studies
SVT	Supplements to Vetus Testamentum
WBC	Word Biblical Commentaries

CHAPTER ONE

INTRODUCTION

A. General Introduction

The book of Ezekiel has always been hard to understand. According to rabbinic tradition, Rabbi Hananiah ben Hezekiah burned three hundred barrels of oil in his lamp before he was fully able to harmonize its laws with those of Moses.[1] His efforts have been dwarfed by those of modern scholarship, yet there remains much that is still obscure in the book ascribed to the son of Buzi. This study represents an attempt to clarify one area of the prophet's thought, namely his attitude towards the various different leadership groups within Judean society: the monarchy, the priests and Levites, the prophets, and the lay leadership (including $z^e q\bar{e}n\hat{i}m$, $\acute{s}\bar{a}r\hat{i}m$ and other ruling classes).[2]

The majority of studies over the years touching on these questions have dealt with Ezekiel's attitude to only *one* of these elements of society, most frequently the monarchy or the priests and Levites. In my opinion such studies, apart from whatever individual defects they may have, have all suffered from a lack of perspective because they have abstracted the prophet's approach to one particular leadership group from his approach to other groups which held positions of authority in the days leading up to the exile. As a result the scope and nature of any change in status experienced by the group in question — whether upwards or downwards — tends either to be exaggerated or totally denied. The proposition is here advanced, however, that there is a coherent and connected attitude taken toward these leadership groups throughout the book: those singled out for the most reproach in Ezekiel's critique of the past are marginalized in his plan for the future, while those who escape blame are assigned positions of honour. Both upward mobility and downward mobility are evident, as he envisages a radically restructured society, designed to avoid repetition of the sins of the past. In the language of the book of Ezekiel: "I will requite their deeds

---

[1] *B. Shab.* 13b. Unfortunately the fruits of his labours have not been preserved for our benefit!

[2] The decision to focus on these particular groups as the representatives of leadership in Israel finds some support in Ezekiel 22:25-29, which R. Hals describes as "from beginning to end an indictment of leaders for their failure" (*Ezekiel*, FOTL 19 [Grand Rapids 1989] 161). In this passage, those addressed are the $n^e\acute{s}\hat{i}'\hat{i}m$ (corrected text; see below, p.19 n.61), the priests, the $\acute{s}\bar{a}r\hat{i}m$, the prophets and the *'am hā'āreṣ*.

upon their heads" (Ezek. 9:10).[3] No one emerges entirely free of blame for
the events which led to the downfall of Judah and so there is a measure of
grace involved for all who are allowed to take part in the restored theocracy; yet there is also a correlation between those identified as chiefly
responsible for the sins which brought about the exile and their status—or
lack of it—in the restored Israel. Moreover, some groups are excluded
entirely from having a share in the Promised Land because of their past
history.

Such a fundamental and far reaching consideration of the structures of
society is one possible response among many to a time of overwhelming
social upheaval such as the exile. Many people—even perhaps most people
—gave up any hope for the future and concerned themselves entirely with
the present, which presented challenges enough of its own. It seems, however, that at least some sought answers to questions such as "Whose fault
is our present distressing situation?" and "How can we avoid it happening
again?".[4] They looked to the past and sought to identify the sins (and the
sinners) that had brought them into exile. They also looked to the future
and vowed "Never again". Similar thoughts are also at work in other
biblical documents of the exilic and post-exilic period, such as the Deuteronomistic History.[5] That each comes to different conclusions as to the causes
and future remedies of the exile shows that history and its analysis is a
complex and multi-faceted affair, especially when it comes to the apportionment of blame.[6]

The chapters of this study each deal with one leadership group identified
by Ezekiel. For each group, we shall examine the ways in which this group
is criticized by Ezekiel for its past activities and the place which it is
assigned in Ezekiel's plan for the future. The results are gathered together
in the conclusion and the implications examined for our understanding of
the book of Ezekiel, and especially of the nature of the central portion of
chapters 40-48. We shall also examine critically in excurses the widely-
held hypothesis of Gese, that there are present in Ezekiel 40-48 two clearly
identifiable literary strata, which he terms the "$n\bar{a}\acute{s}\hat{\imath}$' stratum" and the
"Zadokite stratum".

---

[3] Cf. also Ezekiel 7:3ff.; 11:21; 16:43; 17:19; 22:31; 23:49.
[4] H. McKeating, *Ezekiel*, Old Testament Guides (Sheffield 1993) 103.
[5] Note, for example, the stress on the sins of Manasseh as the cause *par excellence* of
the exile (2 Ki. 23:26f.).
[6] In this context G.H. Matties comments: "World mending is no easy task; the answers
do not always sound the same" (*Ezekiel 18 and the Rhetoric of Moral Discourse*, SBLDS 126
[Atlanta 1990] 220). In particular, it seems probable that the responses to exile on the part of
those actually in exile were very different from those who remained in the land. The writings
of Deutero-Isaiah, among others, suggest that many in exile had given up any hopes of a
return to the land of Israel.

B. The Authorship and Unity of the Book of Ezekiel

1 *An Historical Overview*

It is common in the study of the Book of Ezekiel to assert that there was no significant challenge to the unity of the Book of Ezekiel or its prophetic authorship before the publication by G. Hölscher of *Hesekiel. Der Dichter und das Buch* in 1924. This book is then seen as being responsible for opening the floodgates of criticism, from which no established result has yet emerged.[7] There is some justification for this view: it was certainly the opinion of most scholars of that time. Prior to Hölscher, a series of scholars had made strong statements about the book's unity, notably R. Smend,[8] C. Cornill,[9] A.B. Davidson,[10] S.R. Driver,[11] and G.B. Gray.[12] Further, while few scholars followed Hölscher's method, his work certainly acted as a catalyst for renewed study of the book of Ezekiel. Yet it would be a mistake to think that all scholars before Hölscher were agreed on the unity and prophetic authorship of the book, or that this was universally denied after the publication of his work. In fact, as will be shown below, the *range* of views currently advocated concerning the authorship and integrity of the book is little different from the range extant before Hölscher. What has happened over the years has rather been a fluctuation in the *popularity* of these different views. What Hölscher's work did was not so much to create a new critical perspective on the authorship of the book of Ezekiel as to make such a perspective more fashionable.

The range of opinions which have been advanced on the unity and authorship of the book can best be classified by plotting a graph with two axes, one measuring the unity of the book (largely a unity vs. largely redactional), the other measuring its date (largely exilic vs largely post exilic).

---

[7] For this kind of presentation, see e.g. H.H. Rowley, "The Book of Ezekiel in Modern Study", *BJRL* 36 (1953-54) 150ff. [= *Men of God* (London 1963) 173ff.].

[8] "In einem Zuge niedergeschrieben" (*Der Prophet Ezechiel*, KeH [Leipzig ²1880] xxii).

[9] "Eine...von ihm selbst und nach einem grossartigen und kunstvollen Plane angelegte Sammlung" (*Das Buch des Propheten Ezechiel* [Leipzig 1886] vi).

[10] "Issued in its completed form at once" (*The Book of the Prophet Ezekiel*, CBSC [Cambridge 1892] ix).

[11] "The whole from beginning to end [bears] unmistakably the stamp of a single mind" (*An Introduction to the Literature of the Old Testament* [Edinburgh and New York ⁹1913] 279).

[12] "No other book of the Old Testament is distinguished by such decisive marks of unity of authorship and integrity as this" (*A Critical Introduction to the Old Testament* [London 1913] 198).

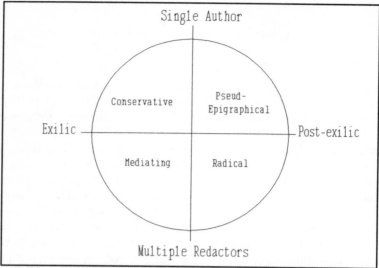

Figure 1: Theories of Authorship of the Book of Ezekiel.

This provides for four basic quadrants of opinion: *conservative* (essentially exilic and a unity), *pseudepigraphic* (essentially post-exilic but a unity), *radical* (essentially post exilic and redactional) and *mediating* (essentially exilic but largely redactional). Of course, within each quadrant there will be a variety of shades of opinion; for example, different mediating scholars will disagree as to exactly how much of the book is redactional, while different radical scholars will disagree as to when in the post-exilic period different portions of the book were written. Nonetheless, the benefit of this four quadrant mapping is that it makes clear that each position at its extremes tends towards two other positions: the radical position may tend towards the pseudepigraphic position if it almost entirely excludes the possibility of any genuine words of the prophet being preserved in the present book, or towards the mediating position if the work of the main redactors is dated early. Similarly, the mediating position may tend towards the conservative position or the radical position, depending on how much of the book is attributed to redactors. Interestingly, in practice at their extremes the conservative position and the pseudepigraphic position touch since both may treat the present text as a unity, albeit a unity attributed to different periods.[13]

---

[13] Compare this classification of different positions with those developed by B. Lang, *Ezechiel. Der Prophet und das Buch* (Darmstadt 1981) 2-17, J. Lust, "Introduction. Ezekiel and His Book" *Ezekiel and His Book*, ——, ed. (Leuven 1986) 1-3; J. Becker, "Ez 8-11 als einheitliche Komposition in einem pseudepigraphischen Ezechielbuch", *Ezekiel and His Book*,

The *conservative* position was most popular prior to the 1920's as the list of scholars noted above indicates. Even scholars such as Kraetzschmar and J. Herrmann, who in many ways prepared for the more radical approach of Hölscher by identifying editorial insertions within the book,[14] would today be regarded as conservatives in view of the extent to which they regard the book as the work of the prophet of the exile. This position has never entirely gone out of fashion, and more recent exponents of this view would include L. Boadt,[15] J. Ebach,[16] R. Hals,[17] C.G. Howie,[18] B. Lang,[19] H.H. Rowley,[20] and J.B. Taylor.[21] Perhaps the best known exponent of this position in recent years has been M. Greenberg.[22]

The *pseudepigraphic* approach found most support after 1930 under the influence of C.C. Torrey, who argued that the book belonged to the period around 230 BC[23] This approach was also followed, though the author was dated to different periods, by N. Messel,[24] L.E. Browne[25] and A. van den Born.[26] It was by no means a new solution, however, having been advanced at least as early as 1832 by L. Zunz.[27] Nor is it yet completely abandoned, having been recently forcefully argued by J. Becker.[28]

J. Lust, ed. (Leuven 1986) 136f. and H. McKeating, *Ezekiel*, 30-61.

[14] See R. Kraetzschmar, *Das Buch Ezechiel*, HK (Göttingen 1900) xiff. and J. Herrmann, *Ezechielstudien*, BWAT 2 (Leipzig 1908) 6.

[15] "Textual Problems in Ezekiel and Poetic Analysis of Paired Words", *JBL* 97 (1978) 490f.

[16] *Kritik und Utopie. Untersuchungen zum Verhältnis vom Volk und Herrscher im Verfassungsentwurf des Ezechiel (Kap. 40-48)*; Ph.D. diss., University of Hamburg 1972, 245-50.

[17] *Ezekiel*, 5f.

[18] *The Date and Composition of Ezekiel* (New Haven 1950) 100-2.

[19] *Kein Aufstand in Jerusalem: die Politik des Propheten Ezechiel* (Stuttgart 1978) 125-7.

[20] "Ezekiel in Modern Study", 190.

[21] *Ezekiel. An Introduction and Commentary*, TOTC (Leicester 1969) 20.

[22] See, for instance, "What are Valid Criteria for Determining Inauthentic Matter in Ezekiel?", *Ezekiel and His Book*, J. Lust, ed. (Leuven 1986) 123-35; *Ezekiel 1-20*, AB (Garden City, NY 1983) 18-27. Even though his "holistic approach" does not presuppose the absence of redactional influence—indeed in places he recognizes such influence—yet his conclusions justify the label "conservative". In his commentary he notes: "A consistent trend of thought expressed in a distinctive style has emerged giving the impression of a single mind…The persuasion grows on one…that a coherent world of vision is emerging, contemporary with the sixth-century prophet and decisively shaped by him, if not the very words of Ezekiel himself" (*Ezekiel 1-20*, 26f.).

[23] *Pseudo-Ezekiel and the Original Prophecy* (New Haven 1930 = New York 1970) 99.

[24] *Ezéchielfragen* (Oslo 1945) 23: ca. 400 BC.

[25] *Ezekiel and Alexander* (London 1952) 2ff.: ca. 300 BC.

[26] *Ezechiël—Pseudo-epigraaf?*, Studia Catholica 28 (1953): "the period of Ezra-Nehemiah".

[27] *Die gottesdienstlichen Vorträge der Juden* (Berlin 1832) 157-62. He sums up his discussion in the following terms: "Vielleicht dürften diese Wahrnehmungen zu der Ansicht berechtigen, dass Ezechiel und seine Vision der persischen Epoche näher stehen, als gemeiniglich geglaubt wird". Cf. also L. Seinecke, *Geschichte des Volkes Israel* (Göttingen 1876) I, 138 and H. Winckler, "Die Zeit der Ezechielprophetie", *Altorientalische Forschungen* 3,1 (1902) 135-55.

[28] "Erwägungen zur ezechielischen Frage", *Künder des Wortes*, L. Ruppert, P. Weimar and E. Zenger, eds. (Würzburg 1982) 137-49.

The *radical* position is usually regarded as the product of Hölscher's work. Yet radical ideas concerning the composition of the book were being advanced (anonymously) at least as early as 1798.[29] Moreover, Hölscher's methods of separating the genuine from the non-genuine have been completely abandoned,[30] with new approaches having been developed to distil out the original "base layer" from subsequent layers, especially in German-speaking scholarship. Some recent examples of this position would be H. Schulz,[31] J. Garscha,[32] H. Simian,[33] G. Bettenzoli,[34] and K. Pohlmann.[35] This position also includes the view of James Smith, that Ezekiel was actually a prophet of the Northern Kingdom during the reign of Manasseh, since he too posits an extensive post-exilic redaction.[36]

Perhaps the only genuinely new approach to appear in the wake of Hölscher's work is the *mediating* position. This position is distinguished from the conservative position in that it sees large portions of the book as due to the work of redactors—typically around one third to a half of the present book.[37] It is equally distinguished from the radical position in that it sees the vast majority of the book as due to exilic authors, sometimes described as the "disciples" or "school" of Ezekiel. Perhaps the first to adopt something like such a position was G. Fohrer,[38] but it has been further developed by W. Zimmerli to such an extent that he is properly regarded as its father.[39] Similar views are advanced by W. Eichrodt,[40]

---

[29] On the basis of stylistic differences between chapters 1-24 and the remainder of the book, an anonymous author ascribed all of Ezekiel 25-32 and parts of Ezekiel 34-39 to Daniel in *The Monthly Magazine* (189f.). For a full discussion of early radical criticism of the book of Ezekiel see S. Spiegel, "Ezekiel or Pseudo-Ezekiel", *HThR* 24 (1931) 246ff. [= *Pseudo-Ezekiel and the Original Prophecy by C.C. Torrey and Critical Articles*, M. Greenberg, ed. (New York 1970) 124ff.].

[30] Indeed they have rarely been taken up by anyone without significant modification!

[31] *Das Todesrecht im Alten Testament*, BZAW 114 (Berlin 1969) 163-87.

[32] *Studien zum Ezechielbuch* (Berne and Frankfurt 1974).

[33] *Die theologische Nachgeschichte der Prophetie Ezechiels. Form und traditionskritische Untersuchung zu Ez 6; 35; 36*, FzB 14 (Würzburg 1974).

[34] *Geist der Heiligkeit. Traditionsgeschichtliche Untersuchung des QDŠ-Begriffes im Buch Ezechiel*, Quaderni di Semitistica 8 (Florence 1979).

[35] *Ezechielstudien*, BZAW 202 (Berlin 1992) 247ff.

[36] *The Book of the Prophet Ezekiel: a New Interpretation* (London 1931). No one appears to have followed Smith.

[37] See Lang, *Ezechiel. Der Prophet und das Buch*, 18 for a table listing the number of verses regarded as original by a variety of commentators.

[38] *Die Hauptprobleme des Buches Ezechiel* (Berlin 1952) 40-2. Lang identifies Fohrer as a conservative (*Ezechiel. Der Prophet und das Buch*, 3f.), but since Fohrer holds almost one third of the book to be redactional (Lang, 17) this seems to be stretching the term unduly, especially since Fohrer consciously distances himself from positions which regard the book as a unity as well as from more radical positions (*Hauptprobleme*, 28, 104).

[39] Lang, *Ezechiel. Der Prophet und das Buch*, 12; for his own statement see Zimmerli, *Ezechiel*, BKAT (Neukirchen-Vluyn 1969) 104*-114* and "Das Phänomenon der 'Fortschreibung' im Buche Ezechiel", *Prophecy. Essays Presented to G. Fohrer*, J.A. Emerton, ed. BZAW 150 (Berlin 1980) 174-191.

[40] *Der Prophet Hesekiel*, ATD (Göttingen 1970) 14*ff.

J. Wevers,[41] F-L. Hossfeld,[42] R.E. Clements,[43] K. Carley,[44] P. Joyce[45] B. Vawter and L.J. Hoppe,[46] and H. McKeating.[47]

This survey of opinions has shown that there is not, and in fact never has been, a true scholarly consensus over the date and composition of the book of Ezekiel, in spite of the confident assertions to the contrary around the turn of the century. While there was a weight of opinion at that time in favour of its unity and exilic authorship, there were always dissenting voices. What has been seen over the past century is a gradual drift in the centre of gravity of scholarly opinion. This drift actually began well before the time of Hölscher, but received substantial impetus from his work, so that in the decade immediately afterward the weight of scholarly opinion probably resided in radical and pseudepigraphic positions. Since the work of Fohrer and Howie the pendulum has swung back somewhat. The mediating position is probably currently numerically the strongest through the widespread influence of W. Zimmerli.[48] Yet there still remains no consensus of opinion: each of the quadrants has found supporters in recent years and there is no obvious trend in any particular direction.[49]

This is not the place to go into an in-depth analysis of the strengths and weaknesses of the different positions. Such is not the purpose of this study and, given the current undecided state of Ezekiel studies, it seems best to refer the reader to the works already cited for a more detailed presentation of these strengths and weaknesses. However, some indication of the position adopted in this study is necessary.[50] We shall therefore present at the outset the general presuppositions which have informed this inquiry. At the end of our investigation, we shall consider to what degree the results obtained support the view we have taken. Such an approach will enable

---

[41] *Ezekiel*, NCeB (London 1969) 22ff.

[42] *Untersuchungen zu Komposition und Theologie des Ezechielbuches*, FzB 20 (Würzburg 1977) 13ff.

[43] "The Ezekiel Tradition", *Israel's Prophetic Tradition: Essays in Honour of P. Ackroyd*, R. Coggins, A. Phillips and M. Knibb, eds (Cambridge 1982) 128, 133.

[44] *The Book of the Prophet Ezekiel*, CBC (Cambridge 1974) 4.

[45] *Divine Initiative and Human Response in Ezekiel*, JSOTS 51 (Sheffield 1989) 31.

[46] *A New Heart. A Commentary on the Book of Ezekiel*, International Theological Commentary (Grand Rapids 1991) 3-10.

[47] *Ezekiel*, 60f.

[48] The next strongest position numerically would be the conservative position. Though radical studies continue to appear with regularity, they seem to have had little impact on the wider scholarly world, and the pseudepigraphic position seems at present to be defended only by Becker.

[49] So Lang, *Ezechiel. Der Prophet und das Buch*, 17.

[50] Note the comment of P.R. Ackroyd: "The complexity of the literary and other problems attaching to the book of Ezekiel is such that any discussion ought ideally to be prefaced by a full-scale consideration of the view that is adopted" (*Exile and Restoration* [London 1968] 103).

those holding different positions to assess how far they must modify their opinions in the light of the findings of this study.[51]

2 *The Approach Taken in This Study*

The starting point adopted in this study is to assume, until proven otherwise, that the book of Ezekiel in its present form is a coherent and consistent whole, written during the time of the exile. That is simply another way of saying that we intend to take the date and time references of the book seriously. Yet some radical critics start from quite the opposite presumption, that the text is non-genuine until proven genuine.[52] Our approach, however, does not suggest a return to the view of Smend, that the whole book was written in a single effort. It seems likely that some passages were reworked and modified, whether by the author himself or by later redactors. In at least one case, it can be demonstrated that an oracle from another prophet has been taken over, reworked and integrated into the language and style of Ezekiel.[53] But it should be noted that if the "original" oracle had not been preserved in another place, it would not be possible to re-create it from the present text of Ezekiel. What is more, even assuming such a reconstitution were possible, by literary critical or other means, replacing the present text with the "original form" of the oracle would, at least in this instance, distort the text rather than clarify it. The text in its present form is the most solid datum that we have available to us[54] and it therefore seems the most appropriate place to begin our investigations.

It seems to me that an attempt to exegete the present text as it stands is, at the very least, a necessary preliminary step to determining what tensions and breaks there may actually be in the text. The concept of a "tension" between two parts presupposes some prior understanding of the shape of the whole. Only on the basis of some such understanding can one address with any confidence the question of which tensions may be regarded as a legitimate part of the original text and which tensions are insurmountable. Such an approach may ultimately conclude that some material has been added

---

[51] It should perhaps be remembered that in the course of recent study only one person has expressed surprise at the results of his work on the book of Ezekiel—M. Burrows in *The Literary Relations of Ezekiel*, (Philadelphia 1925) 105—a surprise which may have been tempered somewhat by knowing that his results fitted perfectly the hypothesis of his thesis supervisor, C.C. Torrey!

[52] E.g. Garscha, *Studien*, 15.

[53] Ezekiel 22:25-28 which is based upon Zephaniah 3:3-4. On the relationship see Zimmerli, *Ezechiel*, 522. Ironically this proves Garscha's dictum (*Studien*, 15 n.49) that it is not sufficient to establish the oldest material and assume it to be authentic—though in a quite different sense to the way Garscha intended it.

[54] This of course presumes, rather than excludes, appropriate use of the versions to establish the text. On this, see M. Greenberg, "The Use of Ancient Versions for Interpreting the Hebrew Text: a sampling from Ezekiel ii 1-iii 11", *SVT* 29 (Leiden 1978) 131-148.

later; however, it does so on the basis of a full attempt to understand the existing text, rather than on the basis of external criteria.

The variety of such external criteria which have been adduced as means of determining what is "original" from what is later highlight the difficulties which beset alternative approaches.[55] A recent example may be found in G. Bettenzoli's attempt to separate out the genuine from the non-genuine by relating the prophecies to two separate law-codes, found in Leviticus 18-20 and 21-22. According to him, this provides:

> ein eindeutiges Kriterium zur Unterscheidung zweier Theologien und zugleich zur Bestimmung der echten Schriften Ezechiels. Denn Ezechiel konnte nur einer bestimmten soziologischen Gruppe angehören und ihre theologische Ansicht vertreten.[56]

This presupposes, however, that these "different theologies" are so obviously contradictory that no one could hold both to be true. But the redactor who, *ex hypothesi*, put Leviticus 18-20 next to 21-22 obviously saw no insuperable contradiction in the traditions, not to mention centuries of readers and commentators down to the present day. If the juxtaposition of these traditions held no contradiction for them (and, on Bettenzoli's hypothesis, for Ezekiel's disciples), then how may we be so sure that they could not equally have been similarly synthesized by someone such as Ezekiel?[57]

In many cases it may prove to be practically impossible to separate out confidently the work of the prophet from the work of his redactors.[58] We are left then with an examination of the present text, and an attempt to understand it as it stands, tensions and all. Such an attempt is what this present study provides. It is hoped that in the process at least some of the tensions of the text in the areas studied will be brought to a new resolution.

---

[55] Not to mention the wide variety of results!

[56] *Geist der Heiligkeit*, 106.

[57] Here the application of Ockham's razor seems in order, though this argument only extends to the authorship of the relevant sections of the book of Ezekiel. The actual composition of Leviticus 18-22 and the possibility in general of multiple authors contributing to a single text is a quite separate question. For a more detailed critique of Bettenzoli, see G. Matties, *Ezekiel 18*, 201ff.

[58] Vawter and Hoppe, *Ezekiel*, 10. In spite of their belief that the book has undergone 'extensive' redaction, they note that "it is often impossible to separate what is 'authentic' from what is 'accretional'". In a similar vein, M. Fishbane writes: "The hope of resolving the historical-theological questions of Ezekiel's prophecies becomes…complicated and well nigh utopian. It is enough for us here to confront the issues squarely and acknowledge that most solutions must remain tentative or arbitrary" ("Sin and Judgement in the Prophecies of Ezekiel", *Interp.* 38 [1984] 146).

CHAPTER TWO

KINGS AND PRINCES

A. Introduction

Ezekiel's view of the monarchy has been extensively investigated. It has long been recognized that Ezekiel used distinctive terminology for the royal figure, preferring the title *nāśî'* (usually translated "prince", "chief") to the usual *melek*.[1] The reason for that choice for the future ruler has been debated ever since: is he king in all but name, a powerful monarch, a descendant of David[2] — or a shadowy figure without real power, simply the patron of the new Temple?[3] Often the choice between these two alternatives has rested upon whether more stress is laid on chapters 34 and 37, where the two terms appear synonymous, or on chapters 40-48 where the *nāśî'* appears confined to a secondary role in the Temple. The tension between these chapters has led some commentators to view the economy described in Ezekiel 40-48 as an interim arrangement, awaiting the fulfilment described in chapters 33-39,[4] while others have attributed the chapters to different authors,[5] or even to a change of mind in the prophet![6] Even the consistency of usage within chapters 40-48 has been questioned by H. Gese, who distinguishes between a *nāśî'* stratum, which speaks of the *nāśî'* positively, as an individual, and the rest of these chapters which speak negatively of plural *nᵉśî'îm* and seek to restrict their power.[7]

A further question arises as to what, if any, is the relationship between the usage of the term *nāśî'* in Ezekiel and its usage elsewhere in the Old

---

[1] See R. Smend (*Ezechiel*, 311) in 1880, followed by E.G. King ("The Prince in Ezekiel", *Old Testament Student* 5 [1885] 111-6) and J. Boehmer ("*MLK* und *NŚY* bei Ezechiel", *Theologische Studien und Kritiken* 73 [1900] 112-7). Many older commentators had thought that the *nāśî'* of chapters 40-48 was actually the High Priest (so e.g. R. Greenhill, *An Exposition of the Prophet Ezekiel, with Useful Observations Thereupon* [London, 1650]).

[2] E.g. E. Hammershaimb, "Ezekiel's View of the Monarchy", *Studia Orientalia, Ioanni Pedersen Septuagenario* (Copenhagen 1953) 138 [= *Some Aspects of Old Testament Prophecy* (Copenhagen 1966) 60].

[3] E.g. O. Procksch, "Fürst und Priester bei Hesekiel", *ZAW* (o.s.) 58 (1940/1) 119; C. Biggs, "The Role of *nāśî'* in the Programme for Restoration in Ez 40-48", *Colloquium* 16,1 (1983) 52f.

[4] So Boehmer, "*MLK* und *NŚY*", 115; Procksch, "Fürst und Priester", 119.

[5] J.B. Harford, *Studies in the Book of Ezekiel* (Cambridge 1935) 63f.; G.R. Berry, "The Authorship of Ezekiel 40-48", *JBL* 34 (1915) 17.

[6] K. Begrich, "Das Messiasbild des Ezechiel", *ZWTh* 47 (1904) 459.

[7] *Der Verfassungsentwurf des Ezechiel (Kap. 40-48) traditionsgeschichtlich untersucht*, BHTh 25 (Tübingen 1957) 110.

Testament?[8] Is Ezekiel's use idiosyncratic—unrelated to that of the rest of the Old Testament, so that *nāśî'* and *melek* are simple synonyms?[9] If not, is it primarily related to the Priestly Stratum's depiction of Wilderness life (the predominant usage numerically)[10] or to the single reference to Sheshbazzar as *nāśî'* of Judah in Ezra 1:8 at the time of the restoration?[11]

Apart from questions of terminology, studies have explored other areas of Ezekiel's involvement with the monarchy. There have been attempts to explain Ezekiel's purpose in the first part of the book in terms of the prevailing political climate of his day[12] and articles dedicated to explaining the task of the *nāśî'* in chapters 40-48.[13] Yet it appears that there has not so far been a comprehensive attempt to draw all of these elements together to give a consistent picture of Ezekiel's attitude towards the monarchy—past and present—such as we shall attempt to do here.

B. *melek* AND *nāśî'* IN THE BOOK OF EZEKIEL

We begin with the question of terminology. It is of crucial importance that we understand first of all the range of usage of the word *nāśî'* outside the book of Ezekiel, and then consider how Ezekiel's usage relates to that, before we make assertions as to the significance of the word. All too often the transition is too quickly made from the observation that Ezekiel eschews the use of the word *melek* in chapters 40-48 to the conclusion that therefore he has in mind something less than a king. Such a conclusion might ultimately be justifiable—but not without a full examination of wider usages.

1 *The Etymology and Derivation of the Word nāśî'*

The etymology of *nāśî'* has been variously explained. Martin Noth thought that it was originally based on a phrase such as *nāśa' qôl* "to raise one's voice, speak up" or *nᵉśû' pānîm* "an honoured person" (i.e. one with lifted countenance).[14] J. van der Ploeg derived it from the passive form of the

---

[8] On this see the studies by E.A. Speiser, "Background and Function of the Biblical *nāśî'*", *CBQ* 25 (1963) 111-7; M. Noth, *Das System der Zwölf Stämme Israels*, BWANT 4,1 (Stuttgart 1930) 151-62; and J. van der Ploeg, "Chefs du Peuple d'Israel et Leurs Titres", *RB* 57 (1950) 40-61.

[9] So Y. Kaufmann, *History of the Religion of Israel*, vol. 7 [Hebrew] (Jerusalem 1955) 566 n.88. Similarly W. Gronkowski, *Le Messianisme d'Ezechiel* (Paris 1930) 78 n. 69.

[10] So e.g. K. Seybold, *Das davidische Königtum im Zeugnis der Propheten*, FRLANT 107 (Göttingen 1972) 139.

[11] So Gese, *Verfassungsentwurf*, 118f.; Hölscher, *Hesekiel*, 211f.; Zimmerli, *Ezechiel*, 1248.

[12] Lang, *Kein Aufstand*.

[13] E.g. Biggs, "*nāśî'*".

[14] Noth, *System*, 151-62.

stem *nāśa'* "to raise", i.e. a leader who had raised himself.[15] In contrast, Speiser explains *nāśî'* as a *qātîl* stem form, which describes a *nomen professionis*.[16] According to Speiser, the full form is *nāśî' bā'ēdâ* (cf. Exodus 34:31) and thus stands for duly elected chieftain.[17] This interpretation as a passive *nomen professionis* has now been supported by the discovery of a semantic equivalent in Ugaritic. Moshe Held has noted that the Ugaritic verb *zbl* "to carry, bring" has a substantive *zbl*, probably to be vocalized *zabūl(u)*, which occurs in synonymous parallelism with *tpt* "ruler" (eight times) and in the idiom *kht zbl* "throne of princeship/royalty" (five times).[18] The democratic overtones which Speiser inferred from his derivation of the word are brought into question by the examples cited by Held, however. In the Baal epic *zbl* is used as a title of Yamm:

> *ylm qdqd zbl ym // bn 'nm tpt nhr*
>
> It [the club] strikes the head of Prince Yamm, on the forehead [it strikes] Ruler Nahar.[19]

In the legend of King Keret, the idiom *kht zbl* has reference to the king's sons:

> *tb bny lmtbtkm // lkht zblkm*
>
> Sit my sons upon your seats [of kingship], upon your thrones of princeship.[20]

It is also used in epithets such as *zbl b'l ars* "the Prince, Lord of the Earth".[21] None of these usages has anything less than a royal significance, so there is nothing inherently democratic or limited in power in the word *zbl*. The fact that its semantic equivalent in Ugaritic frequently bears this royal sense should therefore caution us against inferring "democratic" overtones simply from the derivation of the Hebrew word *nāśî'*. If the connotation of limited authority is to be shown to be valid, then it must be demonstrated from the word's usage, not from its derivation.

2 *The Usage Of nāśî' Outside Ezekiel*

The term *nāśî'* occurs 126 times in the Old Testament. Of these, 36 occurrences are in Ezekiel, 72 in the Hexateuch (Genesis four times, Exodus

---

[15] "Chefs", 50.
[16] "*nāśî'*", 114. Cf. H. Niehr, "*nāśî'*", *Theologische Wörterbuch des Alten Testament*, G.J. Botterweck, H. Ringgren and H.-J. Fabry, eds. (Stuttgart 1986) V, 648.
[17] "*nāśî'*", 114.
[18] M. Held, "The Root *ZBL/SBL* in Akkadian, Ugaritic and Biblical Hebrew", *JAOS* 88 (1968) 91f.
[19] 1.2.IV.24,25. Texts are cited in accord with the KTU system. Translation by Held.
[20] 1.16.V.24,25.
[21] Attested eight times. See Held, "The Root *ZBL/SBL*", 91.

four times, Leviticus once, Numbers 60 times and Joshua 12 times), two in the Books of Kings, six in the Books of Chronicles and one in the Book of Ezra. It will be noted at once that, apart from those in the Book of Ezekiel, the vast majority of these occurrences crop up in descriptions of the period prior to the monarchy. This overwhelming first impression is further strengthened when the usage in the Books of Chronicles is examined: of the six occurrences, one is the parallel to one of the occurrences in the Books of Kings (2 Chr. 5:2), one refers to the wilderness period (1 Chr. 2:10)[22] and one is rather timeless in reference (1 Chr. 7:40).[23] Apart then from the usage in the book of Ezekiel, we are left with only six occurrences during or subsequent to the period of the monarchy. These are as follows:

1 Kings 8:1   The *n'śî'ê hā'ābôt libnê yiśrā'ēl* are summoned along with the elders of Israel and all the heads of the tribes for the bringing up of the ark to the Temple under Solomon.[24] = 2 Chronicles 5:2.

1 Kings 11:34   Solomon is not to be deprived of the kingdom during his lifetime. He will be a *nāśî'* all the days of his life.

1 Chronicles 4:38   A list of the *n'śî'îm* of Simeon during the days of Hezekiah (cf. v. 41).

1 Chronicles 5:6   Beerah, *nāśî'* of Reuben, was taken into exile by the Assyrians.

2 Chronicles 1:2   "Every *nāśî'* of all Israel" (*l'kōl nāśî' l'kol-yiśrā'ēl*) included in the list of dignitaries addressed by Solomon after his accession.

---

[22] According to Numbers 2:3 and Exodus 6:23 (both P) Nahshon was a contemporary of Moses (on this see R.L. Braun, *1 Chronicles*, WBC [Waco 1986] 34).

[23] It is notable that four out of the five non-synoptic occurrences in the Books of Chronicles are in the genealogies (1 Chr. 1-9). This perhaps increases the likelihood of them representing genuine recollections of the past, since has been suggested that the Chronicler had access to authentic source material in this section. See H.G.M. Williamson, *1 and 2 Chronicles*, NCeB (London 1982) 20; S. De Vries, *1 and 2 Chronicles*, FOTL 11 (Grand Rapids 1989) 23ff.

[24] The presence of the *n'śî'îm* is dubbed "artificial and unhistorical" here by De Vries on the basis of its absence from some manuscripts of the LXX (*1 Kings*, WBC [Waco 1985] 124). However, J. Gray notes that the LXX makes a habit of omitting tautological phrases in Kings (*I and II Kings*, Old Testament Library [London ²1970] 204); in view of the full agreement of 2 Chronicles 5:2 it seems likely that this phrase should be retained and understood as being in explanatory apposition to *kol-ro'šê hammaṭṭôt* (I.W. Slotki, *Kings*, Soncino Books of the Bible [London 1950] 57); cf. Joshua 22:30.

Ezra 1:8   Sheshbazzar, the *nāśî'* of Judah receives the Temple vessels from Cyrus to convey them to Jerusalem.

Since there are three occurrences referring to events during the days of Solomon, two around the time of Hezekiah and only one after the exile, the evidence hardly supports Speiser's contention of two separate periods of usage: an early stage starting with the Patriarchs and ending with Joshua and a late stage beginning with Ezekiel.[25] In fact, apart from these few scattered references and Ezekiel's own idiosyncratic usage, *nāśî'* in the Old Testament always refers to a pre-monarchical figure. It is therefore in the accounts of this period that we must seek the definitive meaning of the term *nāśî'*.

In the description of the pre-monarchic days of Israel's history given in the Hexateuch the *nᵉśî'îm* appear to have been tribal leaders, the heads of a patriarchal group (*bêt-'āb*).[26] They were present both at sub-tribal level (cf. Num. 3:30,35) and at the level of entire tribes (cf. Num. 3:32; Jos. 22:14). They correspond to the sheikhs of tribes and sub-tribes, and represented the chief political authority of their day.[27] They had the right to declare war (Jos. 22:14), make treaties (Jos. 9:15) or decide property issues (Num. 36:1). This form of leadership was at least roughly analogous to that of some of the other tribal groups with which Israel came into contact, so that their leaders could also be called *nᵉśî'îm* (Jos. 13:21).[28] Major decisions were probably made by an executive council of the *nᵉśî'îm*, acting as representatives of their tribes.[29] At least on the tribal and clan level there seems to have been a hierarchy of *nᵉśî'îm* (Num. 3:32; 16:2).[30] The Priestly source records that they provided offerings for the tabernacle and for the dedication of the altar (Numbers 7); this does not necessarily make theirs a sacral office, however, nor were they really "patrons of the liturgy".[31] Rather, as figureheads of the community they acted on behalf of their people: the gifts that they brought were really the gifts of those they represented.[32] They do not appear to have any special privileges or particular role

---

[25]   "*nāśî'*", 111.

[26]   Speiser, "*nāśî'*", 113.

[27]   J.L. McKenzie, "The Elders in the Old Testament", *Biblica* 40 (1959) 534; R. de Vaux, "La thèse de l'amphictyonie israelite", *HThR* 64 (1971) 432.

[28]   Cf. also Genesis 34:2.

[29]   B. Halpern, *The Constitution of the Monarchy in Israel*, HSM 25 (Chico 1981) 207.

[30]   Halpern, *Constitution*, 209. Cf. 1 Chronicles 7:40 for another reference to "chief *nᵉśî'îm*" (*ro'śê hannᵉśî'îm*).

[31]   As J.D. Levenson maintains (*Theology of the Program of Restoration of Ezekiel 40-48*, HSM 10 [Missoula 1976] 63).

[32]   Compare the account of Exodus 35:20-29, where their gifts are simply part of a wave of generosity running through the people.

to play in worship.[33] Indeed, in the one incident where it appears they sought a more significant role in the cult (Num. 16:2) this was severely denied. In Leviticus 4, where the various guilt offerings are laid out, it appears that their sin is more important than that of one of the *'am hā'āres*, for the required sacrifice is a male goat rather than a female goat. However, in both cases atonement is only made for the individual involved (Lev. 4:31,35). In contrast, the sin of the anointed priest (*hakkōhēn hammāšîah*) is equivalent to the sin of the whole community (Lev. 4:3): both must be atoned for by the sacrifice of a young bull (Lev. 4:3,14).

When the *nᵉśî'îm* of Israel appear as a group in the Hexateuch, it is noteworthy that they are usually alongside a single leader (Moses or Joshua) and the priest of the day.[34] It would seem that it was these latter individuals who performed the sacral functions of leadership in the cult, a situation which may not have gone unquestioned (cf. Num. 16-18) but which seems to have been upheld. Certainly there is no recorded case in the Hexateuch of a *nāśî'* either offering sacrifice or taking part in the liturgy or being privileged with closer access to God.[35] Far from them being apolitical sacral figures, in the Hexateuch at least it appears that their primary responsibilities are what we would think of as political and military.[36] However, such acts as judging, leading in war, making covenants and alotting the Promised Land[37] (in all of which we find the *nᵉśî'îm* active) would certainly have had a religious side to them in the ancient Near East.[38] As we shall argue further below, it seems unlikely that this depiction is a pure creation of the Priestly school.[39]

In the time of the monarchy, the office of *nāśî'* undergoes an eclipse, as noted above.[40] Although still apparently in existence, the power of the *nᵉśî'îm* was naturally much reduced. Authority was gradually transferred from the representatives of the tribes to the representatives of the king,

---

[33] de Vaux, "Thèse", 432: "Les *nᵉśî'îm* font des offrandes au sanctuaire, ils ne l'administrent pas".

[34] Moses, Aaron and the *nᵉśî'îm* (Ex. 34:31; Num. 1:44; 4:34, 46), Moses, Eleazar and the *nᵉśî'îm* (Num. 27:2; 31:13; 32:2; Jos. 9:15,18), Joshua, Eleazar and the *nᵉśî'îm* (Num. 34:17ff.; Jos. 17:4). Cf. Joshua 22:13f., 32 where Phinehas and the *nᵉśî'îm* are sent to investigate the actions of the Transjordan tribes.

[35] Interestingly, where such access is given those invited are the seventy elders of Israel (*ziqnê yiśrā'ēl*), not the *nᵉśî'îm* (Ex. 24:1,9f.). Of course, some of these may also have been *nᵉśî'îm* but it is not as such that they receive cultic privilege.

[36] Speiser comments: "The *nāśî'* represents [in Ex. 22:27] the chief political authority, comparable to later *melek*" ("*nāśî'*", 115). According to Halpern, "among [their tasks] the military duties would be primary" (*Constitution*, 214).

[37] Cf. e.g. Joshua 17:4; Numbers 1:44; Joshua 9:15,18; Numbers 34:17ff.

[38] In Genesis 23:6 *nāśî'* appears as an honorary title: the Hittites respond to Abraham's description of himself as an alien and a stranger by declaring him a *nᵉśî' ᵉlōhîm* among them. For a different interpretation of this title however, see M.H. Gottstein, "*nᵉśî' ᵉlōhîm*", *VT* 3 (1953) 298-9.

[39] See below, p.17.

[40] See above, p.13. Speiser, "*nāśî'*", 115.

especially in the political and military realms. It seems that their presence
was valued on ceremonial occasions, where they still functioned as representatives of their people (1 Ki. 8:1 = 2 Chr. 5:2; 2 Chr. 1:2), but their
importance must have been much diminished. Though even down to Hezekiah's day, they were still apparently able to lead a tribe in independent
military action (1 Chr. 4:38), this seems to have been the exception rather
than the rule. There are some hints from this period, however, that the
office of *nāśî'* came to be seen as a kind of tribal forerunner to kingship,
so that the old *n^eśî'îm* were thought of as one-tribe kings. Thus, the old
law against cursing the *nāśî'* (Ex. 22:27) is applied to the king and becomes
the basis for the charge against Naboth (1 Ki. 21:13).[41] When considering
rulers of tribal groupings outside Israel, the distinction between a *melek* and
a *nāśî'* was not always clear.[42] In the Chronicler's genealogy of David, it
is surely of significance that his ancestor Nahshon is described as the *nāśî'*
of the people of Judah (1 Chr. 2:10): the status of this ancestor provides
another legitimation of the rule of the Davidides.[43] When because of the sin
of Solomon the continuance of that rule comes into question, it is affirmed
that Solomon will remain a *nāśî'* all the days of his life, and (apparently
with reference to 2 Samuel 7) that one tribe will be left to his sons (1 Ki.
11:34f.). The retention of a Davidic *nāśî'* over Judah is seen as a fulfilment
of the dynastic oracle.[44] After the time of Hezekiah, mention of the office
disappears completely from the historical books until the end of the exile.

Did the old forms of leadership begin to re-emerge after the exile in the
absence of a king? In Ezra 1:8 the leader of the first return to Jerusalem,
Sheshbazzar, is designated *nāśî'* of Judah. In the light of this reference
Hölscher advanced the view that the *nāśî'* was the highest civil personality
of post-exilic Judah.[45] He identified this position with that held by one
Ostanes in the Elephantine Papyri.[46] However, since the latter figure is
given no title, this identification is extremely speculative. Nils Messel
identified the *nāśî'* with the *pehâ*, the governor under the Persians, since
both titles are given to Sheshbazzar (compare Ezra 1:8 and 5:14).[47] However, it is possible that Sheshbazzar was given the designation *nāśî'* of

---

[41] Procksch, "Fürst und Priester", 115.
[42] Cf. Joshua 13:21 and Numbers 31:8, where the leaders of Midian are referred to
respectively as *n^eśî'ê midyān* and *malkê midyān* (cf. Niehr, "*nāśî'*", 650).
[43] There is, however, nothing outside Ezekiel to suggest that the office of *nāśî'* was hereditary (Halpern, *Constitution*, 211).
[44] Levenson, *Theology*, 63.
[45] Hölscher, *Hesekiel*, 211.
[46] Hölscher, *Hesekiel*, 212. Cf. A.E. Cowley, *The Aramaic Papyri discovered at Assuan*
(London 1906) #30. In this, Hölscher has been followed by Gese, *Verfassungsentwurf*, 118.
[47] Messel, *Ezéchielfragen*, 144. Similarly S. Japhet, "Sheshbazzar and Zerubabbel against
the Background of the Historical and Religious Tendencies of Ezra-Nehemiah", *ZAW* 94
(1982) 98.

Judah in the book of Ezra for purely theological reasons. It may be that the writer deliberately used archaic terminology, harking back to the days of the first exodus for terminology to describe the new exodus.[48] Alternatively, in the light of its use in 1 Kings 11, it may be a reference to God's continuing faithfulness to the Davidic covenant. In 2 Samuel 7:11b the building of the Temple is linked with the establishment of the Davidic dynasty. Sheshbazzar, though nowhere given a Davidic genealogy,[49] may perhaps thus be identified as the legitimate successor of Solomon, and hence fitted to begin rebuilding the Temple (Ezra 5:16). He plays a vital role in the returning of the Temple vessels, an important symbol of continuity between the new Temple and that of Solomon.[50] A further possibility is that the usage in Ezra is influenced by Ezekiel 40-48, so that Sheshbazzar is identified as the guarantor of the hopes of Ezekiel.[51] However, in view of the absence of other clear influence by Ezekiel 40-48 on Ezra-Nehemiah, this last alternative seems less likely.

If any such *theological* motivation lies behind the designation of Sheshbazzar as *nāśî'* of Judah in Ezra 1:8, then we are left entirely without evidence for any prominent post-exilic figure bearing the title of *nāśî'*. Indeed the powerful men who appear during this period go rather by the title *pehâ* (Zerubbabel, Hag. 2:21; Nehemiah and his predecessors, Neh. 5:14f.) or *tiršātā'* (Nehemiah, Neh. 10:2). In the lists of Ezra and Nehemiah there is no hint of one or more *nᵉśî'îm*. Only much later, in intertestamental and post-biblical times, does the title enjoy a resurgence.[52] This lack of evidence of a prominent *nāśî'* figure in the early post-exilic period, especially one with the military functions ascribed to the *nᵉśî'îm* by P,

---

[48] H.G.M. Williamson, *Ezra-Nehemiah*, WBC (Waco 1985) 18.

[49] The identification of Shenazzar in 1 Chronicles 3:18 with Sheshbazzar remains a disputed subject. In favour of such an identification are H. Gese (Verfassungsentwurf, 118), Y. Aharoni (*The Land of the Bible* [London 1974] 359), F. M. Cross ("A Reconstruction of the Judean Restoration", *JBL* 94 [1975] 12 n.43), D.J.A. Clines (*Ezra, Nehemiah, Esther* [Grand Rapids & London 1984] 41) and E. Stern (*The Cambridge History of the Bible I: Introduction. The Persian Period*, W.D. Davies and L. Finkelstein, eds. [Cambridge 1984] 70). Those opposed to such an identification include P.R. Berger ("Zu den Namen *ššbsr* und *šn'sr*", *ZAW* 83 [1971], 98-100), S. Japhet, ("Sheshbazzar and Zerubbabel", 95), P.E. Dion ("*ššbsr* and *ssnwry*", *ZAW* 95 [1983] 111-12) and E. Lipiński ("Cambridge History of Judaism" [Review Article], *BO* 42 [1985] 163).

[50] Biggs, "*nāśî'*", 54. On the Temple vessels providing continuity, see P.R. Ackroyd, "The Temple Vessels—a Continuity Theme", *SVT* 23 (1972) 166-81.

[51] L. Rost, *Die Vorstufen von Kirche und Synagoge im Alten Testament*, BWANT 24 (Stuttgart 1938) 75. G.A. Cooke also sees Ezra 1:8 as influenced by Ezekiel (*Ezekiel*, ICC [Edinburgh 1936] 497).

[52] Speiser, "*nāśî'*", 115; S. Zeitlin, "The Titles High Priest and the *nāśî'* of the Sanhedrin", *JQR* n.s. 48 (1957-8) 1-5. Also note the evidence of the Piraeus inscription which comes from the Sidonian diaspora around the end of the Fourth Century BC. It identifies one ŠM'B'L as the *nāśî'* of a sanctuary with a council of *nᵉśî'îm*; cf. KAI 60:2, 4 and M.F. Baslez & F. Briquel-Chatonnet, "Un example d'intégration phénicienne au monde grec: les Sidoniens au Pirée à la fin du IVe siècle", *Atti del II Congresso Internazionale di studi Fenici e Punici*, (Rome 1991) I, 229-240.

makes it unlikely that the concept of the *nāśî'* is a retrojection of the post-exilic situation into the wilderness period by P. Rather, it seems to be a genuine recollection of the past.[53]

We may sum up our discussion of the *nāśî'* outside the book of Ezekiel as follows: the *nāśî'* was a prominent figure of the pre-monarchic period, who acted as the elected (or designated) representative of his tribe or family group in military, political or religious contexts. After the inception of the monarchy, the power of the *nᵉśî'îm* naturally faded though they continued in existence, with at least ceremonial functions. In the immediately post-exilic period, the only solid evidence of a figure with such a title is Ezra 1:8, and the significance of the title there is susceptible of several explanations. Even from earliest times the distinction between the highest level of *nāśî'* (a tribal chief) and a *melek* was not hard and fast.

3 *The Usage of melek and nāśî' in Ezekiel 1-39*

The occurrences of the words *melek* and *nāśî'* in these chapters are shown below:

melek:	Referent	LXX
1:2	King Jehoiachin.	*basileus*
7:27	An unspecified ruler of Judah.	*basileus*[54]
17:12	The king of Babylon.	*basileus*
17:12	The king of Jerusalem (= Jehoiachin).	*basileus*
17:16	The king who caused him [Zedekiah] to reign (= the king of Babylon).	*basileus*
19:9	The king of Babylon.	*basileus*
21:24[19]	The king of Babylon.	*basileus*
21:26[21]	The king of Babylon.	*basileus*
24:2	The king of Babylon.	*basileus*
26:7	Nebuchadnezzar, king of Babylon.	*basileus*
27:33	The kings of the earth.	*basileus*
27:35	The kings of the coastlands.[55]	*basileus*
28:12	The king of Tyre.[56]	*archōn*
28:17	Unspecified kings.	*basileus*
29:2	Pharaoh, king of Egypt.	*basileus*
29:3	Pharaoh, king of Egypt.	*basileus*

---

[53] Halpern, *Constitution*, 213f.; M.Z. Brettler, *God is King: Understanding an Israelite Metaphor*, JSOTS 76 (Sheffield 1989) 37.
[54] Omitted by LXX[B].
[55] Are these *malkê hā'iyyîm* the same as the *nᵉśî'ê hayyām* in Ezekiel 26:16 (note the use of *hā'iyyîm* in Ezekiel 26:15)?
[56] Also designated the *nāgîd* of Tyre in Ezekiel 28:2.

29:18	Nebuchadnezzar, king of Babylon.	*basileus*
29:19	Nebuchadnezzar, king of Babylon.	*basileus*
30:10	Nebuchadnezzar, king of Babylon.	*basileus*
30:21	Pharaoh, king of Egypt.	*basileus*
30:22	Pharaoh, king of Egypt.	*basileus*
30:24	The king of Babylon.	*basileus*
30:25[2]	The king of Babylon.	*basileus*
31:2	Pharaoh, king of Egypt.	*basileus*
32:2	Pharaoh, king of Egypt.	*basileus*
32:10	Unspecified kings "of many peoples".	*basileus*
32:11	The king of Babylon.	*basileus*
32:29	The kings of Edom.[57]	——[58]
37:22	The future ruler of the re-united kingdom.	*archōn*
37:24	The new David.	*archōn*

nāśî':	Referent	LXX
7:27	The *nāśî'* is wrapped in despair.	*archōn*
12:10	The *nāśî'* in Jerusalem (= Zedekiah).	*archōn*
12:12	As 12:10.	*archōn*
19:1	The *nᵉśî'îm* of Israel (= Jehoahaz and Jehoiachin? or Zedekiah?).[60]	*archōn*[59]
21:17[12]	"The *nᵉśî'îm* of Israel are thrown to the sword along with my people".	*aphēgoumenoi*
21:30[25]	Profane and wicked *nāśî'* of Israel (= Zedekiah).	*aphēgoumenos*
22:6	The *nᵉśî'îm* of Israel are guilty of oppression.	*aphēgoumenoi*
22:25	Her *nᵉśî'îm*[61] are guilty of oppression.	*aphēgoumenoi*
26:16	The *nᵉśî'îm* of the coastlands.[62]	*archontes*
27:21	The *nᵉśî'îm* of Kedar.	*archontes*
30:13	There will no longer be a *nāśî'* in Egypt.	*archontes*[63]
32:29	The *mᵉlākîm* and *nᵉśî'îm* of Edom.	*archontes*
34:24	My servant David will be *nāśî'* among them [the future Israel].	*archōn*
37:25	My servant David will be their *nāśî'* forever.	*archōn*

---

[57] "Her kings and her *nᵉśî'îm* ". On the text see below, p.21.
[58] LXX brings together reference to the kings and princes under the term *archontes*.
[59] LXX has singular.
[60] On the identity of these *nᵉśî'îm*, see Zimmerli, *Ezechiel*, 423ff. See further below, p.35.
[61] The MT has *qeśer nᵉbî'êhā* in v.25. However, the prophets are separately indicted in v.28, and the accusation in v.25 seems to fit the *nᵉśî'îm* better (cf. Ezek 19). The LXX *hēs hoi aphēgoumenoi* supports the reading *ʼšer nᵉśî'êhā*. See Zimmerli, *Ezechiel*, 521.
[62] See p.18, n.55 above.
[63] On this plural see below, p.22.

38:2	Gog, chief *nāśî* [64] of Meshech and Tubal.	*archōn*
38:3	As 38:2.	*archōn*
39:1	As 38:2.	*archōn*
39:18	The *n^eśî'îm* of the earth.	*archontes*

Upon examination of the above data, it appears that Ezekiel's usage of *melek* and *nāśî'* has much in common with the usage outside Ezekiel, at least when he is not describing the ruler of Israel. The term *nāśî'* is used to denote the leaders of some of the smaller tribal groupings outside Israel (e.g. Ezek. 27:21; cf. Jos. 13:21). As outside Ezekiel, the distinction between *melek* and *nāśî'* is not hard and fast: the great emperors of Babylon and Egypt are always designated *melek*, but petty kings may go by either title (compare Ezek. 26:16 with Ezek. 27:35; Jos. 13:21 and Num. 31:8). Similarly the ruler of Tyre may be designated either *melek* or *nāgîd* (compare Ezek. 28:2 with Ezek. 28:12).[65]

We also find an apparent example of a hierarchy with a *nāśî'*-in-chief over lesser tribal chieftains (Ezek. 38:2,3; Ezek. 39:1 cf. Num. 3:32; 1 Chr. 7:40).[66] The terminology varies (*n^eśî' rō'š* vs. *n^eśî' n^eśî'ê hallēwî* or *rā'šê n^eśî'îm*) but in each instance there seems to be a hierarchy of rank. As these examples show, *rō'š* is not to be understood here as an adjective ("chief prince")[67] but as a noun in its own right ("prince of the chiefs"). The construction remains difficult, but in the absence of solid evidence of a country by the name of Rosh which might have been connected with Tubal and Meshech, this interpretation remains the preferable choice.[68]

Outside Ezekiel, we also found the *n^eśî'îm* active to some degree as a separate body alongside the monarchy (1 Ki. 8:1 = 2 Chr. 5:2; 2 Chr. 1:2). This is consistent with the present text of Ezekiel 7:27 and 32:29:[69]

---

[64] On this translation see below, p.20.

[65] P. Cheminant suggests that the choice of *nāgîd* (from the root *ngd*, "to be lifted up, exalted") may have been prompted by the *gābah libb^ekā* which follows it (*Les Prophéties d'Ézéchiel contre Tyr (26-28:19)* [Paris 1912] 66).

[66] LXX takes *rō'š* as the name of a country. The translation given here is supported by the Vulgate, the Targum and the massoretic accentation, and partially by the Peshitta, which interprets the phrase *nśy' r'š* as two parallel titles by adding a copula. See Zimmerli, *Ezechiel*, 925.

[67] So J.D. Price, "Rosh: An Ancient Land Known to Ezekiel", *Grace Theological Journal* 6 (1985) 75ff.

[68] L.C. Allen, *Ezekiel 20-48*, WBC (Waco 1990) 199; R.H. Alexander, "A Fresh Look at Ezekiel 38 and 39", *JETS* 17 (1974) 161 n.2. Cf. GKC § 130f. Tubal and Meshech occur together also in Ezekiel 27:13; 32:26. Aside from any possible use in the construction in question, Rosh is nowhere found in the Old Testament as a place name.

[69] Brettler, *God is King*, 38. Ezekiel 21:17[12] ("[My sword] is against all the *n^eśî'ê yiśrā'ēl*; they are delivered over to the sword with my people") could also conceivably fall into this category. However, it seems more likely that this is simply another reference to the historical fate of the latter kings of Judah (Zimmerli, *Ezechiel*, 479).

The king (*melek*) mourns, the prince (*nāśî'*) is wrapped in despair, the hands of the people of the land are palsied by terror. (Ezek. 7:27)

Edom is there, her kings and all her princes (*neśî'êhā*), who for all their might are laid with those who are slain by the sword; they lie with the uncircumcised, with those who go down to the Pit. (Ezek. 32:29)

The text in both cases is differently rendered in some manuscripts of the Septuagint: LXX[B] omitted the phrase "The king mourns" in Ezekiel 7:27, and in Ezekiel 32:29 the LXX renders the phrase "Edom is there, her kings and princes" by *edothēsan hoi archontes Assour*, apparently uniting the two groups into one.[70] On the basis of this, Zimmerli has suggested that in Ezekiel 7:27 the MT contains a later addition,

da Ez für den König von Juda den Titel *nāśî'* braucht und da an der vorliegenden Stelle zudem das Nebeneinander von *nāśî'* und *melek* eine sachliche Verlegenheit bedeutet.[71]

However, Ezekiel is by no means insistent on denying the ruler of Judah the title of king. He allows it to stand for Jehoiachin in Ezekiel 17:12 and it is implied as a legitimate title for Zedekiah in the phrase *hammelek hammamlîk 'ōtô* ("the king [Nebuchadnezzar] who caused him [Zedekiah] to be king"; Ezekiel 17:16). Given that, and what we have seen of the existence of the *neśî'îm* alongside the monarchy elsewhere, the parallelism becomes much less problematic. Nor do we need to collapse the references to *melek* and *nāśî'* into one another as "impressionistic parallelism":[72] in fact, the triad "king, prince, people of the land" forms a neat foil for the triad "prophet, priest and elders" in the preceding verse.[73] In Ezekiel 32:29 the absence of the copula before *melākêhā* is certainly unusual but by no means unique.[74] Gesenius notes that there are exceptions to the usual rule.[75] The formula "There are X and all her Y" is repeated in this chapter with numerous variations, and this may simply be another variation on the theme.[76]

---

[70] Clearly the text of the LXX involves more than a simple omission. For an interpretation of the history of the text see L.C. Allen, *Ezekiel 20-48*, 135.

[71] Zimmerli, *Ezechiel*, 165; similarly F. Hitzig, *Der Prophet Ezechiel*, KeH (Leipzig 1847) 56.

[72] So Levenson, *Theology*, 64. Similarly, Kimhi; van der Ploeg, "Chefs", 48; Wevers, *Ezekiel*, 76. Levenson argues that "We know of no state official, no prime minister or viceroy, with that title". In view of the evidence adduced above this is hardly convincing. In favour of a distinction, see Hammershaimb, "Monarchy", 54; Halpern, *Constitution*, 212.

[73] Cooke, *Ezekiel*, 84; Greenberg, *Ezekiel 1-20*, 156.

[74] It is supplied by Peshitta and Vulgate; Targum follows the MT.

[75] GKC § 154 a. Cf. Genesis 10:1; 14:1 and Jeremiah 2:26 for examples.

[76] V.26 shows a similar lack of a copula between the first and second items. However, this is probably due to Meshech-Tubal being considered as a single unit.

Another verse of interest in this context is found in Ezekiel 30:13. The text of this verse may have been partially corrupted in transmission and may be reconstructed as:

> I shall make an end of rulers from Memphis and no leader (*nāśî'*) will arise any more from Egypt.[77]

This could be read two ways: it could be synonymous parallelism, so that the *nāśî'* would be equivalent to the "rulers" of the A verset. In that case this verse would be another witness to a rank of *nāśî'* below that of *melek*.[78] However, the force of the parallelism could be: "I shall make an end of the rulers...and *what is more* there will no longer be [even] a *nāśî'* in the land of Egypt".[79] On this interpretation, the devastation wreaked on Egypt will be such that, far from the present situation in which Egypt's ruler rightly bears the rank of *melek*, in those days there will not even be a *nāśî'* [= petty tribal king].[80] The choice of interpretation lies largely with the decision on whether to follow the singular of the MT or the plural of the LXX.[81]

This raises the question of the usage of the LXX: is the LXX itself a neutral witness in its translations of *melek* and *nāśî'*? The LXX uses three terms for *melek* and *nāśî'* in Ezekiel 1-39: *basileus*, *archōn* and *aphēgoumenos*. As well as representing *melek* and *nāśî'*, *archōn* is also used to translate *śar* in Ezekiel 17:12, 22:27 (and 27:8?[82]), *nāgîd* in Ezekiel 28:2, *'ēl* in Ezekiel 31:11, and *nāśîk* in Ezekiel 32:30. An examination of the data does not support the conclusion reached by F. Raurell, that the LXX uses *archōn* in chapters 1-39 to stress the pejorative aspects of kingship,

---

[77] For this translation, see L. Allen, *Ezekiel 20-48*, 112. The MT has an additional clause at the beginning, *wᵉha"badtî gillûlîm* ("and I shall destroy the idols") which is absent from the LXX. The next clause reads in the MT *wᵉhišbattî "lîlîm minnōp* ("I will put an end to the images of Memphis"). *"lîlîm* is unique here in the book of Ezekiel, and could be a corruption of *'ēlîm*, which appears elsewhere in the sense of "leaders". *'ēlîm* also fits better as a parallel to *nāśî'* in the next clause. LXX lends weight to this supposition with its reading *megistanas*. This corruption would then have been secondarily glossed by the first clause. That the MT *nāśî'* is due to loss of the *mem* from an original *nᵉśî'îm* due to haplography (cf. LXX *archontas*, so Wevers, *Ezekiel*, 230) is possible but not required (see discussion below). However, L. Boadt defends the existing text of the entire verse in the MT, seeing in *gillûlîm* a reference to Leviticus 26 (*Ezekiel's Oracles against Egypt. A Literary and Philological Study of Ezekiel 29-32*, Biblica et Orientalia 37 [Rome 1980] 77).

[78] This interpretation would favour the plural of the LXX rather than the singular of the MT.

[79] On this kind of parallelism see J. Kugel, *The Idea of Biblical Poetry* (New Haven 1981) 8.

[80] Boadt, who retains the MT, seems to be moving in this direction when he states that this verse "accents the diminution of Pharaoh from a king-divinity to a mere tribal chief" (*Oracles against Egypt*, 77).

[81] It should be noted that elsewhere in Ezekiel the LXX does not always agree with MT as to the number of the term *nāśî'* even where the MT is not in doubt (cf. Ezek. 19:1; 48:22).

[82] So Zimmerli, *Ezechiel*, 628. G. Fohrer & K. Galling assume the loss of *nᵉśî'ê*; (*Ezechiel*, HAT [Tübingen ²1955] 153); L. Allen (*Ezekiel 20-48*, 81) suggests *śābê*, "elders". MT has *yōšᵉbê*.

depicting the ruler of Judah as a foreign tyrant, unjust and ungodly, avoiding the title *basileus* for polemical reasons.[83] This false conclusion is reached by placing undue stress on the two instances in chapter 37 where the LXX translates *melek* by *archōn*. In fact, the LXX of Ezekiel consistently translates *melek* by *basileus*, *except* where *melek* is found together with *nāśî'* or *nāgîd*. Where they are found in close proximity, the LXX harmonized the two terms, understandably in the light of Ezekiel's own usage, and translated both by *archōn*. Only this explanation can account for the omissions in Ezekiel 7:27 and 32:29 and the harmonizing of Ezekiel 28:12 with 28:2, and Ezekiel 37:22 and 24 with 34:24 and 37:25. What polemical purpose can be discerned in the translation of the *melek* of Tyre as an *archōn* (Ezek. 28:12)? The simple answer is that there is no polemical purpose: it serves rather to harmonize the description with Ezekiel 28:2 where the same individual is called a *nāgîd* by the MT, already translated *archōn* by the LXX. In addition, by the time of the LXX remembrance of an office of *nāśî'* distinct from the executive of the day had faded, so Ezekiel 7:27 and 32:29 were understood as synonymous parallelism. If this much is true, then there is equally little reason to see a polemical purpose behind the choice of *archōn* in Ezekiel 37:22 and 24. The individual in question here is designated *nāśî'* by the MT in Ezekiel 34:24 and 37:25, and in the interests of harmonization the LXX translates throughout by *archōn*. One consequence of this is that there is no reason to emend the MT reading of *melek* here to *nāśî'*, as has been done by many commentators.[84]

If we can see a harmonistic purpose behind the occasional use of *archōn* to translate *melek*, there seems no readily discernible distinction between *archōn* and *aphēgoumenos* as translations of *nāśî'*. Both appear in the singular and the plural, and in negative and positive (or at least neutral) contexts. It is striking that *aphēgoumenos* appears as the exclusive translation in chapters 20-25 (in four occurrences between Ezekiel 21:17[12] and 22:25). The only instance where there seems a definite motivation at work is in chapter 22, where the translator needed to distinguish between *n°śî'îm* (for which he chose *aphēgoumenoi*) in Ezekiel 22:25 and *śārîm* (*archontes*) in 22:27.[85] It appears that Lust may well be right in attributing some of the variations to inconsistency on the part of the translator;[86] however, the

[83] F. Raurell, "The Polemical Role of the *APXONTEΣ* and *AΦHΓOYMENOI* in Ez LXX", *Ezekiel and His Book*, J. Lust, ed. (Leuven 1986) 87.

[84] E.g. K.H. Bernhardt, *Das Problem der altorientalischen Königsideologie im Alten Testament*, SVT 8 (Leiden 1961) 116 n.5.; J. Herrmann, *Ezechiel, übersetzt und erklärt*, KAT (Leipzig 1924) 234; A. Bertholet & K. Galling, *Hesekiel*, HAT (Tübingen 1936) 128; Fohrer & Galling, 211; W. Eichrodt, *Der Prophet Hesekiel*, ATD (Göttingen 1970) 358.

[85] On the text of Ezekiel 22:25 see above, p.19 n.61.

[86] "Exegesis and Theology in the Septuagint of Ezekiel: The Longer 'pluses' and Ezekiel 43:1-9", *VIth Congress of the International Organization for Septuagint and Cognate Studies*, SCS 23 (Atlanta 1987) 219.

apparent inconsistency is reduced if McGregor's division of the LXX translation between three translators is accepted.[87] He identified these translators as S1 (chapters 1-25), S2 (chapters 26-39) and S3 (chapters 40-48). On this scenario, S1 used *archōn* consistently for *nāśî'* in chapters 1-20 and then appears to have switched to *aphēgoumenos* for the remainder of his work,[88] while S2 translated *nāśî'* by *archōn* throughout. McGregor's S3, on the other hand, avoided the translation *archōn* for *nāśî'* altogether; instead he alternated between *hēgoumenos* and *aphēgoumenos* without apparent distinction.[89]

Having surveyed Ezekiel's usage of *melek* and *nāśî'* as they pertain to the situation external to Israel we may now return to the more fundamental issue, regarding his usage of these terms to describe the ruler (past or future) of Israel. Even if it is true that the LXX has no pejorative purpose in its translation, is it also true that Ezekiel has no pejorative purpose in mind in his usage in chapters 1-39?

Ezekiel uses *melek* of the reigning king of Israel in three instances (Ezek. 1:2; 7:27 and 17:12) and of the future king twice (Ezek. 37:22, 24). The first instance is part of the date formula: "It was the fifth year of the exile of King Jehoiachin". Because of the formulaic nature of this usage, it is not of great significance: *nāśî'* would simply not have fitted the context here. The second instance deals with the ineffectiveness of the leadership in general in face of the coming crisis, and includes the office of *melek* as one of those who will be found helpless in that day. It is not clear which king in particular is in mind, nor that there is any blame attached to the holder of the office; he is simply an example of the coming powerlessness of all the authority figures of the land.[90] The third instance records how Jehoiachin was taken into exile by Nebuchadnezzar. Here, there may possibly be an implied contrast between *melek* and *nāśî'*. If exile was the fate of Jehoiachin when he fought against Nebuchadnezzar, though he merited the more exalted title *melek*, what are the prospects for Zedekiah, who is never explicitly termed *melek* by Ezekiel, and who owes his very throne to Nebuchadnezzar (Ezek. 17:16)? Zimmerli, however, thinks that the use of the title *melek* here was simply due to the historical narrative character of Ezekiel 17:12b-15a.[91]

---

[87] L.J. McGregor, *The Greek Text of Ezekiel: an Examination of its Homogeneity*, SCS 18 (Atlanta 1985) 95ff.

[88] The phenomenon of "progression of translation" is discussed by McGregor (*Greek Text*, 43). Perhaps the translator was influenced by his use of *archōn* also to translate *śārîm* (Ezek. 17:12; 22:27)?

[89] On the usage of S3 (chapters 40-48) see further below, p.27.

[90] Mentioned alongside the *melek* are the *nāśî'* and the *'am hā'āres*.

[91] Zimmerli, *Ezechiel*, 384.

We have discussed above[92] the textual questions surrounding the usage of *melek* to describe the future ruler of Israel in Ezekiel 37:22,24. The choice of *melek* here is very probably conditioned by the context: if the two *kingdoms* (*mamlākôt*; LXX *basileias*) are to be rejoined into one, who should reign over them but a *melek*?[93] The title does not focus on his rulership over them so much as the unification of the two kingdoms under one king.[94] Nonetheless, its use here shows that there was no overriding theological objection attached to the term as a means of denoting the future ruler.

Ezekiel is equally able to give the same future ruler the title *nāśî'* (Ezek. 34:24; 37:25). In neither passage is particular weight placed on this title, however, as if by it Ezekiel were introducing some new limitation on the future king. Rather, in both passages the stress falls on the other appellations bestowed upon this figure: "My servant, David" (Ezek. 34:23f.; 37:24f.) and "one shepherd" (Ezek. 34:23; 37:24). The message Ezekiel is conveying here seems not to be that the future ruler will be a *nāśî'* (as opposed to a *melek*) but rather that the future *nāśî'* will not be like the rulers of the recent past.[95]

We may therefore properly speak of a *preference* for the term *nāśî'* to describe the reigning and future Davidic ruler, but we should not absolutize it: Ezekiel was free to use whichever term best fitted the context.

4 The Usage of melek and nāśî' in Ezekiel 40-48

Thus far in our investigation of terminology we have only dealt with chapters 1-39. We have left chapters 40-48 to this point because they present their own special problems.

To begin with the simplest aspect of these chapters, *melek* only appears in one passage, Ezekiel 43:7-9 (three times).[96] Here it has reference to the former rulers of Israel who were guilty of defiling Yahweh's name through their (spiritual) prostitution and by the fact that they not only failed physically to separate the Temple from the palace but actually set up memorial stelae there to themselves.[97] We noted above that the title *melek* was not entirely denied to Judah's former rulers in Ezekiel 1-39;[98] here, however,

---

[92] See above, p.23.
[93] Zimmerli, *Ezechiel*, 905.
[94] D. Baltzer, *Ezechiel und Deuterojesaja*, BZAW 121 (1971) 139.
[95] On these passages see below, sections C.5, D.4 and D.5.
[96] LXX translates each occurrence by *hēgoumenoi*.
[97] On the text see below, p.41.
[98] See above, p.24.

the term may have been chosen because it has a historical reference stretching back further than Israel's immediate past to rulers who genuinely merited the title *melek*. It was, after all, Solomon who initially located the Temple next to the palace (cf. 1 Kings 6f.). But even while this passage has reference to past sins, it is not simply a record of the past but a command for the future. Thus, contained within the discontinuity, there is also an implied continuity between the future rulers and the past "kings": the *n⁰śî'îm* of days to come, described in the rest of these chapters, are the legitimate successors of the *m⁰lākîm* of the past.[99] This continuity further underlines the importance of not constructing artificially precise boundaries between the terms *melek* and *nāśî'* in Ezekiel.

Apart from this passage, all references to past and future rulers of Israel in Ezekiel 40-48 use the term *nāśî'*. These are as follows:

nāśî':	Referent	LXX
44:3[2]	The future ruler (positive)	*hēgoumenos*
45:7	The future ruler (positive)	*hēgoumenos*
45:8	The past rulers (negative)[100]	*aphēgoumenoi*
45:9	The past rulers (negative)	*aphēgoumenoi*
45:16	The future ruler (positive)	*aphēgoumenos*
45:17	The future ruler (positive)	*aphēgoumenos*
45:22	The future ruler (positive)[101]	*aphēgoumenos*
46:2	The future ruler (positive)	*aphēgoumenos*
46:4	The future ruler (positive)	*aphēgoumenos*
46:8	The future ruler (positive)	*aphēgoumenos*[102]
46:10	The future ruler (positive)	*aphēgoumenos*
46:12	The future ruler (positive)	*aphēgoumenos*
46:16	The future ruler (neutral)[103]	*aphēgoumenos*

[99] Note especially v.7b: "The house of Israel shall no more defile my holy name, neither they, *nor their kings*...", which seems to imply that the future rulers will indeed be kings!
[100] MT has *n⁰śî'ay* "my princes", which some emend to *n⁰śî'ê yiśrā'ēl* on the basis of LXX. So e.g. Zimmerli, *Ezechiel*, 1142; Ebach, *Kritik und Utopie*, 75. But see Cooke, *Ezekiel*, 496 for a defence of the MT as it stands. Whichever alternative is chosen, the other reading is probably due to the scribal practice of abbreviation whereby *n⁰śî'ê yiśrā'ēl* could be written *n⁰śî'ê y*'' (G.R. Driver, "Abbreviations in the Massoretic Text", *Textus* 1 (1961) 121).
[101] Cf. also vv. 23-25 where his responsibilities are detailed.
[102] Note however that P. 967 has *hēgoumenos* for *aphēgoumenos* in Ezekiel 46:8,12,17, 18; 48:21,22. It is probably impossible to determine which was original. Cf. McGregor, *Greek Text*, 147.
[103] Gese thinks this passage to be dependant upon Ezekiel 45:8f., and therefore to display a negative tone of voice (*Verfassungsentwurf*, 88). Certainly Ezekiel 46:18 does suggest that the past rulers abused their powers. However, if regulations designed to avoid the repetition of past abuses are construed as having a negative tone then Ezekiel 44:23f. must be extremely antagonistic towards the Zadokite priesthood (cf. Ezek. 22:26)! Rather than having a negative tone, this passage seems simply to indicate that the future rulers, like most other sectors of society, will operate under a different set of rules in the future.

46:17	The future ruler (neutral)	*aphēgoumenos*
46:18	The future ruler (neutral)	*aphēgoumenos*
48:21²	The future ruler (positive)	*aphēgoumenos*²
48:22²	The future ruler (positive)¹⁰⁴	*aphēgoumenoi*²

It may be seen from this summary that these chapters use *nāśî'* of the future ruler almost entirely in the singular, and in a positive sense: they are concerned with his privileges and responsibilities in the cultic sphere. Where the plural form is used and there is a negative connotation (Ezek. 45:8f.), the focus is on the abuses of the past, providing a parallel to the rebuke of the *m°lākîm* in Ezekiel 43:7ff.[105] In contrast to Ezekiel 1-39, there is no apparent instance of the *n°śî'îm* as a separate entity, distinct from the ruler. As in chapters 1-39, there is no hard and fast distinction between *melek* and *nāśî'*: both may be used to describe the rulers of the past. However, the future ruler is described as the *nāśî'* with a consistency which was lacking in chapters 1-39.

The usage of the LXX in chapters 40-48 supports the hypothesis of a different translator for these chapters (McGregor's translator S3).[106] *archōn* is not used to translate *nāśî'*; instead *hēgoumenos* and *aphēgoumenos* are used without apparent distinction.

Excursus: The So-Called *nāśî'* Stratum in Ezekiel 40-48

The examination of the tradition-history of Ezekiel 40-48 published by H. Gese in 1957 has had an enormous impact on the study of these chapters.[107] J. Levenson terms the study "a model for form-critical work in its exactitude and its sobriety of judgement".[108] Zimmerli deems it "wertvolle Vorarbeit".[109] While Gese's approach has not been entirely exempt from criticism[110] and some of the details of his analysis have been questioned,[111]

---

[104] Zimmerli wishes to omit the second occurrence in this verse (*Ezechiel*, 1209), though it is present in the versions, except the Peshitta which has a tendency to abbreviate. In support of Zimmerli's position, it does seem out of place here and may perhaps be due to vertical dittography (L. Allen, *Ezekiel 20-48*, 276).

[105] Though as we noted in that context, interest in the past is only for the sake of the "no more" of the future. See above, p.26.

[106] See above, p.24.

[107] *Der Verfassungsentwurf des Ezechiel (Kap. 40-48) traditions-geschichtlich untersucht*, BHTh 25 (Tübingen 1957).

[108] Levenson, *Theology*, 1.

[109] Zimmerli, *Ezechiel*, 1240.

[110] Cf. M. Greenberg, "The Design and Themes of Ezekiel's Program of Restoration", *Interp.* 38 (1984) 189ff.; J.G. McConville, "Priests and Levites in Ezekiel: a Crux in the Interpretation of Israel's History", *TynB* 34 (1983) 11ff.; M. Haran, "The Law Code of Ezekiel 40-48 and its Relation to the Priestly School", *HUCA* 50 (1979) 46ff. See also H.H. Rowley "H. Gese, 'Der Verfassungsentwurf des Ezechiel'" [Review], *JTS* n.s. 9 (1958) 340-2.

the essential outlines of his conclusions have remained largely unchallenged in critical circles.[112] This is all the more astonishing when one considers the rapid proliferation of tradition-historical studies on Ezekiel 1-39 in recent years.[113] In view of the influence Gese's studies have had, one particular aspect of them, the so-called "*nāśî*' stratum", is worthy of closer examination here.[114]

In brief, Gese's thesis is that in addition to a base layer and numerous glosses and expansions, two principal strata can be identified in chapters 40-48 , the "*nāśî*' stratum" and the "Zadokite stratum". According to Gese, these strata were originally totally unrelated.[115] The "*nāśî*' stratum" consists of Ezekiel 44:1-3, 45:21-25, 46:1-10,12. It speaks of the *nāśî*' as the leader of the cultic congregation and with the *'am hā'āreṣ* at his side; elsewhere, outside the *nāśî*' stratum, the people are simply designated *'am*.[116] It always uses the singular of *nāśî*' and speaks positively of him, in contrast to those pieces which restrict his role (Ezek. 45:8b-9; 46:16-18).[117] In content, the *nāśî*' stratum deals with the sacrifice regulations for the congregation and the *nāśî*'. It is not confined to Ezekiel 40-48, but is closely linked literarily to Leviticus 4, which also connects the *nāśî*' and the *'am hā'āreṣ*.[118] The "Zadokite stratum", on the other hand, consists of Ezekiel 44:6-16, (44:17-27), 44:28-30a and 45:13-15. Its characteristics are the "You (pl.)" address to Israel, the restricting of the priesthood to Zadokites, and the degrading of other priests to ancillary personnel in the Temple (Levites).[119]

According to Gese, these two independent strata were brought together later and harmonized, though not completely successfully.[120] The competing claims to the sacrificial gifts of the people were resolved by the insertion of Ezekiel 45:16f. between Ezekiel 45:13-15 (Zadokite stratum) and 45:21-25 (*nāśî*' stratum). However, the harmonizer spoke only of *hā'ām* in Ezekiel 45:16, which was later glossed with *hā'āreṣ* to bring it into line with the terminology of the *nāśî*' stratum, at the expense of grammatical propriety.[121] The cultic place of the *nāśî*' is retained which the acceptance of the offering

[111] E.g. whether his "Zadokite Stratum" is not rather a single insertion (Ezek. 44:6-16) which has then influenced the rest of Ezekiel 40-48 by "metastasis" (so A.H.J. Gunneweg, *Leviten und Priester*, FRLANT 89 [Göttingen 1965] 188).

[112] An exception is the unpublished 1972 dissertation by J.H. Ebach, *Kritik und Utopie*, 20ff. However, Ebach's conclusions appear to have gone largely unnoticed in the scholarly world. See also Hals, *Ezekiel*, 287f.

[113] For example, the works by Bettenzoli, Garscha, Hossfeld and Simian listed in the bibliography.

[114] His so-called "Zadokite stratum" will be examined in more detail below. See p. 87ff.

[115] *Verfassungsentwurf*, 110.

[116] *Verfassungsentwurf*, 85, 110.

[117] *Verfassungsentwurf*, 85.

[118] *Verfassungsentwurf*, 110.

[119] *Verfassungsentwurf*, 111.

[120] *Verfassungsentwurf*, 113.

[121] *Verfassungsentwurf*, 72.

gifts carries over to him; however, at the same time a strong polemic posture against the *nāśî'* institution is noticeable which wishes to confine his possible power.[122]

If Gese's analysis is correct,[123] there are competing attitudes towards the *nāśî'* in Ezekiel 40-48: the *nāśî'* stratum is entirely positive, while later additions are more negative. Clearly it is of some importance to our study to examine whether Gese's theory can stand or not.

The first aspect of Gese's thesis to be examined is the connection he identifies between the *nāśî'* and the *'am hā'āres*. According to Gese, it is a distinguishing mark of the *nāśî'* stratum that it always links these two entities; elsewhere in chapters 40-48 the talk is simply of *'am* or *'ammî*.[124] But on closer inspection this is not a sufficiently distinctive feature: *nāśî'* and *'am hā'āres* also occur in a common context in Ezekiel 7:27, 12:12-19 and 22:25-29. It turns out that of the eight undisputed uses of this phrase in Ezekiel[125], six occur in passages which also relate to the *nāśî'*.[126] This connection is therefore scarcely a distinctive mark of the *nāśî'* stratum, since only three of the six[127] concurrences in Ezekiel are within this layer.

Gese goes on to argue for a tradition-historical connection of the *nāśî'* stratum with Leviticus 4, where the terms *nāśî'* and *'am hā'āres* are also linked in a cultic context. On the basis of this he suggests:

> es muß ein Stadium in der Arbeit an den kultischen Gesetzen gegeben haben, in dem der Begriff *'am hā'āres* die kultische Gemeinde umschreiben könnte, an deren Spitze der *nāśî'* stand.[128]

But this is not at all clear from a comparison of Ezekiel 45f. with Leviticus 4. Certainly the two passages have many connections but they do not prove what Gese seeks to demonstrate. Instead, the passage in Leviticus actually undermines Gese's position. There the head of the cultic community – the definite individual who acts on behalf of the community as well as himself in making atonement with a bull as a sin offering – is the anointed priest

---

[122] *Verfassungsentwurf*, 113.
[123] With respect to the *nāśî'* stratum, it has been supported by most recent commentators, including Zimmerli (*Ezechiel*, 1245) and L. Allen (*Ezekiel 20-48*, 253).
[124] *Verfassungsentwurf*, 85. For more on the relationship of *'am hā'āres* and *'am* in Ezekiel see below, p.120f.
[125] Not including the apparent reference in Ezekiel 45:16, where the MT *hā'am hā'āres* is anomalous grammatically. The latter word is normally thought to be an explanatory gloss; it is absent from LXX*. Note, however, that a similar confusion exists in a very similar context of sacrificial offerings in 2 Kings 16:15, where MT has *'am hā'āres* but some MSS have *hā'ām* and LXX has *ho laos*. If Ezekiel 45:16 is also a genuine occurrence of *'am hā'āres* then the correlation rises to seven out of nine, for the *nāśî'* is also present in this verse. For a further consideration in favour of an original *'am hā'āres* see below, p.120.
[126] Ezekiel 7:27; 12:19 (cf. 12:10,12); 22:29 (cf. 22:27; on the text, see p.19, n.61) 45:16; 45:22; 46:3; 46:9. The others are Ezekiel 33:2 and 39:13.
[127] Or four of the seven including Ezekiel 45:16.
[128] *Verfassungsentwurf*, 111.

(hakkōhēn hammāšîah) and not the nāśî'.[129] Indeed Leviticus knows nothing of the nāśî'; only of one among several.[130] To be sure, a nāśî' in Leviticus 4 is more important than the average member of the community:[131] his sin requires a male goat (v.23) as opposed to a female goat required for a member of the 'am hā'āreṣ (v.28).[132] But those who act to represent the whole community (kol-'ʿdat yiśrā'ēl) when it sins are not the nᵉśî'îm but the elders of the community (ziqnê hā'ēdâ). Moreover, the passage in Leviticus 4 transgresses Gese's distinction between the 'am hā'āreṣ and 'am as designations of the cultic community. According to Gese, in Ezekiel 40-48 these terms mark out distinctively different strata.[133] But Leviticus 4 can alternate between 'am (v.3), 'ēdâ (v.13ff.), qāhāl (v.13ff.) and 'am hā'āreṣ (v.27) for the cultic community without apparent distinction.[134] A similar flexibility of expression is evident in Ezekiel 39:7-13, where the inhabitants of Israel are variously described as "my people Israel" ('ammî yiśrā'ēl, v.7), the house of Israel (bêt yiśrā'ēl, v.12) and "the people of the land" ('am hā'āreṣ, v.13).[135]

The other distinction which Gese seeks to make between his nāśî' stratum and the rest of Ezekiel 40-48 is the attitude towards the nāśî'. According to Gese, nāśî' does occur outside the nāśî' stratum, but only in contexts which limit his power or also speak only of the nᵉśî'îm.[136] This claim too fails to stand up to close examination. Certainly there are passages which seem to envisage a dynastic succession of nᵉśî'îm and legislate to prevent abuses by them (Ezek. 45:8,9; 46:16-18). But do they thereby conflict with the outlook of the "nāśî' stratum"? The "nāśî' stratum" itself certainly contains no hint of eternal life for the nāśî'. Yet if the nāśî' is not to live forever then would it not be natural—or at least thinkable—that a dynastic succession should be envisaged? Equally the "nāśî' stratum" does not present the nāśî' as a sinless being. Indeed, that seems to be excluded by his need to offer a sin offering for himself as well as the people (Ezek. 45:22). So why should there be no need to warn against the

---

[129] Compare Leviticus 4:3 with Ezekiel 45:22.
[130] Contrast the lack of the definite article in Leviticus 4:22 with the definite form in Leviticus 4:3.
[131] Assuming that this is what the 'am hā'āreṣ represents in Leviticus 4. A full discussion of the usage of 'am hā'āreṣ in the book of Leviticus is outside the scope of this study. For further discussion, see the works cited in chapter 5.B.5.
[132] On the grading of sacrificial materials see P.P. Jenson, Graded Holiness. A Key to the Priestly Conception of the World , JSOTS 106 (Sheffield 1992) 174-7.
[133] Verfassungsentwurf, 85.
[134] Note the comment of Ebach (Kritik und Utopie, 70): "'am hā'āreṣ in Lev. 4 kommt sehr in der Nähe der Begriffe qāhāl, 'ēdâ, und 'am".
[135] On 'am hā'āreṣ in Ezekiel see further below, p.120f.
[136] Verfassungsentwurf, 110.

repetition of past sins?[137] The only passage showing a truly negative attitude towards the *nᵉśî'îm* (Ezek. 45:9) is just such an appeal to give up the sins of the past. The limitations imposed by Ezekiel 46:16-18 are no more indicative of a negative attitude to the *nāśî'* than are the limitations of Ezekiel 44:17ff. of a negative attitude towards the Zadokite priesthood.[138] Moreover, there are several passages outside the *nāśî'* stratum which do show an extremely positive attitude towards the *nāśî'*, notably the gift provisions of Ezekiel 45:16f. and the land distribution of Ezekiel 45:7 and 48:21f. Because of their positive attitude towards the *nāśî'*, Gese is forced to admit that these are related to the *nāśî'* stratum.[139] But ultimately he denies them to the *nāśî'* stratum because of their lack of the terminology *'am hā'āres*.

The result of this examination has been to show that there are no solid distinguishing marks by which the so-called "*nāśî'* stratum" may be separated from its surroundings. Neither the attitude towards the *nāśî'* nor the correlation of *nāśî'* and *'am hā'āres* is a distinct mark of a separate stratum. All that we are left with is common content: these are simply the passages which deal with the responsibilities of the *nāśî'*, especially in the cultic realm. The common content is enough to account for all the similarities between them, without recourse to literary stratification; the tension between privilege and restriction is a necessary part of Ezekiel's plan for the future.[140] The so-called "*nāśî'* stratum" is a myth.

5 Conclusions on the Usage of melek and nāśî' in Ezekiel

As we noted above, Ezekiel's preferred term to describe the Israelite king, whether past or future, is *nāśî'*. This is not a hard and fast rule, but simply a predilection. This lack of consistency suggests that for the author of the book of Ezekiel there was not the strong significance which some have seen in the word itself. But Ezekiel's usage in this one area is so different from the general Old Testament usage which we examined above that it demands some explanation. Several alternatives have been advanced. Some have suggested that it may have been felt to express the vassal state of the Judean kings: in contrast to the great emperors of Babylon and Egypt, the

---

[137] This is especially true if a dynastic succession is under consideration. After all, it only took one full generation for the original Davidic dynasty to move from the faithfulness of a David (1 Ki. 3:6) to the divided heart of a Solomon (1 Ki. 11:3ff.). From there onwards, according to the Books of Kings, the progression of the monarchs was mostly downhill.

[138] Note especially Ezekiel 44:23f., which contain an implicit rebuke with their direct reference to Ezekiel 22:26.

[139] *Verfassungsentwurf*, 112f.

[140] "Der scheinbare Widerspruch zwischen kultischen Priviligien und politisch-sozialen Einschränkungen des Herrschers ist m.E. für den Verfassungsentwurf Ez. 40-48 konstitutiv" (Ebach, *Kritik und Utopie*, 24). This will emerge even more clearly as this study progresses.

ruler of Judah was merely a *nāśî'*, a second-rate king.[141] Others have found
in the term an appeal to the wilderness period for a leader who is an
apolitical sacral figure.[142] Still others have seen his use of the term as
influenced by post-exilic realities.[143] In view of what we saw above concerning the absence of any important figure with that title in the immediately
post-exilic situation, we can discount the last opinion.[144] There is, however,
an element of truth in both of the other conceptions. Certainly the term
nāśî' when used to describe the kings of Judah of the immediate past was
an accurate representation of their status in the world. Zedekiah was a
vassal king under the king of Babylon, dependent upon him for his throne,
a status that is suitably underlined by the term *nāśî'*.[145] Elsewhere, Ezekiel
is eager to emphasize the fate that befalls such a ruler when he rebels
against his overlord.[146] The idea of the future ruler as a dependant of
Yahweh would also not have been foreign to Ezekiel. It is surely contained
in his description of the future ruler as Yahweh's "servant" (Ezek. 34:23f.;
37:24f.). Further, Yahweh's kingship is clearly stressed in Ezekiel 20:33:[147]

> "As I live," says the Lord God, "surely with a mighty hand and an outstr-
> etched arm, and with wrath poured out, I will be king ('emlôk) over you".

It is also unlikely that Ezekiel's usage of the term is pure creation,[148] so we
should expect to find in it some reflection of the usage outside Ezekiel, and
especially of the wilderness period since that is when it predominates.[149]
However, we have already seen that the depiction of the *nāśî'* of this period
is hardly the apolitical sacral figure that Levenson is looking for. Quite the
reverse: the major responsibilities of the *nāśî'* of the wilderness period
included waging war and concluding covenants with other nations.[150] But the
political power of the *n^e śî'îm* during this period was a *limited* power,
derived from their representation of the people. In view of the abuses of
power perpetrated by the monarchy in the past, it is reasonable to suppose
that Ezekiel intended by the term *nāśî'* to convey a ruler with limited

---

[141] Procksch, "Fürst und Priester", 178.
[142] Levenson, *Theology*, 66ff.
[143] Hölscher, *Hesekiel*, 211.
[144] See above, p.16.
[145] Note the apparent contrast in Ezekiel 17 between Jehoiachin, who is likened to a cedar
sprig (v.4), and Zedekiah, who is likened to a low spreading vine (v.6).
[146] Ezekiel 17:13ff.; 19:5ff. Whether these are intended as a warning before the event (so
Lang, *Kein Aufstand*, 51, 113) or an explication after the event is not important here.
[147] H. Reventlow, *Wächter über Israel—Ezechiel und seine Tradition*, BZAW 82 (Berlin
1962) 86; W. Zimmerli, "Das Gotteswort des Ezechiel", *ZThK* 48 (1951) 258 [= *Gottes
Offenbarung* (Munich   1963) 143 = [ET] *Journal for Theology and Church* 4 (1967) 10];
"Deutero Ezechiel?", *ZAW* 84 (1972) 509; A. Graffy, *A Prophet Confronts His People: The
Disputation Speech in the Prophets*, Analecta Biblica 104 (Rome 1984) 67.
[148] *Contra* Lang, *Kein Aufstand*, 180.
[149] See above, p.14f.
[150] See above, p.15.

authority, genuinely representative of the people. In the words of Allen, the designation *nāśî'*

> underlines the monarch's subordination to Yahweh...[and] emphasizes the king's links with the people.[151]

As we shall see in the rest of this chapter, these are themes which Ezekiel brings to expression in other ways also. By using the same title for the rulers of the immediate past and for the rulers of the future, there is an implicit criticism of the past kings: though they bore the title *nāśî'*, it should be clear to all that they failed to live up to the responsibilities of that title.

Nevertheless, the fact that Ezekiel is still able to alternate between *melek* and *nāśî'* at will and that he also uses *n^eśî'îm* to designate a group of leaders in the past separate from the king suggests that the terminology is not all important. Ezekiel's message concerning the monarchy cannot be determined simply from his use of *nāśî'* in preference to *melek*. To do that we shall have to examine the passages which bring it into focus.

C. The Critique of Royal Leadership in the Book of Ezekiel

The book of Ezekiel contains a critique of the royal leadership of Judah in a variety of forms: there is both pictorial speech[152] (Ezek. 17:2ff.; 19:1ff.; 34:1ff.) and direct address (Ezek. 22:6, 25;[153] 43:7ff.; 45:8f.). Our primary concern in this section is not with the form of the critique, however, but with its content: what are the specific charges brought against the royal leadership? The following constitute all the passages in Ezekiel critical of the monarchy.

1 *Ezekiel 17*

The first passage critical of royal leadership is to be found in chapter 17. This chapter contains a fable of a great eagle and a small cedar sprig and a vine (vv. 1-10), the interpretation of the fable (vv. 11-21) and a re-application of the imagery of eagle and cedar twig to the future (vv. 22-24). Each of these sections is separated to some degree from what has gone before by a new introduction, yet there is a common theme running

---

[151] L. Allen, *Ezekiel 20-48*, 194; cf. Lang, *Kein Aufstand*, 180.
[152] B. Willmes comments: "Am besten benutzt man vorläufig den hebräischen Terminus *māšāl*, der zur Bezeichnung bildlicher Reden sehr verschiedener Art dient" (*Die sogenannte Hirtenallegorie Ez 34: studien zum Bild des Hirten im AT*, Beiträge zur biblischen Exegese und Theologie 19 [Frankfurt 1984] 274).
[153] On the text of the latter verse see p.19, n.61.

throughout the chapter: the source of power and security for king and nation.

In the fable, the great eagle takes a sprig from the top of a mighty cedar and carries it off to "a land of trade and a city of merchants" (i.e. Babylon).[154] In place of the cedar sprig (Jehoiachin), he plants a sapling of a different order which grows only into a low spreading vine (Zedekiah).[155] Although situated in a prime location (v.5) where it could thrive and reach its full potential,[156] the vine is faithless to the eagle which planted it and turns instead towards another eagle (Egypt). The point of the fable is driven home by a rhetorical question: "Will it thrive?" — to which the answer is clearly "No!".[157] Like the parables of Jesus, the message of the fable may seem clear enough in itself; but as with some of Jesus' parables an interpretation has been attached (cf. Matthew 13). Whether this full interpretation was given to the same audience to which the fable had been related or (as often in the New Testament) to a smaller audience of "disciples", we are not told.[158] The interpretation makes explicit the offence of the king (Zedekiah): he has broken his (Nebuchadnezzar's) covenant and despised his oath (v.15f.). In v.19 this offence is developed further by noting that it was not simply Nebuchadnezzar's covenant and oath which he despised but "My (Yahweh's) oath" and "My covenant" which he had broken. This may have reference to the practice attested in Hittite suzerainty treaties of requiring the vassal king to swear an oath of self-imprecation of which his own gods would be witnesses,[159] a practice which appears to have been adopted by the Babylonians.[160] The offence with which Zedekiah is charged is not simply rash political intrigue but rebellion against Yahweh. The prophet is not concerned with practical politics — the arguments in favour of and against siding with Egypt or Babylon — but rather with the inevitable

---

[154] Cf. Ezekiel 16:29. The ambiguities inherent in the MT *way'bî'ēhû 'el 'eres K'na'an* ("he brought him to the land of Canaan [= traders]") are noted in Greenberg, *Ezekiel 1-20*, 310, 321.

[155] Zimmerli, *Ezechiel*, 380f.

[156] As Greenberg comments: "Nothing in vss. 5-7 suggests that the first eagle begrudged the vine anything that would enhance its glory — as a vine" (*Ezekiel 1-20*, 312). The image of a vine is not in itself necessarily negative, especially when it is that of a vine planted beside water (cf. Ezek. 19:10).

[157] Lang, *Kein Aufstand*, 47.

[158] W.H. Brownlee favours the latter alternative (*Ezekiel 1-19*, WBC [Waco 1986] 268).

[159] V. Korošec, *Hethitische Staatsverträge. Ein Beitrag zu ihrer iuristischen Wertung*, LRWS 60 (Leipzig 1931) 21-35.

[160] G.E. Mendenhall, "Puppy and Lettuce in Northwest-Semitic Covenant Making", *BASOR* 133 (1954) 30 n.16; M. Tsevat, "The Neo Assyrian and Neo Babylonian Vassal Oaths and the Prophet Ezekiel", *JBL* 78 (1959) 199f.; C.T. Begg, "*b'rît* in Ezekiel", *Proceedings of the Ninth World Congress of Jewish Studies* (Jerusalem 1986) 77; Zimmerli, *Ezechiel*, 386. This interpretation is questioned by Greenberg (*Ezekiel 1-20*, 322), who understands "My covenant" as literally Yahweh's covenant with Israel (cf. Ezek. 16:59). If Nebuchadnezzar will punish a rebel, how much more Yahweh! Cf. Hals, *Ezekiel*, 117.

consequences of disobedience.[161] The one who chooses the greener grass on the other side of the fence will find, to his cost, that Yahweh has the power to make green grass brown and vice versa (cf. v.24). Judgement on the one who has transgressed is inevitable.

2 *Ezekiel 19*

This chapter contains a lament for the $n^e\acute{s}\hat{i}'\hat{i}m$ of Israel. Again the language is pictorial, using the images of a mother lion and two lion cubs and of a vine. The vexed question of the identity of the mother lion and of the identities of the cubs has been much discussed.[162] The first of the lion cubs, deported to Egypt in v.4, is clearly Jehoahaz.[163] The choice for the second lion cub, deported to Babylon in v.9 is usually seen as lying between Jehoiachin or Zedekiah.[164] In favour of the latter choice, it has been argued that the "mother" in Ezekiel 19 is a reference to the queen mother, Hamutal, who was the mother of both Jehoahaz and Zedekiah.[165] However, in considering kings who had suffered deportation it seems unlikely that Ezekiel would have left out any reference to the king with whom he had shared this fate.[166] It seems therefore best to identify the "mother" as Israel, as is certainly the case in v.10, and the two kings as Jehoahaz and Jehoiachin. Their behaviour is described in v.3 and v.6f. Of the first lion, it is simply said: "He learned to catch prey and he devoured men". Of the second lion cub the verdict is fuller:

> He learned to catch prey; he devoured men. ⁷And he ravaged[167] their strongholds [or "He did evil to their widows"?],[168] and laid waste their cities; and the land was appalled and all who were in it at the sound of his roaring.

---

[161] Eichrodt, *Hesekiel*, 142f.; Hammershaimb, "Monarchy", 57.

[162] For a discussion of the alternatives, see Zimmerli, *Ezechiel*, 423f.; Eichrodt, *Hesekiel*, 162; C.T. Begg, "The Identity of the Princes in Ezekiel 19; Some Reflections", *EThL* 65 (1989) 358-69.

[163] He was deported to Egypt by Pharaoh Neco according to 2 Kings 23:33.

[164] However, Begg prefers a third option, Jehoiakim ("Princes in Ez 19", 368).

[165] Cf. 2 Kings 23:31; 24:18. So e.g. C. von Orelli, *Das Buch Ezechiel und die zwölf kleinen Propheten* (Nördlingen 1888) 73; Fohrer & Galling, *Ezechiel*, 106; I. Kottsieper, "'Was ist deine Mutter?' Eine Studie zu Ez 19:2-9", *ZAW* 105 (1993) 456.

[166] So Zimmerli, *Ezechiel*, 423; Greenberg, *Ezekiel 1-20*, 356. Cf. Fishbane, "Sin and Judgement", 144.

[167] Reading *wayyāra'* (Hiph. of *r''*) for *wayyēda'*. Cf. Zimmerli, *Ezechiel*, 418; Kottsieper, "Ez 19:2-9", 448.

[168] Zimmerli suggests reading *'alm'nôtām* for *'alm'nôtāyw*, understanding *'alm'nôt* as the same as *'arm'nôt*, "citadels" (*Ezechiel*, 418; Cf. Isa. 13:22). Against this see C.F. Keil, *Biblischer Commentar über den Propheten Ezechiel* (Leipzig ²1882) 161. However, in favour of understanding *'alm'nôt* in its more usual sense of "widows" compare with Ezekiel 22:25. This verse seems to be a kind of parallel to Ezekiel 19:6 and describes the activities of the $n^e\acute{s}\hat{i}'\hat{i}m$ (see p.19, n.61) as "like a roaring lion tearing the prey; they have devoured people; they have taken treasure and precious things; they have made many widows (*'alm'nôtêhā*) in her midst". Greenberg takes the MT as it stands as "He knew (i.e. he had experience of) his widows" (*Ezekiel 1-20*, 351).

It has been suggested that the carnivorous blood lust exhibited by these young lions is not to be understood as a blameworthy feature, but rather as describing the normal growth and development of the king within the chosen metaphor.[169] That seems unlikely in view of the use to which this same metaphor is put in Ezekiel 22:25 (cf. Jer. 2:15). Rather, it seems probable that Ezekiel exploited the ambiguity which is inherent within the metaphor.[170] The comparison of kings and lions was old and well established, yet contained within that imagery is the possibility of powerful men acting like wild beasts which have the capacity to empty the land (cf. 2 Ki. 17:26). A poetic figure which in some contexts is strongly positive (Gen. 49:9; Deut. 33:20) can equally in other contexts become a figure of fierce cruelty (Prov. 28:15; Nah. 2:12-14).[171] As in the fable of chapter 17, judgement is coming—a judgement which rests in this case, however, upon the whole series of kings from Jehoahaz on. If the language of verses 3 and 6 is stereotyped, it is because the sins of these kings are similarly stereotyped, no longer now the political sins of chapter 17 but the moral sin of oppressing their people.[172]

The latter part of Ezekiel 19 compares the last ruler of Judah to a stem of a vine:

> [10]Your mother was like a vine in a vineyard transplanted by the water, fruitful and full of branches by reason of abundant water. [11]Its strongest stem became a ruler's sceptre; it towered aloft among the clouds;[173] it was seen in its height with the mass of its branches. [12]But the vine was plucked up in fury, cast down to the ground; the east wind dried it up; its fruit was stripped off, its strong stem was withered; the fire consumed it. [13]Now it is transplanted in the wilderness, in a dry and thirsty land. [14]And fire has gone out from its stem, has consumed its branches and fruit, so that there remains in it no strong stem, no sceptre for a ruler. This is a lamentation, and has become a lamentation.

The sin attributed to the vine branch is pride (v.11).[174] It had exalted itself among the clouds and was conspicuous for its height (compare the similar condemnation of Egypt in Ezekiel 31:10f.).[175] This bough is the last king of Judah, and thus represents Zedekiah. The result of such hubris will be to bring disaster upon the whole nation. Thus Ezekiel 19 adds the charges of pride and oppression to the register of the offences of the monarchy,

---

[169] Zimmerli, *Ezechiel*, 425.
[170] Hals, *Ezekiel*, 129.
[171] Greenberg, *Ezekiel 1-20*, 357; R.W. Klein, *Ezekiel: the Prophet and his Message* (Columbia 1988) 120.
[172] Lang, *Kein Aufstand*, 106.
[173] Hebrew *ʿăbōtîm*; RSV translates: "thick boughs". For the rendering given here, see Greenberg, *Ezekiel 1-20*, 353.
[174] Greenberg, *Ezekiel 1-20*, 353.
[175] Klein, *Ezekiel*, 120.

with pride being particularly associated with Zedekiah while the charge of
oppression is more broadly aimed at two of the last kings of Judah.

3 Ezekiel 21:30-32[25-27]

This is a curse oracle addressed to Zedekiah as reigning nāśî' of Israel:[176]

> And you, O unhallowed wicked one, nāśî' of Israel, whose day has come,
> the time of your final punishment,[26]thus says the Lord God: "Remove the
> turban, and take off the crown; things shall not remain as they are; exalt that
> which is low, and abase that which is high.[27]A ruin, ruin, ruin I will make
> it; there shall not be even a trace of it until he comes to whom judgement
> belongs,[177] and to him I will give it".

Zedekiah's sins are not spelled out in detail in this passage. However, the
description of Zedekiah as a "profane and wicked one" (ḥalāl rāšāʿ)[178]
would seem most probably to have reference to the oathbreaking cited in
chapter 17.[179] He has committed sacrilege by profaning a holy oath: thus he
is named ḥālāl: godless.[180] The result will be not only disaster for the king
but the upheaval of the order of society. The king will be stripped of his
insignia, the turban (miṣnepet)[181] and the crown (ʿᵃṭārâ), and will be cast
off his throne. This is, however, merely symptomatic of a more general
turning of social relationships on their heads, whereby the low become
exalted and the lofty are brought low.[182] Unlike chapter 17, this oracle
closes with no word of hope: the final word is God's judgement, given over
into the hands of the Babylonians. Zedekiah was the last straw in the
iniquity of Israel's rulers.[183] To rub in the point, Ezekiel reshapes the old
saying of Genesis 49:10: the sceptre will never depart from Judah until...
Nebuchadnezzar comes![184]

---

[176] Zimmerli states that with the nāśî' of Israel "nur Zedekia gemeint sein kann" (Ezechiel, 492).

[177] RSV "whose right it is". For mišpāṭ as "judgement" rather than "right", cf. the similar use of nātattî mišpāṭ in Ezekiel 23:24. Cf. W.L. Moran, "Gen 49:10 and its Use in Ez 21:32", Biblica 39 (1958) 422-5; L. Allen, Ezekiel 20-48, 28.

[178] Zimmerli prefers to take it as a construct phrase, pointed ḥᵃlal rāšāʿ, on the basis of v.34.

[179] Vawter & Hoppe, Ezekiel, 108. As a further link between these chapters, note also the common themes of exalting the low and abasing the high in Ezekiel 17:24 and 21:31[26].

[180] Lang, Kein Aufstand, 117.

[181] This was also apparently part of the dress of the High Priest, according to Exodus 28f.; Leviticus 8.

[182] Eichrodt, Hesekiel, 198; L. Allen, Ezekiel 20-48, 28.

[183] Gronkowski, Messianisme, 40.

[184] On this see Moran, "Ez. 21:32", 405-425; A. Caquot, "Le Messianisme d'Ezechiel", Semitica 14 (1964) 15.

4 *Ezekiel 22*

In Ezekiel 22 we encounter a catalogue of the crimes of Jerusalem. Prominent among those accused of wrongdoing are the *neśî'îm* (vv. 6 and 25).[185] The plural form (*neśî'ê yiśrā'ēl*, v.6; *"šer neśî'êha*, v.25) raises the question of whether those so designated are a series of the former kings or the lesser rank of *neśî'îm* which we found in Ezekiel 7:27 and 32:29.[186] The commentators mostly choose to identify them as the former kings of Judah, often without even considering the other option.[187] This is not without some justification; the former identification is almost certainly the correct one, as may be seen by comparing Ezekiel 22:25 with Ezekiel 19:1,6f., where the *neśî'ê yiśrā'ēl* are definitely the former kings of Judah. Yet a neglected corollary of this identification is the historical nature of the condemnation in this chapter which it implies. If not only Zedekiah is in view but also his predecessors, then it is not simply the present sins of Jerusalem which are under indictment but also the sins of at least the recent past. This suggests that the Hebrew perfect tenses of v.6f. should all be translated by English perfects: "In you, there have been...". Most commentators and translations translate at least some of these as present tenses without any justification.[188] If a present tense is understood then the *neśî'îm* must surely be understood in the lower sense of "members of the royal house", an interpretation which we have rejected above.

The crimes with which the former kings are charged are once more bloodshed and judicial robbery: "each has used his power to shed blood in you" (v.6) and

> her princes (*neśî'îm*) in the midst of her are like a roaring lion tearing the prey; they have devoured human lives; they have taken treasure and precious things; they have made many widows in the midst of her (v.25).

Here the latter verse simply repeats with greater detail the allegations of v.6. We saw a similar charge made against the *neśî'îm* in chapter 19;[189] it is one which was frequently made elsewhere in the Old Testament.[190] Quite

---

[185] On the text of v.25 see p.19, n.61.
[186] See above, p.20.
[187] E.g. Zimmerli, *Ezechiel*, 524; L. Allen, *Ezekiel 20-48*, 36. But see Hitzig, *Ezechiel*, 161; Cooke, *Ezekiel*, 244 for the latter interpretation, at least as regards v.25. The language of some commentators is unclear and could support either interpretation, e.g. Eichrodt, *Hesekiel*, 209.
[188] NKJV translates v.6-8 by perfects and 9ff. by present tenses; RSV, L. Allen translate v.6 and 8 as perfect, v.7,9ff. as present; NIV translates v.7f. as perfect, v.6,9ff. as present; Eichrodt (*Hesekiel*, 203) treats them all as present (omitting v.8); Zimmerli (*Ezechiel*, 502) treats only v.6 as perfect.
[189] See above, p.35.
[190] Cf. 2 Kings 21:16; 24:4; Jeremiah 22:13-19.

simply, the former kings of Judah have abused their position for their own material gain, even at cost of the lives of others.

5 *Ezekiel 34:1-16*

In Ezekiel 34:2, the prophet is commanded "to prophesy against the shepherds of Israel". Who is denoted by the term "shepherds"? The title "shepherd" is a commonplace for both kings and gods in the ancient Near East. For example, Hammurabi describes himself as "the shepherd who brings salvation and whose staff is righteous" and Merodach-baladan II is called "the shepherd who gathers together again those who have strayed".[191] The protective king stood as the representative of the divine shepherd who appointed him.[192] In this picture, however, Yahweh is coming in judgement upon his shepherds because of their failure to fulfil this role properly. This passage seems to have been brought over and expanded from Jeremiah 23.[193] The central thrust remains the same as in Jeremiah, where the former kings of Judah, Jehoiakim and Zedekiah, are held responsible for the deportation of 597 BC and subsequent events because of their wrongdoing.[194] They have ruled harshly and brutally, feeding only themselves, not the flock, and even slaughtering the choicest animals (Ezek. 34:2ff.). Lemke has pointed out that "to rule with harshness" (*rādâ b*'*pārek*) is only found in two other passages in the Old Testament: in Exodus 1:13f. it refers to the manner in which the Egyptians treated their Hebrew slaves, and in Leviticus 25:43,46 it is forbidden to treat a fellow Israelite in this manner. Ezekiel thus accuses the rulers of doing what their own history should have taught them to abhor and what the law of Moses expressly forbade.[195]

In at least some passages in the Old Testament the term "shepherds" seems to take on a wider connotation, indicating a broader spectrum of leadership than just the ruling king. Thus according to Willmes:

---

[191] L. Dürr, *Ursprung und Ausbau der israelitisch-jüdischen Heilandserwartung; ein Beitrag zur Theologie des Alten Testamentes* (Berlin 1925) 118f.

[192] Zimmerli, *Ezechiel*, 835.

[193] J.W. Miller, *Das Verhältnis Jeremias und Hesekiels sprachlich und theologisch untersucht* (Assen 1955) 106; Zimmerli, *Ezechiel*, 835; B. Gosse, "La Nouvelle Alliance et les Promesses d'Avenir se Référant à David dans les Livres de Jérémie, Ezéchiel et Isaie", *VT* 41 (1991) 424. For a contrary view, seeing merely dependence on the same broad stream of tradition, see Hals, *Ezekiel*, 251; W. Gross, "Israel's Hope for the Renewal of the State", *JNSL* 14 (1988) 125.

[194] W. McKane, *Jeremiah 1-25*, ICC (Edinburgh 1986) 555, 559.

[195] W. Lemke, "Life in the Present and Hope in the Future", *Interp.* 38 (1984) 173 n.10.

> Neben Jahwe werden auch die politischen Führer im AT häufiger als Hirten
> bezeichnet...Meist sind es Gruppen, die führenden Kreise, die als "Hirten"
> bezeichnet werden.[196]

In Jeremiah 25:34ff. the "shepherds" (hārō'îm) are found in parallel with
the phrase "leaders of the flock" ('addîrê haṣṣō'n) and act together as a
group, wailing, finding no place to flee and being slaughtered. The implication seems clear that at least in that passage a wider circle of leadership
than simply kings is under consideration.[197] Is the same also true of Ezekiel
34? Should we see in the condemnation a word against the leadership of
Israel in its entirety, at least in a secondary sense?[198] Such a possibility is
made less likely by two considerations in regard to Ezekiel 34. First, in
addition to the oracle against the shepherds, there is also an oracle against
the fat sheep which seems directed at the other persons with authority in
Judah, the whole ruling class.[199] Second, the solution to the problem of bad
shepherds is one good shepherd, the new David, who acts as the true
earthly representative of the divine shepherd (v. 23f.).[200] We shall have
more to say concerning this new political leader below;[201] for now suffice
it to note that he is a single ruler, "one shepherd", rather than a group
(contrast Jer. 23:4!). Therefore it seems best to understand the "shepherds"
as having reference to the former kings of Judah.[202]

The condemnation of the shepherds is for similar offences to those we
have already seen: self-interest, oppression of the people and a lack of
concern for them. For that they will be held accountable by Yahweh and
removed from office (v.10) so that they can be replaced by a shepherd after
God's own heart, the new David.

6 Ezekiel 43:7-9

Chapters 40-48 of the book of Ezekiel are normally described as Ezekiel's
constitutional design for the future. However, this future orientation is in
no way divorced from the past; in fact, as we shall see, its shape is strong-

---

[196]   Hirtenallegorie, 311.
[197]   Similarly in Zechariah 11:4ff., a passage which seems to owe something to Ezekiel 34.
Cf. P. Lamarche, Zacharie 9-14. Structure Littéraire et Messianisme (Paris 1961) 66ff.
[198]   Thus Klein, Ezekiel, 121; A. Cody, Ezekiel, Old Testament Message (Wilmington
1984) 164; Hitzig, Ezechiel, 262; Hossfeld, Untersuchungen, 257.
[199]   Willmes, Hirtenallegorie, 511. On this passage see below, p.121f.
[200]   These verses are often seen as an expansion, with the setting of a man alongside the
divine judge being thought "überraschen[d]" (Zimmerli, Ezechiel, 841). In view of the
evidence which Zimmerli adduced earlier for a close connection between the divine shepherd
and the protective king (835), it is rather Zimmerli's own position which is surprising! H.
Gottlieb remarks: "YHWH der Besitzer der Herde ist, der den König als seinen Hirten
eingesetzt hat" ("Die Tradition von David als Hirten", VT 17 [1967] 196).
[201]   See below, p.47.
[202]   Hölscher, Hesekiel, 169; D.M.G. Stalker, Ezekiel, Torch Biblical Commentaries
(London 1968) 242; J. Blenkinsopp, Ezekiel, Interpretation (Louisville 1990) 156.

ly influenced by the contours of past events. Just as in chapters 1-24 his condemnation of the past is laced with a thin thread of hope for the future, so in these chapters his hope for the future includes elements which explicitly or implicitly condemn the past—always, however, in the context of a statement that things in the future will no longer be as they were in the past. The first of these elements is found in Ezekiel 43:7-9, a passage strongly condemnatory of the people of Judah, and with them their former kings:

> [7]And he said to me, "Son of man, this is the place of my throne and the place of the soles of my feet, where I will dwell in the midst of the people of Israel for ever. And the house of Israel shall no more defile my holy name, neither they, nor their kings, by their harlotry, and by the memorial stelae[203] of their kings,[204] [8]by setting their threshold by my threshold and their doorposts beside my doorposts, with only a wall between me and them. They have defiled my holy name by their abominations which they have committed, so I have consumed them in my anger.[9]Now let them put away their idolatry and the memorial stelae of their kings far from me, and I will dwell in their midst for ever."

The first thing to notice about this passage is that it is only parenthetically critical of the former kings: the primary object of critique is *the people*. It is "the house of Israel" which is charged with defiling the divine name by their harlotry (*z'nûtām* = idolatrous worship[205]): the memorial stelae of their kings (*pigrê malkêhem*) merely serve as an example of this faithlessness. The setting up of a memorial stele to the dead king by his son appears to have been part of a "cult of the dead", known from Ugarit.[206] To find such within the Temple area itself was a double abomination. Yet even this sin is not charged simply to the former kings: the responsibility for keeping the *pigrê malkêhem* away from Yahweh is assigned to the *people*, not to the priests or *n'śî'îm* (v.9). It may be that the people are being charged with too close an identification of the king with Yahweh, an identification which resulted in Yahweh's holy name being defiled by the king's detestable practices (v.8). It was an identification which was encouraged by the

---

[203] RSV: "dead bodies". On the *pigrê malkêhem*, see D. Neiman, "*PGR*: A Canaanite Cult Object in the Old Testament", *JBL* 67 (1948) 55-60; Zimmerli, *Ezechiel*, 1082; K. Galling, "Erwägungen zum Stelenheiligtum von Hazor", *ZDPV* 75 (1959) 11f.; for an alternative explanation of *pigrîm* as offerings for the dead, see J.H. Ebach, "*PGR* = (Toten-)Opfer", *UF* 3 (1971) 365-8. The most recent treatments of the subject maintain a diversity of views: T.J. Lewis mentions Ebach's view favourably, but retains Neiman's rendition as "memorial stelae" (*Cults of the Dead in Ancient Israel and Ugarit*, HSM 39 [Atlanta 1989] 141), while E. Bloch-Smith takes it as a literal reference to corpses, as in the RSV (*Judahite Burial Practices and Beliefs about the Dead*, JSOTS 123 [Sheffield 1992] 116, 119).

[204] In favour of revocalizing MT *bāmôtām* ("their high places") as *b'môtām* ("at their death") see L. Allen, *Ezekiel 20-48*, 243; Zimmerli, *Ezechiel*, 1082; J. Ebach, "*PGR* = (Toten-)Opfer", 368.

[205] Zimmerli, *Ezechiel*, 1083.

[206] See Lewis, *Cults of the Dead*, 95-97, 174.

location of the old Temple as part of the palace complex (v.8); this too will change in Ezekiel's plan. The former kings certainly do not escape reproach here—they too were guilty of harlotry (v.7) and it was Israel's kings who were responsible for locating the Temple and palace together in the first place—yet their condemnation is parenthetical rather than central to the thrust of this passage. In the future the kings of Israel will be put in their place—but only as part of a comprehensive programme of putting the whole of the House of Israel in its place (v.10f.).

This is the only passage in chapters 40-48 which uses the word *m^elāk-îm*, "kings", rather than *nāśî'*. The exact reasoning behind the choice of word here cannot be determined with certainty. Most likely it is due to the historical nature of the charges brought: this was not simply a problem during the last days of the monarchy, when vassal kings reigned, but throughout the history of the monarchy, even during the days of those who merited the title *melek*. But again it needs to be emphasized that Ezekiel's usage is capable of alternating between these terms without particular distinction.

This passage thus adds the charge of cultic abominations to the account of the former kings, along with the political and moral sins noted earlier. Yet that charge is itself only an aside in a word against the people of Israel as a whole, including the former kings in the sins of the people rather than singling them out for special blame as they are for the other sins.

7 *Ezekiel 45:8-9*

> My princes[207] shall no more oppress my people; but they shall let the house of Israel have the land according to their tribes. [9]"Thus says the Lord God: Enough, O princes of Israel! Put away violence and oppression, and execute justice and righteousness; cease your evictions of my people, says the Lord God.

These verses follow the summary of the distribution of the land in Ezekiel 45:1-7, which concludes with the allocation for the *nāśî'*. This allocation itself stimulates the remembrance of past abuses by the *n^eśî'îm* which will become but a memory in the future state, just as consideration of the entrances and exits of the Temple in Ezekiel 44:5 leads to discussion of past abuses in that area. The abuses of the *n^eśî'îm* are familiar enough from the earlier chapters: oppressing the people by taking their land in v.8, violence and oppression in v.9 and use of crooked measures in v.10ff.[208] A similar note is sounded again in Ezekiel 46:18 with its insistence that the

---

[207] Perhaps read "the princes of Israel" (*n^eśî'ê yiśrā'ēl* instead of *n^eśî'ay*)? See above, p.26 n.100.
[208] On this last offence see below, p.52 n.268.

nāśî' shall not take any of the inheritance of the people, displacing them by force. These themes are so familiar from elsewhere in the prophetic books that there is no need to place the origin of these verses in a supposed desire to limit the power of an historical figure in exilic or post-exilic history.[209] The criticism is rather directed at the final kings of Judah: the charge is oppression, injustice and violence.[210]

We have thus found a consistent pattern of offences stressed throughout the book of Ezekiel, especially violence, oppression, and injustice. The former kings are judged to have ruled harshly and out of self-interest, at the expense of the people. Zedekiah is singled out for particularly strong criticism, and accused of sacrilegious oath-breaking and pride. The result of these offences was the overthrow of the kingdom and the downfall of the monarchy. The exalted had been brought down: things would no longer be the same. We may note in passing, however, what things the kings are *not* accused of: there is no accusation of responsibility for cultic sin or idolatry, except for the parenthetical inclusion of the former kings in the abominations of the people in Ezekiel 43:7-9. In particular, they are strikingly absent from chapters 8-11 where that accusation is centred.

D. The Future of Royal Leadership in the Book of Ezekiel

What then of the future? Standing at the null-point of the exile and envisioning the future shape of the nation of Israel, what was Ezekiel's conception of the future of royal leadership? As was the case with his criticism of royal leadership, his affirmations concerning the future of that institution are scattered throughout the book. In the following sections we shall examine all the relevant passages.

1 *Ezekiel 12:10-14; 21:29-32[24-7]: The Fate of Zedekiah*

These two passages spell out the outlook for Zedekiah personally. Ezekiel 12:10-14 is addressed to "the *nāśî'* in Jerusalem", i.e. Zedekiah. In it, he is promised exile to Babylon and death there along with his people. The king's fate had been intertwined with that of his city for a long time in the ancient Near East, so this message would hardly have come as a surprise.[211] Ezekiel is simply underlining the fact that the future for Zedekiah is bleak,

---

[209] So Gese, *Verfassungsentwurf*, 116.
[210] Levenson, *Theology*, 113.
[211] Lang, *Kein Aufstand*, 21.

as it is also for Jerusalem. The reasons for that bleak outlook are not stated in this section.

Ezekiel 21:29-32[24-7] is similarly vague about the nature of Zedekiah's offences,[212] but equally sure about the outcome: personal—and deserved—disaster for the one whose day of final punishment has come (v.30[25]). The symbols of royalty will be removed and he will be handed over for judgement into the hands of Yahweh's instrument of wrath.

2 Ezekiel 17:22-24

A note of hope is added in these verses to the fable of the two eagles. Just as in the fable an eagle came and carried off a cedar sprig, planting a low spreading vine in its place—depicting Nebuchadnezzar's installation of Zedekiah as a vassal king—so Yahweh himself will install a vassal king on "a high and prominent mountain", which can only be Mt. Zion.[213] The note of reversal of what has gone before is very clear: the future will not be like the past. The high tree will be brought down and the low tree exalted (v.24). In contrast to the vine which rebelled and will wither (vv. 7-10), the cedar of Yahweh's planting will thrive and bear fruit (v.23).[214] Nor is it simply a matter of rescuing the cedar sprig which has been carried off to Babylon and restoring Jehoiachin to the throne.[215] Yahweh will go back to the source, as it were, for a new shoot (v.22). A fresh start will be made—though still from the same cedar tree.[216] As in chapters 12 and 21, no hope is held out for the vine—Zedekiah. He is condemned to die in Babylon (v.16). Yet, for Ezekiel, the death of the contemporary Davidides does not mean the end of the road for the Davidic monarchy. A new sprig from that same tree will be planted and will flourish under the blessing of Yahweh's protection.

According to Levenson, the reversal envisaged here includes a diminution of the office of kingship. He sees the essence of this passage as a formal analogy: "YHWH is to the messiah as Nebuchadnezzar is to Zedek-

---

[212] Ezekiel 21:29[24] says simply: "you have made your guilt to be remembered,...your transgressions are uncovered, so that in all your doings your sins appear", without describing the nature of the offences more closely.

[213] Levenson, *Theology*, 7; Hitzig, *Ezechiel*, 121; Eichrodt, *Hesekiel*, 141; Keil, *Ezechiel*, 151.

[214] S. Herrmann identifies the cedar as the Temple rather than as a king (*Die Prophetischen Heilserwartungen im Alten Testament*, BWANT 5 [Stuttgart 1965] 256); similarly Ebach, *Kritik und Utopie*, 275f. However, in order to do this he has to suppose that these verses are unrelated to what has gone before, which seems rather unlikely.

[215] *Contra* e.g. R.S. Foster ("A Note on Ezekiel xvii:1-10 and 22-24", *VT* 8 (1958) 379) who sees the prophet's hope as lying in a restoration of Jehoiachin.

[216] Compare this conception with Isaiah 11:1, where a shoot is expected "from the stump of Jesse". Even while the royal house may stand condemned, the hope of a new David is kept alive. Cf. O. Kaiser, *Der Prophet Jesaja. Kapitel 1-12*, ATD (Göttingen ²1963) 125f. Note also the similarity of Isaiah 10:33b and Ezekiel 17:24.

iah".[217] On this conception the messiah becomes simply a figurehead king
with no effective power: He is "the king who holds office by virtue of the
stipulations of the covenant only, the inhabitant of Zion whose office is
valid only to the extent to which it is governed by Sinai".[218] The analogy
which Levenson points out certainly underlies the passage, but it is doubtful
that such a radical re-writing of Israelite kingship should be read into it.
The understanding of the king as Yahweh's vassal would hardly have been
viewed as an innovation:[219] it is, for example, the understanding behind the
law of the King in Deuteronomy 17:14ff. What is more, such a diminished
conception of the office of king hardly seems to do justice to the imagery
of the passage itself. If the cedar sprig is the coming king, then the projected growth into a majestic cedar which provides shade for birds of all kinds
surely suggests the greatness of this king, a greatness at least comparable
to the greatness of the kings of old.[220] If there is an analogy between the
status of the future king and of Zedekiah in that each is the vassal of a
more exalted figure, there is also a crucial difference: in circumstances
suitable for maximal growth, Zedekiah only became a low vine (v.6)
whereas the coming king will become a lofty tree.[221] Though compared to
Yahweh the coming king will be a vassal, compared to the kings of the
earth he will be recognized as a mighty figure (v.24).

The thrust of this oracle is very straightforward: in spite of the failure
of the individual Davidic kings and the doom which has been pronounced
upon them, there remains a future for the Davidic line. The concrete details
of the shape of that future are, however, not spelled out in this passage.[222]

3 Ezekiel 19

The opening and closing verses of this chapter indicate the fundamentally
negative outlook envisaged for the $n^e\acute{s}\hat{i}'\hat{i}m$: this chapter is "a lamentation
($q\hat{i}n\hat{a}$) for the $n^e\acute{s}\hat{i}'\hat{e}\ yi\acute{s}r\bar{a}'\bar{e}l$" (Ezek. 19:1,14). A lamentation is only appropriate in the context of death;[223] it means in this context the death of hope
not simply for Jehoiachin (Ezek. 19:9),[224] but a judgement upon all existing

---

[217] Levenson, *Theology*, 80.

[218] Levenson, *Theology*, 81.

[219] Cf. K. Seybold, *Das davidische Königtum im Zeugnis der Propheten*, FRLANT 107 (Göttingen 1972) 139.

[220] Compare the similar imagery used in Daniel 4 to depict the exalted status of Nebuchadnezzar.

[221] C. Feinberg, *The Prophecy of Ezekiel* (Chicago 1969) 98.

[222] Lang, *Kein Aufstand*, 86.

[223] Note the comment of Hals (*Ezekiel*, 130): "To conduct a dirge beside the hospital bed of a still living patient would be incredibly crass".

[224] Zimmerli notes: "Indem Ez die Deportation Jojachins mit derjenigen des Joahas in einer einzigen Klage zusammenbindet, verkündet er über Jojachin, was Jer 22:10 in früherem Zeitpunkt über Joahas sagte: 'Er kehrt nicht mehr zurück'" (*Ezechiel*, 428).

members of the Davidic dynasty. Of the vine it must now be said: "There remains in it no strong stem, no sceptre for a ruler" (Ezek. 19:14). Thus this passage joins in the condemnation of the existing Davidic kings which we saw above in chapter 17. There is, however, in this chapter no mention of the hope of a positive future which was expressed in that context.

Because of that absence of hope, some commentators have seen in this chapter the complete end of the monarchy, never to return. Vawter & Hoppe express this viewpoint in the following terms:

> What is obvious is that Ezekiel is writing the *finis* to the Davidic dynasty... With [Jehoiachin] the dynasty ended. As we shall see, in the ideal Israel of the future Ezekiel makes room, as a matter of protocol, for a Davidic "ruler".[225]

Such a perspective is unduly negative about the role assigned to the *nāśî'* in the future, as we shall demonstrate below. Moreover, it is particularly inappropriate to argue for such a distinction in status between the past kings of Judah and the future "rulers" on the basis of a chapter which uses precisely the same terminology for the former kings of Judah (*nᵉśî'ê yiśrā'ēl*) as the rest of the book does for those future rulers of the restored people (cf. Ezek. 45:9)! To be sure, an end is spoken of for the Davidic dynasty, just as we have seen elsewhere in Ezekiel. However, it is an end which does not inherently rule out the possibility of a new beginning by means of divine intervention and for the sake of the divine name,[226] though to be sure such a new beginning is not explicitly promised here.[227]

4 Ezekiel 34:23-24

Ezekiel 34 presents the same general progression of thought as chapter 17: the failure of the past rulers, the divine response of punishing those responsible, and divine intervention to reverse the failure of the past.[228] Unlike chapter 17, however, the focus of attention in this chapter is not the monarch's external political relationships, but rather his actions towards his own people. Ezekiel 34:23f. affirms that the oppression and misrule of the former kings will not be repeated in the days to come. The text is as follows:

> ²³And I will set up over them one shepherd, my servant David, and he shall feed them: he shall feed them and be their shepherd. ²⁴And I, the Lord, will

---

²²⁵ Vawter & Hoppe, *Ezekiel*, 101.
²²⁶ Cf. Ezekiel 37:1-14 where a scene redolent with death gives way to unexpected new life through the intervention of the spirit of Yahweh.
²²⁷ Zimmerli, *Ezechiel*, 431.
²²⁸ Levenson, *Theology*, 86.

be their God, and my servant David shall be prince among them; I, the Lord, have spoken.

According to Ezekiel 34, the expected change in Israel's governance will be accomplished not so much through a change in the nature of the *office* but through a change in the nature of the *occupant*. Future Israel is to be led by a shepherd, as was supposedly the case in the past. The contrast will be in the way in which he carries out his role. In the past, the shepherds abdicated their proper responsibilities of nurturing the weak of the flock and protecting them from the strong (v.4,8). Zedekiah's rulership was not marked by political strength but rather by political weakness. This can be illustrated in a variety of ways from the book of Jeremiah. For example, he is unable to carry through the covenant of freedom for the slaves against the opposition of the royal officials (*haśśārîm*)[229] and the people (Jer. 34:10). When the officials (*haśśārîm*) come to him later and demand the death of Jeremiah, his answer is revealing: "Behold he is in your hands; for the king can do nothing against you" (Jer. 38:5). Later in that same chapter, Zedekiah warns Jeremiah not to tell the officials (*haśśārîm*) what their conversation was about, lest the officials kill Jeremiah (v.24ff.). The picture we gather is of a man unable to control his own officers,[230] perhaps because he was regarded by many as simply the regent for Jehoiachin.[231] In the light of this past history, what Judah requires is not a weak, depoliticized king but a strong shepherd.

It is no coincidence, therefore, that the announcement of the new earthly shepherd in Ezekiel 34:23 follows directly after the proclamation of divine intervention to judge between sheep and sheep, in order to protect the weak from the strong (vv. 20-22). Only the stronger can protect against the strong. Strength and service are the two features emphasized in the description of the new ruler.[232] The strength of his position is made clear first: "I will set up over them one shepherd, my servant David" (v.23a). He will be "established" (Hifil of *qwm*), a term with monarchical overtones connected to the traditions of the election of David.[233] His position will be "over them [i.e. the people]" (*ʿlêhem*), that is, in a position of authority and

---

[229] On the meaning of this term see below, p.110.
[230] T. Overholt, *The Threat of Falsehood. A Study in the Theology of the Book of Jeremiah*, SBT 16 (London 1970) 32.
[231] Zimmerli, *Ezechiel*, 44.
[232] Note the comment of D.R. Yates: "*ʿebed* suggests that the new Davidic leader is a *servant* of a new covenant, whereas *nāśîʾ* helps to retain the idea of princely dignity on the part of Israel's new ruler" (*The Eschatological Message Concerning Man in the Book of Ezekiel*; Ph.D. diss., Boston University 1972, 182).
[233] For hifil of *qwm* with the promise to David cf. 2 Samuel 7:12,25; 1 Kings 9:5; Jeremiah 33:14; Amos 9:11. For hifil of *qwm* with shepherds in the sense of rulers cf. Micah 5:4ff.

strength.[234] The uniqueness of his position is further underlined by the description of him as "*one* shepherd"; this is in contrast not simply to the two shepherds of Israel and Judah, as in chapter 37,[235] but to the many shepherds of the opening verses of the chapter. In contrast to the many shepherds, who have failed the flock repeatedly down through the history of Judah, will come one shepherd singlehandedly able to meet the needs of the flock.

That there is no diminution of power in this office may further be seen by the king identified by Ezekiel as the model of this kind of kingship: the new king will be another David. The name "David" had powerful overtones for Ezekiel's hearers. It spoke of the time when Israel's greatness was at its zenith and when the country was united.[236] The name of David was associated with preparations for the construction of the first Temple.[237] It was also associated with Yahweh's election of Israel: the promise of permanence for the ruling house in 2 Samuel 7 became linked with Yahweh's commitment to his chosen people.[238] More even than that, however, was the recollection of David as the one king who, if not perfect, was the archetypal man of integrity (1 Ki. 3:6; 9:4), the man "after Yahweh's own heart" (1 Sam. 13:14). He is the picture of a strong king who ruled with justice and fairness.[239]

This clear affirmation of the power of the coming ruler should serve as a balance against the common tendency to focus exclusively on the servant nature of this coming king. Such a viewpoint is typified by Zimmerli, who sees in the terminology *hannāśî' ᵃšer bᵉtôkām* ("the prince who is in their midst") one who holds office in Israel but is not Israel's ruler, and raises the question of whether this does not betray already a step along the road to the conception of the *nāśî'* of chapters 40-48.[240] Similarly, Klein lays great stress on the preposition *bᵉtôk*:

---

[234] Cf. Ezekiel 37:24, where David my servant is said to be "king over them" (*melek ᵃlêhem*).

[235] So Zimmerli, *Ezechiel*, 841f.

[236] Cody, *Ezekiel*, 166; Lemke, "Life in the Present", 180.

[237] Especially in the presentation of the Chronicler, who goes into great detail to show the importance of David's role in having the Temple built. On this see Biggs, *nāśî'*, 53.

[238] G. von Rad, *Deuteronium Studien*, FRLANT 58 (Göttingen 1947) 52-64.

[239] J.D. Pleins, "From the Stump of Jesse: the Image of King David as a Social Force in the Writings of the Hebrew Prophets", *Proceedings of the Eastern Great Lakes and Midwest Bible Society* 6 (1986) 162; Taylor, *Ezekiel*, 223; J. Herrmann, *Ezechielstudien*, 123.

[240] Zimmerli, *Ezechiel*, 844. Similarly, with reference to this chapter, W. Kessler comments: "Eine selbstständige Rolle spielt dieser Messias keineswegs, er ist nur eine Figur auf dem Schachbrett, die — wenn sie auch die vornehmste ist — letztlich doch nur ein willenloses Werkzeug in der Hand des allein waltenden Gottes ist" (*Die innere Einheitlichkeit des Buches Ezechiel*, Berichte des theologischen Seminars der Brüdergemeine 11 [Herrnhut 1926] 81). So also Ebach, *Kritik und Utopie*, 277.

> This prince...will rule *among*, rather than over, the people. The oppressive shepherds, of course, had ruled *over* the people.[241]

Such a stress fails to note that the new shepherd too is placed *over* the people (v.23).[242] His relationship to them is not simply *primus inter pares* but shepherd to sheep, a relationship which involves authority as well as service.[243]

Yet the aspect of service *is* stressed here, along with that of authority, simply because it is the area where the former shepherds had failed so badly. They had failed to tend the flock as shepherds; instead they had ruled harshly and arbitrarily, motivated by their own gain to acts of violence and oppression. Therefore they will be replaced in the future by a good shepherd, one who is free of precisely the faults they exhibited, who will tend the sheep rather than exploit them. Once again the promise of restoration represents a conscious repairing of the flaws of the past.[244]

5 *Ezekiel 37:22-5*

This passage forms part of a pericope whose concern is for the future unity of Israel and Judah. As part of that unity, they will have only one king over them.[245] That king is identified as the one shepherd of chapter 34 and given the same symbolic title, "my servant David". Little new information is given regarding this figure. What there is, however, tends to confirm the impression made by chapter 34 of his greatness: he shall be "king over them",[246] and their *nāśî'* forever (*lᵉ'ôlām*). In this last statement is perhaps a recognition of the problem with the original David and all of the "good" kings: ultimately each one died and their sons and grandsons rarely walked in their ways.[247] In the future this failure of godly succession too will be remedied.[248]

---

[241] Klein, *Ezekiel*, 123 (emphasis original). Compare T. Krüger, *Geschichtskonzepte im Ezechielbuch*, BZAW 180 (Berlin 1989) 453; D. Baltzer, *Ezechiel und Deuterojesaja*, BZAW 121 (1971) 139.

[242] Compare Ezekiel 37:24f. where the future ruler is described both as *melek* over them (*ᵃlêhem*, v.24) and as *nāśî'* (v.25).

[243] Since "shepherd" is inherently an image which combines service with authority, we should avoid the common tendency to set these in opposition, as does e.g. Hals, *Ezekiel*, 254. For a more balanced picture, see Yates, *Eschatological Message*, 182.

[244] Levenson, *Theology*, 94; Hals, *Ezekiel*, 288.

[245] Compare the statement in Hosea 1:11 that Israel will be regathered under one *rō'š*.

[246] Some have argued on the basis of the LXX (*archōn*) that the MT originally read *nāśî'* (J. Herrmann, *Ezekiel*, 234; Procksch, "Fürst und Priester", 116; Bernhardt, *Der altorientalischen Königsideologie*, 116). However, the correspondence with *mamlākôt* later in the same verse, and the fact that the same LXX translator also renders *melek* by *archōn* in Ezekiel 28:12 suggests that *melek* is in fact original and the LXX is due to assimilation to Ezekiel 34:24 (Zimmerli, *Ezechiel*, 905).

[247] Cf. e.g. 1 Kings 11:4; 15:3; 2 Kings 14:3; 16:2.

[248] One should not regard this as a statement of expectation of eternal life for the future ruler. The title "my servant David" carries with it "etwas von der Zeitlosigkeit einer Chiffre" (Zimmerli, *Ezechiel*, 918). The expectation is expressed of a continuing state of righteous rule,

6 *Ezekiel 40-48*

The most fundamental fact to be noted about the future ruler in chapters 40-48 is that he is a single individual who rules all twelve tribes, without being identified with any.[249] His land is separate from that of the twelve tribes (Ezek. 48:21), as is that of the Temple complex and the City.[250] This clearly distinguishes him from the *nᵉśî'îm* of the wilderness period, who were distinctively tribal chiefs.[251] Ezekiel's future *nāśî'*, on the other hand, by being distinguished from the tribes becomes a visible symbol of inter-tribal unity in chapters 40-48, like the coming David of Ezekiel 37:22-25.[252] Unlike the historical kingdom of Israel, whose unity had been broken by the misrule of two of its kings, Solomon and Rehoboam,[253] the future kingdom would be united behind a single king. Another contrast with the *nᵉśî'îm* of the Hexateuch is that the office envisaged by Ezekiel appears to be hereditary, with his land being passed down from father to son (Ezek. 46:16).[254] This presumably implies what also appears to be the case in Ezekiel 34 and 37: that here we have to do with a Davidide—for what other ruling family would have been conceivable to an orthodox Judahite?[255]

It is thus already clear that we have to do with an exalted figure, far greater than any *nāśî'* of the period of the Hexateuch and more akin to the pre-exilic kings. This picture is further defined, both positively and negatively, in the allocation of the land. Negatively, the Temple is no longer to be simply part of a larger palace complex, as Solomon's Temple had been (Ezek. 43:8): instead it will be surrounded by a priestly area to avoid all danger of defilement. Further the city is no longer the king's private pres-

---

utilizing the theme word of this section (*'ōlām*) which occurs five times in vv. 25-28. How precisely this is to be accomplished is not in view here.

[249] *nāśî'* occurs in the plural in these chapters only in Ezekiel 45:8f. There it probably should be seen as having reference to a succession of *nᵉśî'îm* rather than several at once. It may be an allusion to the abuses described in chapter 22, where the *nᵉśî'îm* also appear in the plural.

[250] Ebach, *Kritik und Utopie*, 187ff.

[251] According to Levenson: "the primary distinction [between *nāśî'* and *melek*] is between rule over a single tribal unit and rule over a kingdom of many tribes" (*Theology*, 63). Cf. Speiser, "*nāśî'*", 113.

[252] Zimmerli, *Ezechiel*, 539; King, "Prince", 116.

[253] Cf. 1 Kings 11f. However, the historical forces behind this breakup were probably more complex than might appear from this account.

[254] We have argued above that Ezekiel elsewhere sometimes used the plural *nᵉśî'îm* when describing the past succession of Davidides (cf. Ezek. 19:1; 22:6,25 [corrected text]). See above, p.38.

[255] Gese, *Verfassungsentwurf*, 118; J. Skinner, *The Book of Ezekiel*, Expositor's Bible (New York 1901) 447; G. Ch. Macholz, "Noch Einmal: Planungen für den Wiederaufbau nach der Katastrophe von 587", *VT* 19 (1969) 342; By contrast, K. Begrich argues that Ezekiel's failure to designate the *nāśî'* of Ezekiel 40-48 a Davidide is a deliberate attempt to distinguish him from the messianic figure of the earlier chapters ("Das Messiasbild des Ezechiel", *ZWT* 47 [1904] 455).

erve, as was Jerusalem ("the City of David"): the new city will belong to the whole house of Israel (Ezek. 45:6; 48:19).[256] Positively, however, the nāśî' is allocated a large portion of land within the consecrated area (t'rûmâ),[257] closer to the Temple than anyone else except the priests and Levites. This is a gracious gift indeed, considering the past history of the former kings.

The purpose of this gracious gift is to prevent the abuses with which the monarchy was charged in the earlier chapters from being repeated in future. The nāśî' will not be tempted to oppress the people by stealing their land because he will have sufficient land of his own (Ezek. 45:8; 46:18).[258] His possession of the land will not be "freehold": it is not his to dispose of as he wills for ultimately it belongs to the Lord. Thus he must not give it permanently to his "servants" ("bādîm; i.e. those personally bound to him).[259] At the "year of liberty" (š'nat-hadd'rôr) it will revert to the nāśî' so that it may remain within his family (Ezek. 46:17). This too removes a source of temptation to acquire ever greater quantities of land with which to reward his followers.[260]

The status of the nāśî' is confirmed when we turn to the cultic realm and look at his responsibilities there. We saw above that the tribal n'śî'îm had no special tasks or privileges in the cult.[261] By contrast, Ezekiel's nāśî' is a central figure in the worship of the new Temple. To be sure he is not a priest and is thus not permitted to enter the inner court or offer sacrifices, as some of the pre-exilic kings seem to have done.[262] He is, however, the foremost layman, with unique responsibilities and privileges with respect to the cult.[263] He alone is permitted to eat bread in the presence of the Lord inside the closed east gate of the Temple, which is especially holy because the Lord has passed through it (Ezek. 44:1-3).[264] In a situation in which

---

[256] Macholz, "Planungen", 344.

[257] On the terminology t'rûmâ see below, p.128 n.145.

[258] Macholz, "Planungen", 337.

[259] Zimmerli, Ezechiel, 1177; U. Rüterswörden, Die Beamten der israelitischen Königszeit. Eine Studie zu śr und vergleichbaren Begriffen, BWANT 117 (Stuttgart 1985) 19.

[260] Macholz, "Planungen", 339f.; M. Greenberg, "Idealism and Practicality in Numbers 33:4-5 and Ezekiel 48", JAOS 88 (1968) 64. On this practice, see T.N.D. Mettinger, Solomonic State Officials. A Study of the Civil Government Officials of the Israelite Monarchy (Lund 1971) 80-110. See further below, p.130.

[261] See above, p.14.

[262] Cooke, Ezekiel, 497; however, it seems that the later kings may not have exercised the same rights in the Temple (Skinner, Ezekiel, 458f.).

[263] W. Zimmerli, "Planungen für den Wiederaufbau nach der Katastrophe von 587", VT 18 (1968) 245 [= [ET] "Plans for Rebuilding after the Catastrophe of 587" I am Yahweh, W. Brueggemann, tr. D.W. Stott, (Atlanta 1982) 123]; Biggs, "nāśî'", 49. Seybold notes the desire "den nāśî' zwar als vornehmstes Glied der Gemeinde zu würdigen, ihn aber nur bis zur Chorschranke des inneren Vorhofs dem k'bôd yhwh nahekommen zu lassen" (Davidische Königtum, 150).

[264] This closed gate thus becomes a kind of cult room. On this, see Zimmerli, Ezechiel, 1112; Biggs, "nāśî'", 48.

one's status is especially defined by one's relationship to the Temple this is no small privilege.[265]

The *nāśî'* of Ezekiel 40-48 is also the figurehead of the people in worship. The gifts and offerings required of the people[266] were to be gathered up from the people of the land,[267] so that all might participate in the *t'rûmâ* of the *nāśî'* (Ezek. 45:16). This privilege of the *nāśî'* also has its own temptations: it would be easy for the *nāśî'* to extort additional amounts from the people by using corrupt measures. This appears to be what is forbidden in Ezekiel 45:9-12.[268] As we saw also in Numbers 7, the *nāśî'* is acting as representative on behalf of the people.[269] But whereas the former was a unique event, the dedication of the altar, in Ezekiel's vision the *nāśî'*'s representative function is continual. He is to provide the cereal offering (*minhâ*), sin offering (*hattā't*), burnt offering ('*ôlâ*) and fellowship offering (*š'lāmîm*) "to make atonement (*l'kappēr*) for the house of Israel" (Ezek. 45:17). This responsibility extends to the New Moons and Sabbaths (Ezek. 45:17) and especially to the two great annual feasts (Ezek. 45:21-25), and is no small privilege in view of the central importance of atonement in Ezekiel 40-48.[270] It is a contribution expected of the former kings of Israel (cf. 1 Ki. 9:25), just as elsewhere in the ancient Near East (cf. Ezra 7:17-23).[271] This wider representative responsibility clearly distinguishes him from the *n'śî'îm* of Leviticus: their responsibility to make atonement only extended to their own sin (cf. Lev. 4:26). In Leviticus, only the Aaronic priesthood "makes atonement" (*l'kappēr*) for others (cf. Lev. 10:17; 14:29; 16:33). However, provision of an offering to atone (*l'kappēr*) for all Israel *is* recorded of at least one pre-exilic king, Hezekiah (2 Chr. 29:23f.) in a ceremony which shows certain similarities to Ezekiel 45.[272] Even the use of a bull (*par*) as a sin offering illustrates the greater importance of Ezekiel's *nāśî'* in comparison to those of the Pentateuch.

---

[265] S. Niditch, "Ezekiel 40-48 in a Visionary Context", *CBQ* 48 (1986) 219.

[266] One sixtieth of the wheat and barley, one hundredth of the oil and one two-hundredth of the sheep.

[267] On the construction *hā'ām hā'āreṣ* see above, p.29, n.125. It is doubtful that great emphasis should be laid on whichever term is preferred since comparison of Ezekiel 44:19 with Ezekiel 46:3 shows that both terms can designate the cultic congregation, worshipping in the outer court. Note also the apparently similar confusion in the Hebrew mss of 2 Kings 16:15. On the distinction between *'am* and *'am hā'āreṣ* in Ezekiel 40-48 see further below, p.120f.

[268] Thus Levenson seems to be incorrect in calling this "the *nāśî'*'s one non-temple duty" (*Theology*, 114). What is envisaged here is most likely not the establishment of a national standard of weights and measures but the use of accurate measures to determine the portions given by the people to the *nāśî'* for the *t'rûmâ* (so Haran, "Law Code", 57).

[269] See above, p.14.

[270] Ebach, *Kritik und Utopie*, 272.

[271] K. Galling, "Königliche und nichtköniglicher Stifter beim Tempel von Jerusalem", *ZDPV* 68 (1951) 137.

[272] Though this may represent post-exilic practices.

For the latter, a male goat ($\acute{s}^e$'$\hat{i}r$) as a sin offering was sufficient (Lev. 4:23; Num. 7:16,22,28,34,40,46,52,58,64,70,76,82). A bull as sin offering was only required for events of special importance, involving the priesthood or the whole community.[273]

When it comes to the actual offering of his sacrifices the $n\bar{a}\acute{s}\hat{i}$' again appears as a person of privilege. The ordinary lay worshippers are only permitted to come to the entrance of the inner east gate (Ezek. 45:3). Even if they were permitted to climb the steps, the view of the inner court must have been extremely restricted, down a corridor some ninety feet long.[274] The $n\bar{a}\acute{s}\hat{i}$', on the other hand, was permitted to come right to the threshold of the gateway, from where he would have had a good view of everything which transpired in the inner court (Ezek. 46:2). Like the pre-exilic kings before him, he acts as a focus for the worshipping community.[275] On other occasions, however, the $n\bar{a}\acute{s}\hat{i}$' appears not so much at the head of the people as in their midst, with them when they go into the Temple and with them when they go out (Ezek. 46:10). This too is significant: it is as the representative of the people that the $n\bar{a}\acute{s}\hat{i}$' gains his importance, rather than due to a special standing as "son of God" which seems to have been ascribed to the pre-exilic kings.[276]

So great is the $n\bar{a}\acute{s}\hat{i}$''s involvement with the cult that some scholars have seen him as a purely sacral figure, a "*Kirchenpatron*".[277] But this fails to take account of the essentially Temple-centred nature of Ezekiel 40-48. *Everything* is viewed from a cultic perspective.[278] If the $n\bar{a}\acute{s}\hat{i}$' is portrayed as a purely sacral figure, then so also is the entire lay congregation. They too have no non-cultic tasks described, except perhaps for those who are fishing in the transformed Dead Sea (Ezek. 47:10)! Omission does not imply annulment: Ezekiel is highly selective in what he discusses. Therefore, in considering the limitations which Ezekiel places upon the $n\bar{a}\acute{s}\hat{i}$', it is necessary to pay attention to what *is* said rather than what is not said.

---

[273] These are limited to the sin of the anointed priest (Lev. 4:3), or of the community as a whole (Lev. 4:14); the ordination of Aaron and his sons (Ex. 29:14; cf. Lev. 8:2); the day of atonement (Lev. 16:6 – but note this is only required for the sins of Aaron and his household; the sins of the community are atoned for by two male goats (v.5)); the setting apart of the Levites (Num. 8:8). For all other occasions the use of male goats seems to have been standard (eg. Num. 29:11,16; 2 Chr. 29:21; Ezra 8:35).

[274] Zimmerli, *Ezechiel*, 1171.

[275] Cf. 2 Samuel 6:12-15; 1 Kings 8:62-64; 2 Chronicles 29:20ff.

[276] As in Psalm 2:7. On this see J. Day, *Psalms*, Old Testament Guides (Sheffield 1990) 99f.

[277] Begrich, "Messiasbild", 454; Procksch, "Fürst und Priester", 116. Levenson's apolitical messiah, whom he describes as "a figure of great honour, but impotent" (*Theology*, 113) seems close to this in practice.

[278] Skinner, *Ezekiel*, 448. Cooke comments that Ezekiel "hardly mentions the secular side of the nation's life" ("Some Considerations on the Text and Teaching of Ezekiel 40-48", *ZAW* 42 [1924] 114).

One restriction which is sometimes thought to be placed upon the *nāśî'* lies in the area of responsibility for the administration of justice: advocates of this position point in particular to Ezekiel 44:24, where the priests are now assigned to act as judges in any dispute (*rîb*).[279] The priests had been involved in judicial activities for a long time, especially in cases requiring a divine decision.[280] Previously many areas, especially royal matters, had apparently been outside their jurisdiction (2 Chr. 19:11). The king (or his delegate) seems to have acted as final court of appeal (2 Sam. 15:3f.; 1 Ki. 3:16ff.; Jer. 22:15f.). It is suggested, on this interpretation, that this final court of appeal has been removed and now the priests are left in sole charge of the judicial system. But was this actually what Ezekiel envisaged? In Ezekiel's scheme the *nāśî'* is still held responsible for "doing justice and righteousness" (*mišpāṭ ûṣᵉdāqâ ᵃśû*; Ezek. 45:9). This quality is exactly that which is affirmed of Josiah in Jeremiah 22:15: he "did justice and righteousness" (*'āśâ mišpāṭ ûṣᵉdāqâ*), which is explained in the next verse as having "judged the cause of the poor and needy" (*dān dîn-'ānî wᵉ'ebyôn*). Similar qualities are expected by Jeremiah of the coming "righteous Branch of David": "he shall reign as a king and deal wisely and shall execute justice and righteousness (*'āśâ mišpāṭ ûṣᵉdāqâ*) in the land (Jer. 23:5). It thus seems likely that the *nāśî'*'s responsibilities in the administration of justice have not been significantly curtailed. Instead, as will be argued below, Ezekiel 44:24 acts rather as a restriction on the powers of the leaders of the laity.[281]

However, it is certainly true that the *nāśî'* is no longer responsible for the administration of the cult. This is already implied in the separation of the Temple from the palace (Ezek. 43:8): the Temple will no longer be a royal chapel. In the past the kings had the power to appoint or dismiss priests, to organize and reform the worship in the Temple and were responsible for repairing it when necessary.[282] Significantly it is Yahweh who builds this Temple, reforms its worship and organizes its priesthood. In the organization of the renewed cult, no less than in the organization of the renewed kingdom, the *nāśî'* has no active part to play. This fits entirely

---

[279] A. Bertholet, *Der Verfassungsentwurf des Hesekiel in seiner religionsgeschichtliche Bedeutung* (Freiburg and Leipzig 1896) 12; Zimmerli, *Ezechiel*, 1135. This verse clearly contradicts the idea of J. Klausner (*The Messianic Idea in Israel*, tr. W.F. Stinespring, [London 1956] 132) that the absence of a judging role in the restored community is due to the lack of any wilful transgressions on the part of the people requiring judgement.

[280] Cf. Exodus 22:8. A. Cody, *A History of Old Testament Priesthood*, Analecta Biblica 34 (Rome 1969) 72.

[281] See below, p.131.

[282] Solomon dismissed Abiathar for supporting Adonijah's claims to the throne (1 Ki. 2:26); the organization of the entire Temple service by David is a favourite theme of the Chronicler; Josiah is the ultimate authority driving reform through during his reign (2 Ki. 22,23)–note that it is he who orders the celebration of the Passover (2 Ki. 23:21). Cf. Galling, "Stifter", 134f.

with the role of the future *nāśî'* in chapter 34. The Lord will act on his own to rescue Israel, and only after that does he place at their head his undershepherd, the *nāśî'* (Ezek. 34:23f.).[283]

Another area which is now the object of direct divine intervention is the distribution of the land. This is especially significant since this was a task explicitly alotted to the *n̆śî'îm* in the days of Joshua, according to Numbers 34:18. In Ezekiel's vision, however, the re-allocation of the land has already taken place by divine decree (Ezekiel 48): the only responsibility of the *nāśî'* in this regard is not to obstruct its implementation (Ezek. 45:8).

E. Conclusions

Ezekiel's vision of the future for the monarchy may be summed up under two separate aspects: the future for the existing rulers of Judah and the future of the Davidic line as a whole. With regard to the first aspect, he is wholly negative: there is no future to be expected for either Zedekiah or Jehoiachin. Zedekiah can expect nothing but exile and death.[284] Nor should any hope be placed in a restoration of Jehoiachin.[285] The epitaph on the existing *n̆śî'îm* of Israel has already been written:

> Fire has gone out from [the vine's] stem, [and] has consumed its branches and fruit, so that there remains in it no strong stem, no sceptre for a ruler.[286]

On the other hand, however, the end for the current Davidides does not mean the end for the Davidic dynasty. That much is clear already in outline form in Ezekiel 17:22-4,[287] and the picture is developed further in Ezekiel 34, 37, and 40-48.[288] There will be a future *nāśî'* to replace the past *n̆śî'îm*.

Ezekiel's future *nāśî'* appears in these chapters as a man of great — but limited — power and privilege. He is a powerful ruler, but at the same time a gentle shepherd.[289] In the area of the cult he has an honoured position at the head of the people, yet he holds that position as representative of the people. He is a man with lands and servants, prestige and influence. Yet he is not an absolute ruler. He possesses no final authority in the ordering

---

[283] It is perhaps suggestive in the light of the comments above that a similar emphasis is placed on the priority of Yahweh's judicial acts in Ezekiel 34. This is an area where the former shepherds have clearly failed in the past: Yahweh's response is to state three times that he will personally judge the sheep (v.17: *hinᵉnî šōpēt bên śeh lāśeh*; cf. v.20, 22).

[284] Cf. Ezekiel 12:10-14; 17:12-21; 19; 21:30-2[25-7].

[285] Cf. Ezekiel 17:22; 19:9. See also the comments above, pp.35, 44.

[286] Ezekiel 19:14.

[287] See above, p.44.

[288] See above, pp.48, 50.

[289] See above, p.47.

of the cult, nor does he possess the authority to appropriate or redistribute the land.[290]

When we compare these privileges and limitations to the criticisms of the monarchy in the earlier chapters, some striking parallels appear. The good shepherd David represents a reversal of the wicked shepherds in chapter 34.[291] Further, in chapters 40-48, we find the chief limitations are on the *nāśî*'s role in the administration of the cult and against moves to appropriate the land of others, areas which were the object of major criticisms of the former *n^eśî'îm* of the past. The concern for protecting the sanctity of the cult is provided for by relocating the Temple away from the palace and the direct influence of the *nāśî'*, while the *nāśî*'s land hunger is curbed by restricting his ability to dispose of land. Yet the *nāśî*'s own privileged role within the cult and within society is retained. This continued privilege in the cult would be hard to explain if his predecessors had been held responsible for the introduction of cultic abuses in the past. However, others are held responsible for those sins by Ezekiel, as we shall see later.

The purpose of these provisions is that the *n^eśî'îm*, like the rest of the people of Israel, might see in the Temple vision with its walls and restrictions, as well as its rewards, a mirror to the past and might "be ashamed of their sins" (Ezek. 43:10). Law and grace go hand in hand in these chapters: alongside the affirmations that things will no longer be as they were, provisions are made and laws enacted specifically designed to prevent a recurrence of the sins noted in the earlier portion of the book.

Having completed our discussion of the privileges and responsibilities of the *nāśî'* we may return to the question: "Why does Ezekiel choose this particular term?" It is usually asserted that Ezekiel selected it because of its old associations, seeking a return to Sinai. Thus Speiser thinks that Ezekiel preferred the more modest status of the elected *nāśî'* to the fleeting grandeur of the hereditary *melek*.[292] Coppens suggests that in using the term Ezekiel may have a return to the amphictyonic union in mind.[293] Levenson asserts: "In terming his head of state *nāśî'*, Ezekiel sought to bring the institution of the monarchy under the governance of the Sinaitic covenant".[294] The problem with such a position, however, is that from our study

---

[290] See above, pp.45, 47, 50ff.

[291] Hals, *Ezekiel*, 249.

[292] Speiser, "*nāśî'*", 116. In view of the significance attributed to keeping the possession of his land within his family however it seems at least probable that Ezekiel thought of the *nāśî'* as holding a hereditary position. So Gese, *Verfassungsentwurf*, 118; Raurell, "Polemical Role", 85; Seybold, *Davidische Königtum*, 146; Ebach, *Kritik und Utopie*, 161.

[293] J. Coppens, "L'esperance Messianique royale a la vielle et au lendemain de l'exil", *Studia Biblica et Semitica T.C. Vriezen dedicata* (Wageningen 1966) 56.

[294] Levenson, *Theology*, 69; Similarly, Greenberg describes it as an "archaism" ("Design", 197 n.33), Haran assumes that it "has entered Ezekiel's language from the heritage of the

it appears that Ezekiel's *nāśî'* has almost no similarities to the old tribal *n^eśî'îm*. They were tribal figures; he is pan-Israelite. Their tasks were involvement in judging, making covenants and distribution of the promised land; he has no part in these. They had no special cultic tasks or responsibilities; he has great privileges and responsibilities in the cult.

Given these great and thoroughgoing differences it is clear that what Ezekiel envisaged was not a return to Sinai. His plan is not to *replace* the king by an old-style *nāśî'*. Indeed, his *nāśî'* is a lot more like the former kings than he is like the *n^eśî'îm* of the wilderness days, which is why he can at times use the terms *nāśî'* and *melek* interchangeably. Ezekiel did envisage a modified kingship, but his model is not the old form of tribal leadership. If a forerunner is to be sought for Ezekiel's usage, it is rather to be found in 1 Kings 11:34, the only place outside Ezekiel where *nāśî'* clearly denotes a king. There Jeroboam is promised rule over all but one of the tribes which make up Solomon's kingdom. But the Lord also affirms:

> I will not take the whole kingdom out of Solomon's hand; I will make him a *nāśî'* all the days of his life for the sake of David my servant, whom I chose and who observed my commands and statutes.

The importance of this passage lies in the way in which it ties together fulfilment of the promise to David with modification of the kingly office under the distinctive title *nāśî'*.[295] The Davidic kings would henceforth only rule over a fraction of their former empire because of their sins. Yet that diminished responsibility is still affirmed as the fulfilment of the dynastic promise to David. So also in Ezekiel, the office of king has been modified and its scope limited[296] because of past sins. Yet precisely in the choice of the word *nāśî'* God's faithfulness to his dynastic promise to the Davidides is affirmed. As Levenson puts it:

> The gracious thought behind the gift of the monarchy and dynasty has not been withdrawn. The form of the gift has been changed to prevent further abuse.[297]

Priestly school" ("Law Code", 57 n.24) and Hals comments: "One might even dare to see in the prince of chs. 40-48 a return to the pre-monarchic era of the confederacy, where the prince appears in a less lofty role" (*Ezekiel*, 288).

[295] Levenson comments: "This passage considers the office of *nāśî'* a continuing fulfilment of the promise to David....The actual political arrangement is of lesser importance" (*Theology*, 63). Compare it particularly to Ezekiel 34 and 37 where we have the same confluence of ideas: modified kingship, David and *nāśî'*.

[296] But his *nāśî'* does not become an "apolitical messiah" any more than Rehoboam became an apolitical king!

[297] Levenson, *Theology*, 67.

CHAPTER THREE

PRIESTS AND LEVITES

A. INTRODUCTION

Ezekiel's attitude towards the priests and Levites has been the subject of
much discussion since Wellhausen made it pivotal to his reconstruction of
the history of the priesthood in Israel. According to Wellhausen, the
distinction between priests and Levites is an innovation of the prophet
Ezekiel. Before Ezekiel's time all Levites were regarded as priests, whether
they served at the high places dotted around the countryside or in Jerusalem. With Josiah's reform, the levitical priests from the country high
places were effectively made redundant; Deuteronomy 18 had made provision for them to come up to Jerusalem, but this provision was blocked in
turn by the Jerusalemite priests, a situation recorded, in Wellhausen's
opinion, in 2 Kings 23:9. As one of the Jerusalemite priests, Ezekiel "hängt
bloss der Logik der Tatsachen einen moralischen Mantel um", explaining
why this *de facto* situation should prevail *de jure*.[1] This interpretation of
Ezekiel 44:6ff. has had an enormous influence which continues, with some
minor modifications, down to the present day.[2] Of course, Wellhausen's
views have not been without opposition; on the one hand, for example,
Gunneweg has posed the question of whether the identification Levites =
priests is true for the older period,[3] and on the other Wellhausen's interpretation of Ezekiel 44 has been challenged in a variety of ways by Abba,
Duke, Greenberg, McConville and Hals.[4]

Since the work of Gese, it has also become a commonplace to identify
Ezekiel 44:6ff. as part of a "Zadokite stratum" or as a "Zadokite section",
one of the latest additions to chapters 40-48, which affected other parts of

---

[1] J. Wellhausen, *Prolegomena zur Geschichte Israels* (Berlin [3]1886) 124f.
[2] Cf. e.g. N. Allan, "The Identity of the Jerusalem Priesthood During the Exile", *Hey J*
23 (1982) 259f.; J. Bowman, "Ezekiel and the Zadokite Priesthood", *TGUOS* 16 (1955-6) 2.
[3] Gunneweg, *Leviten und Priester*, 220.
[4] Cf. R. Abba, "Priests and Levites in Ezekiel", *VT* 28 (1978) 1-9; R.K. Duke,
"Punishment or Restoration: Another Look at the Levites of Ezekiel 44:6-16", *JSOT* 40
(1988) 61-81; M. Greenberg, "A New Approach to the History of the Israelite Priesthood",
JAOS 70 (1950) 41-7; and J.G. McConville, "Priests and Levites in Ezekiel: a Crux in the
Interpretation of Israel's History", *TynB* 34 (1983) 3-32. Note especially the categorical
conclusion of Hals: "Although it would be wonderful to have historical information on the
details of the rise to power of Zadokites and their relationship with both the menial Levites
of priestly tradition and the powerful Levitic leaders spoken of by the Chronicler, this text in
Ezekiel neither provides us with such information nor helps in the reconstruction of it, for it
has a far different intention" (*Ezekiel*, 321).

these chapters by the addition of a string of harmonizing glosses.[5] This stratum is still seen as having a strong polemical intent as part of the Zadokite "battle programme",[6] just as in Wellhausen's thought, but now the Zadokite polemicist is separated from the prophet Ezekiel. What cements this separation for most interpreters is precisely an apparent contradiction between the prophecies of the first part of the book and chapter 44. For example, it is considered by Zimmerli "undenkbar" that one who described the state of affairs in the Temple in chapter 8 could exonerate the Zadokites from blame in Ezekiel 44:15.[7] A thorough examination of the connection between the critique of priestly leadership and its future is needed to determine if this apparent contradiction is really valid.

EXCURSUS: IS THERE A HIGH PRIEST IN THE BOOK OF EZEKIEL?

The apparent absence of the figure of the High Priest from Ezekiel 40-48 has often been noted, with a variety of explanations.[8] Yet the apparent absence of the High Priest from chapters 1-39 is perhaps equally striking, if seldom commented upon, in view of the cultic abuses which are described. Certainly it is not because such a figure did not yet exist: an institution such as the late pre-exilic Temple would have required a body of priests with the concomitant necessity for organization.[9] Evidence for such organization is not lacking in the biblical documents.

In the early days of the Temple, a simple familial structure would have sufficed with all the priests being under the authority and discipline of the family head, who was simply referred to as "The Priest" (*hakkōhēn*). This title persisted even after the organizational structure of the Temple became more complicated: throughout the Old Testament it is the most common title for the High Priest.[10] Alongside this title, other titles began to develop, notably *kōhēn hārō'š*,[11] *hakkōhēn hārō'š* and *hakkōhēn haggādōl*. The former title is used by the Chronicler of Amariah, priest of the days of

[5] For the latter view, see Gunneweg, *Leviten und Priester*, 188.

[6] German "Kampfprogramm"; Gunneweg, *Leviten und Priester*, 188.

[7] Zimmerli, *Ezechiel*, 1128. Cf. Eichrodt, *Hesekiel*, 399; N. Allan, "Jerusalem Priesthood", 262.

[8] Compare e.g. Zimmerli, *Ezechiel*, 1248; Greenberg, "Design", 208; S. Zeitlin, "Titles", 2; Lang, *Kein Aufstand*, 139; C. Mackay, "Why Study Ezekiel 40-48?", *EvQ* 37 (1965) 159; G.C.M. Douglas, "Ezekiel's Temple", *ET* 9 (1898) 420; D. Lane, *The Cloud and the Silver Lining* (Welwyn 1985) 143.

[9] T. Chary, *Les Prophètes et le Culte à Partir de l'Exil* (Tournai 1955) 50.

[10] J. Bailey, "Usage of Post Restoration Period Terms Descriptive of Priest and High Priest", *JBL* 70 (1951) 217.

[11] This is an exception to the general rule that the substantive and its adjective agree as to article. According to GKC § 126 w, however: "The article is...not infrequently used...with the attribute alone, when it is added to an originally indefinite substantive as a subsequent limitation".

Jehoshaphat, in the context of Jehoshaphat's judicial reform (2 Chr. 19:11).[12] Indeed, according to Bartlett, it may well have been because of the leading priest's role in judicial affairs that this title was given to him.[13] The same title is bestowed upon Jehoiada in 2 Chronicles 24:11[14] and on Azariah in 2 Chronicles 26:20. Another Azariah (his grandson?)[15] is later described as *hakkōhēn hārō'š* in 2 Chronicles 31:10.[16] This is also the title given to Aaron in Ezra 7:5. In this last case there has been some debate as to whether the correct translation is "chief priest" or "first priest". The Septuagint translation *tou hiereōs tou prōtou* is often adduced in favour of the latter translation.[17] However, since the Septuagint translates *kōhēn hārō'š* in precisely the same way in 2 Chronicles 26:20, where Azariah is indicated, the translation "chief priest" seems justified.[18] The chief priest at the time of the exile, Seraiah, one of those executed by Nebuzaradan after the fall of Jerusalem, is called *kōhēn hārō'š* in 2 Kings 25:18 (= Jer. 52:24).

The other title for High Priest, *hakkōhēn haggādôl* is found three times in the Hexateuch (Num. 35:25, 28; Jos. 20:6) in passages dealing with the cities of refuge. Its roots can perhaps be seen in the phrase in Leviticus 21:10: *hakkōhēn haggādôl mē'eḥāyw* ("the priest who is greater than his brothers").[19] Elsewhere in the Old Testament, *hakkōhēn haggādôl* is used of Jehoiada in 2 Kings 12:11, of Hilkiah in 2 Kings 22:4,8 (= 2 Chr. 34:9) and 2 Kings 23:4, of Eliashib in Nehemiah 3:1,20; 13:28, and of Joshua ben Jehozadak in Haggai 1:1,12,14; 2:2,4; and Zechariah 3:1,8; 6:11. Only in these last two books is it used exclusively; elsewhere it is used synonymously with *hakkōhēn*.[20]

---

[12] In view of the evidence for comparable titles such as *kōhēn mišneh* during this period (cf. 2 Ki. 23:4; 25:18), there seems no reason to doubt the historical accuracy of the Chronicler's usage. See below, p.61.

[13] J. Bartlett, "The Use of the Word *rō'š* as a Title in the Old Testament", *VT* 19 (1969) 1-6.

[14] Note 2 Chronicles 24:6 where Jehoiada is termed simply *rō'š* (of the priests and Levites, cf. v.5).

[15] J. Morgenstern, "A Chapter in the History of the High Priesthood", *AJSL* 55 (1938) 13 n.39.

[16] In 1 Chronicles 27:5 a Jehoiada of the time of King David is called *hakkōhēn rō'š*. No grammatical explanation has yet been advanced for the lack of the article on the attribute. It is possible that *rō'š* is a gloss here; alternatively, since some similar attribute is presupposed by LXX *ho hiereus ho archōn*, perhaps we should read *hakkōhēn hārō'š* and find here another attestation of this title.

[17] E.g. L.W. Batten, *A Critical and Exegetical Commentary on the Books of Ezra and Nehemiah*, ICC (Edinburgh 1913) 304; Bartlett, "*rō'š*", 7.

[18] Cf. the LXX of 2 Kings 25:18 = Jeremiah 52:24; though here the contrast with the "second priest" may be responsible for the translation (Bailey, "Priest and High Priest", 223). Note also that in 1 Kings 2:35 where David makes Zadok priest (*hakkōhēn*) in place of Abiathar, the LXX translates *hierea prōton* which must in this context have the force of "chief priest" rather than "first priest" in any chronological sense.

[19] B. Levine, *Leviticus*, JPS Torah Commentary (Philadelphia 1989) 144.

[20] Cf. 2 Kings 12:9; 22:10; 2 Chronicles 34:14; Nehemiah 13:4.

On the basis of this evidence, J. Morgenstern has argued in an influential article that every occurrence of the title *hakkōhēn haggādōl* is a late editorial interpolation.[21] He points to the infrequency with which the title appears, the alternation between the titles *hakkōhēn haggādōl* and *hakkōhēn* and the fact that while Joshua ben Jehozadak is invariably designated *hakkōhēn haggādōl* in Haggai and Zechariah, he is never so designated in Ezra and Nehemiah. On the other hand, Morgenstern does admit the possibility that the more modest title *hakkōhēn hārō'š* was in existence in pre-exilic times.[22] However, it is then hard on his theory to account for the predominance of the "later" term in the books of Kings (4 to 1) and the "earlier" term in the books of Chronicles (5 to 1). The one use of *hakkōhēn haggādōl* in Chronicles (2 Chr. 34:9) reflects its usage in a parallel passage in Kings. Even more difficult to explain on Morgenstern's theory is why 2 Chronicles 24:11 replaces the "later" title found in its *Vorlage* with the "earlier" title. Further, while Joshua ben Jehozadak is not named *hakkōhēn haggādōl* in Ezra and Nehemiah, in line with a general tendency of these books to avoid titles,[23] his descendant Eliashib *is* so designated.[24] The data thus do not support Morgenstern's theory of late editorial insertions. Rather, they are most easily accounted for by assuming that both terms were current from at least the time of the writing of the books of Kings and that usage was a matter of personal preference. We may well accept that the diversity of titles in use gives evidence that there was no *established* title for the chief priest, other than the simple term *hakkōhēn*, even down to the time of the Chronicler. But the growing complexity of operations evidenced by the titles of other Temple officials in the late pre-exilic period, as we shall see below, would have provided the conditions under which we would expect to see these titles for the chief executive officer emerging. Certainly the growing authority of the High Priest in the post-exilic era gave impetus to this trend but there is no reason to doubt that these titles had been in use in an earlier time.

Alongside the various terms for chief priest, we find another priestly title: *kōhēn mišneh* ("the second priest"). This title occurs usually in conjunction with, and presupposes, a title for "chief priest". In 2 Kings 23:4 several "second priests" (*kōhᵃnê hammišneh*), alongside the chief priest (*hakkōhēn haggādōl!*) and the doorkeepers, are mentioned as involved in

[21] Morgenstern, "History", 3.
[22] "History", 13.
[23] J. VanderKam, "Joshua the High Priest and the Interpretation of Zechariah 3", *CBQ* 53 (1991) 553; Japhet, "Sheshbazzar and Zerubbabel", 80ff.
[24] Compare Nehemiah 13:28 with 12:10.

Josiah's reform.[25] In 2 Kings 25:18 (= Jer. 52:24) it is the title of one
Zephaniah, who was executed at Riblah along with Seraiah the chief priest
(kōhēn hārō'š) and three unnamed doorkeepers (šōm'rê hassap). There is
no clear indication of the duties of the second priest; it seems likely that he
would have taken over the role of the chief priest in the event of his being
incapacitated, whether due to age or some other reason.[26] Some support
may be found for this view in the letter addressed to "Zephaniah ben
Maaseiah, the priest" by Shemaiah the Nehelemite, recorded in Jeremiah
29:25ff.

> [26]The Lord has made you priest instead of Jehoiada the priest (hakkōhēn),
> that there may be guards[27] in the house of the Lord over every madman who
> prophesies, to put him in the stocks and the collar. [27]Now why have you not
> rebuked Jeremiah of Anathoth who is prophesying to you?

Here Zephaniah is addressed by the title hakkōhēn, which we saw above
often has the force "chief priest" and is identified as occupying the place
once held by Jehoiada, also called "the priest". The reference appears to
be to Jehoiada's authority over the Temple guards (2 Ki. 11:4ff.), which
Shemaiah wishes to see similarly exercised by Zephaniah in the case of
Jeremiah. The implication is that Zephaniah possesses the power to act as
chief priest. It is clear that he never attained to that office in his own right,
however, since it is still held by Seraiah at the time when both are put to
death by Nebuchadnezzar after the fall of Jerusalem. Zephaniah was apparently not unfriendly to Jeremiah's cause (cf. Jer. 29:24-32), yet it is a mark
of the lack of power of the priesthood of those days that elsewhere in the
book of Jeremiah he appears simply as a messenger sent by the king to
inquire of Yahweh through Jeremiah (Jer. 21:1; 37:3). On both of these
occasions he is mentioned after officials (śārîm) of the king (compare with
Jer. 38:1,4). He seems impotent to effect reform or even to protect Jeremiah against these officials. Thus, in Jeremiah 38:1-13 it is left to an
Ethiopian eunuch, Ebed-melech, to rescue Jeremiah from the cistern into
which he had been thrown by the śārîm.

Not all the priests were as sympathetic to Jeremiah: one Pashhur ben
Immer, also a priest and pāqîd nāgîd ("leading officer") of the house of
Yahweh appears to have had a similar responsibility of disciplining "men

---

[25] Though Targum has singular (followed by, e.g., J. Gray, The Book of Kings, Old
Testament Library [London ²1970] 730). Morgenstern also reads the singular and uses the
title as a springboard for his speculations on the significance of the instances in the Old
Testament where two priests function together as chief priest ("History", 14f.).

[26] There appears to have been an analogous office in the royal household mišneh hammelek
("second to the king"); cf. 2 Chronicles 28:7.

[27] RSV: "to have charge". RSV is following the versions, which appear to read the singular; MT has the plural.

who rave and prophesy" (Jer. 20:1f.). He followed a course of action much more conducive to the thinking of Shemaiah and put Jeremiah in the stocks. The Chronicler describes several *n^egîdîm* with responsibilities in the Temple: a *nāgîd* over the gatekeepers (1 Chr. 9:20),[28] a *nāgîd* over the treasuries (1 Chr. 26:24; cf. 2 Chr. 31:12), and a *nāgîd* of the house of God, which seems to have been another title for the chief priest[29] (1 Chr. 9:11; 2 Chr. 31:13).[30] On a similar note, Zadok is called the *nāgîd* of the Aaronites in 1 Chronicles 27:16f. We find a number of *p^eqîdîm* under a *nāgîd* in 2 Chronicles 31:12f., and this may have been the rank held by Pashhur, as member of a senior priestly family.[31]

Our survey of the priestly titles in the late pre-exilic era[32] thus shows us a picture of increasing complexity in the organization of the Temple, a complexity which would have required an individual who acted as "chief priest". It is thus no surprise that titles such as *(hak)kōhēn hārō'š* and *hakkōhēn haggādôl* begin to appear at this time. The titles do not appear to have been matched by an equal power, however. We find the chief priests subject to the will of the king in the running of the Temple throughout the pre-exilic era, as may be seen, for example, in the erection of Ahaz's new altar by Uriah in 2 Kings 16:10ff. As Morgenstern aptly puts it: "The king was regularly the superior officer of the chief priest even in matters pertaining directly to the Temple cult and the formal and official worship of Yahweh".[33] Reforms as well as abuses were introduced at the bidding of the king, not the chief priest.[34] Perhaps the only instance recorded of a chief priest willing to stand up to a king is Azariah's rebuke of Uzziah in 2 Chronicles 26:16ff. Though the office of chief priest clearly existed, it was far from exerting the kind of power available to the high priests of the post-exilic era.

Seen in this light, we should not expect to find a chief priest who is a dominant figure in the book of Ezekiel. If there is a chief priest in the book

---

[28] Was this office the same as the then current chief (*rō'š*) of the gatekeepers (1 Chr. 9:17)?

[29] H.G.M. Williamson, *Ezra-Nehemiah*, WBC (Waco 1985) 351. If this office was the same as the *n^egîd habbayit* mentioned in 2 Chronicles 28:7 then at least one holder was not the chief priest. However, in a context describing people related to the king, it seems more likely that the *bayit* in question is the royal household (I. Slotki, *Chronicles*, Soncino Books of the Bible [London 1952] 291).

[30] Apparently the same individual is called Azariah in 1 Chronicles 9:11 and Seraiah in Nehemiah 11:11, perhaps due to orthographic confusion of '*z* and *š* (on this see R.L. Braun, *1 Chronicles*, WBC [Waco 1986] 83) compounded by the existence of a (more recent) chief priest by the latter name.

[31] For the family of Immer, cf. 1 Chronicles 9:12; 24:14.

[32] Of course, it cannot simply be assumed that the portrait depicted by the Chronicler necessarily corresponds to the pre-exilic reality. Nonetheless, enough other evidence has been adduced to suggest that at this point the Chronicler's picture was fairly realistic.

[33] "History", 10. Cf. Fohrer, *Hauptprobleme*, 152.

[34] Note where the motivating force comes from in the reforms of 2 Chronicles 31 and 34.

he is more likely to appear as *primus inter pares*, the head of the priestly family, rather than as a figure set apart, a man of a higher grade of sanctity than the other priests. The most likely title for him to bear will be simply *hakkōhēn*, "The Priest". As we shall see in what follows, such a figure may perhaps be glimpsed in the book of Ezekiel. In Ezekiel 45:19 there is reference to the role of one called "The Priest" (*hakkōhēn*) in Ezekiel's spring atonement ritual[35] and in Ezekiel 44:30 the first of the ground meal is to be brought to "the priest" (*lakkōhēn*). In the latter case, it may be that a distinction is intended between firstfruits in general, which belong to "the priests" (*lakkōhᵃnîm*) and the first of the ground meal which is reserved for "The Priest" (*lakkōhēn*). However, this last clause could simply be an addition to bring Ezekiel 44 into line with Nehemiah 10:38.[36] But the former ritual may be compared with Leviticus 4, where the one carrying out the blood rites (already described as "the anointed priest" in v.3,5) is simply called "The Priest". It would seem that, at least in this instance, there *is* a chief priest in the book of Ezekiel.[37]

B. THE CRITIQUE OF PRIESTLY LEADERSHIP IN THE BOOK OF EZEKIEL

In spite of the aspersions often cast by commentators upon the character of the late pre-exilic priesthood, it is remarkable how rarely they are singled out for blame in Ezekiel's oracles of judgement.[38] The word *kōhēn* only occurs twice in chapters 1-33: in Ezekiel 7:26 where the context is a listing of the calamities which the future holds, with no implied criticism, and Ezekiel 22:26 where the priests are condemned along with the other leadership groups in society in terms borrowed from Zephaniah 3. Strikingly, they are nowhere mentioned in the vision of cultic abuses in the Temple in chapters 8-11, as we shall see. This infrequency of criticism is in itself a significant piece of data when we compare it with the frequency with which the other leadership groups are singled out for condemnation by Ezekiel: we may deduce from it that the priesthood was not a primary

---

[35] The identity of the other figure, simply addressed as "you", is unclear. In its present context, it appears to be addressed to the *nāśî'* (Biggs, "*nāśî'*", 51; H.G. May, *The Book of Ezekiel*, The Interpreter's Bible [New York and Nashville 1956] 319).

[36] So Zimmerli, *Ezechiel*, 1139; Gese, *Verfassungsentwurf*, 63; L. Allen, *Ezekiel 20-48*, 264. On the other hand, G.R. Berry saw the High Priest in this figure ("The Authorship of Ezekiel 40-48", *JBL* 34 [1915] 39).

[37] Cooke, *Ezekiel*, 502. Ebach (*Kritik und Utopie*, 115) suggests this possibility, but then rejects it on the grounds that these chapters "das Amt des Hohenpriesters nicht kennt"! The vast majority of recent commentators (e.g. Wevers, Allen, Zimmerli, Eichrodt, Carley) do not even address the issue of the identity of "the priest".

[38] *Contra* e.g. R. Brunner: "Man sich erinnert, in wie großem Ausmaß der Prophet gerade auch die Priester am Elend seines Volkes für schuldig hält" (*Das Buch Ezechiel*, Zürcher Bibelkommentare [Zürich ²1969] 2, 136).

target of his critique.[39]

1 *Ezekiel 7:26*

> Disaster comes upon disaster, and rumour follows rumour They seek a vision from the prophet, but instruction[40] (*tôrâ*) perishes from the priest, and counsel from the elders.

This verse is clearly connected with Jeremiah 18:18, where those plotting against Jeremiah are depicted as saying to one another:

> Instruction shall not perish from the priest, nor counsel from the wise, nor the word from the prophet.

In spite of minor differences in wording and in order, the similarities are striking. It seems most likely that the negative form preserved in Jeremiah is closer to the original saying of the people. Ezekiel would then have taken this citation and reversed it, as he did with other affirmations of the people.[41]

There is no critique of the priesthood in this verse; rather, just as it was the proper function of the prophet to provide a vision and for the elders to provide counsel, so the proper task of the priests was to provide instruction (*tôrâ*).[42] The loss of *tôrâ* is due in this case not to any fault on the part of the priesthood but to the bloodshed which filled the land and the violence which filled the city (v.23). Like the doomed Saul in his last days (1 Sam. 28:6), the nation will find no means of obtaining an answer from Yahweh when it seeks one.[43]

2 *Ezekiel 8-11*

The Veracity of Ezekiel's Vision

Before we begin our discussion of these chapters, it should be noted that the accuracy of Ezekiel's claims concerning the state of the cult in his day has been challenged. It was first suggested by C.C. Torrey that the depiction of cultic abuse in chapters 8-11 owes more to the sins of Manasseh's day than the time of Ezekiel, since such a deplorable state of affairs is

---

[39] *Contra* e.g. R.E. Friedman's summary statement: "Jeremiah attacks those who ignore the Deuteronomic Torah, Ezekiel attacks priests who have done violence to the Priestly Torah and have ignored its precepts" (*The Exile and Biblical Narrative: The Formation of the Deuteronomistic and Priestly Works*, HSM 22 [Chico 1981] 75).

[40] Rather than "the law" (so RSV; Cooke, *Ezekiel*, 83).

[41] E.g. Ezekiel 12:22; 18:2; 37:11. Cf. M. Greenberg, "The Citations in the Book of Ezekiel as a Background for the Prophecies", *Beth Mikra* 50 (1973) 276f.

[42] Cf. Haggai 2:11; Malachi 2:7.

[43] Cf. Ezekiel 14:1-11.

unmentioned by Jeremiah and Kings.[44] This suggestion has been taken up
and refined in the light of Fohrer's criticisms of Torrey's thesis[45] by M.
Greenberg.[46] The key points of the argument are as follows: The heathen
worship of Ezekiel 8 does not fit the time of Jehoiakim and Zedekiah,
according to the witness of the Books of Kings and of Jeremiah. The
former lays the blame for Judah's exile on the sins of Manasseh's age,
which clearly implies that he knew of no comparable guilt under Jehoiakim
or Zedekiah. The latter kings are simply censured in the stereotyped phrase
"they did evil in the sight of Yahweh" (2 Ki. 23:37; 24:19). Likewise,
Jeremiah never depicts the Temple as a desecrated, God-forsaken sanctuary
or calls for its cleansing. To be sure, there is enough evidence to show an
apostasy by Judah in post-Josianic times: it seems that the high places were
revived (Jer. 13:27; 17:1-4), along with other idolatries (Jer. 19:2-13;
32:35). But it is argued that these abominations were limited to privately
sponsored, clandestine cults and did not affect the public, officially sponsored cult.[47] For these reasons, Greenberg discounts Ezekiel's visions as
"untrusty [sic] witnesses to current Temple practice".[48]

Greenberg's analysis has not gone unchallenged. Morton Smith has
argued that the Book of Kings only blames Manasseh for the calamity of
597 BC, not that of 587 BC which it attributes to the sins of Zedekiah (2
Ki. 24:19ff.). Moreover, he has suggested that Jeremiah 44:15ff., with its
emphasis on what *"you"* as well as "your fathers" and "your kings" have
done, actually provides evidence that the exercise of the idolatrous cult of
the Queen of Heaven continued both in private and in public down to the
beginning of the siege in 587 BC. According to Smith, only with the onset
of the siege were the sacrifices to non-Yahwistic cults suspended, hence
the Judean's claim that *ever since* they gave up the cult of the Queen of
Heaven disasters have plagued us.[49]

---

[44] C.C. Torrey, *Pseudo-Ezekiel*, 48. A similar motivation leads R.S. Foster to locate a
sitz im leben for these abominations in the pre-Nehemiah period, i.e. mid 5th century BC (*The
Restoration of Israel. A Study in Exile and Return* [London 1970] 181f.).

[45] *Hauptprobleme*, 164-77.

[46] M. Greenberg, "Prolegomenon", *Pseudo-Ezekiel and the Original Prophecy by C.C.
Torrey and Critical Articles*, ——, ed. (New York 1970) XVII-XXVII. In agreement with
Greenberg in placing the sins described in Ezekiel 8 in Manasseh's era are Fishbane ("Sin and
Judgement", 135) and Matties (*Ezekiel 18*, 151).

[47] "Prolegomenon", XX-XXII.

[48] "Prolegomenon", XXII. Fishbane characterizes Ezekiel's vision as a "propaganda
document" ("Sin and Judgement", 135). I.M. Zeitlin speaks of Ezekiel's "feverish
imagination" (*Ancient Judaism. Biblical Criticism from Max Weber to the Present* [Cambridge
1984] 251f.). For a contrary opinion, see G.W. Ahlström (*Royal Administration and National
Religion in Ancient Palestine* [Leiden 1982] 70 n.129), R.H. Lowery (*The Reforming Kings.
Cult and Society in First Temple Judah*, JSOTS 120 [Sheffield 1991] 172) and J. McKay, who
thinks that Ezekiel 8 "seems to give a picture of paganism in Jerusalem after 597 BC...well
after Josiah's reforms" (*Religion in Judah under the Assyrians*, SBT 26 [London 1973] 68).

[49] "The Veracity of Ezekiel, the Sins of Manasseh and Jer. 44:18", *ZAW* 87 (1975) 14f.
Smith compares this with the events at the time of the fall of Jerusalem in AD 70.

This presentation of the evidence on both sides, it seems to me, misses the purpose of Ezekiel's vision. The agenda has been directed in the wrong course by those earlier critics who saw in the visions of Ezekiel 8-11 evidence that Ezekiel prophesied in Jerusalem.[50] The question then becomes the veracity, or otherwise, of Ezekiel's witness.[51] Indeed, it seems sometimes to be forgotten that what Ezekiel saw was a *vision*: a stylized presentation of reality intended to make a particular point.[52] In such a vision, tensions and anachronisms are perfectly possible.[53] Surely the practices listed in Ezekiel 8 bear the same relationship to reality as does the description of the destruction of Jerusalem in chapters 9 and 10.[54] Hengstenberg appropriately described it as:

> [Alles] was von abgöttischen Elementen im Lande vorhanden war, zu einem Totalbilde vereinigt und in den Tempel versetzt.[55]

Greenberg's distinction between public and private cults—the basis for distinction being the presence or absence of a clergy[56]—is an interesting one because it highlights the possibility of cultic abuses which did not necessarily involve the priesthood. However, it is hardly a distinction that the prophet Ezekiel would have recognized as a valid defence against the charge of cultic abominations—though it might have appealed to some of his hearers! It would have been inadequate for Ezekiel's audience to argue that none of the things described had occurred in the Temple since the time of Manasseh. Reference to Manasseh is, in fact, more of a hindrance than a help, for even in Manasseh's day it is unlikely that a brief tour of the Temple area would have yielded precisely the combination of sights which

[50] E.g. James Smith (*The Book of the Prophet Ezekiel: a New Interpretation* [London 1931] 29): "an account obviously by an eye witness of the various idolatries practised in the Temple". Similarly Bertholet & Galling, *Hesekiel*, 29; Herntrich, *Ezechiel*, 86ff., and more recently Brownlee, *Ezekiel 1-19*, 129.

[51] Note how this viewpoint is the starting point for Y. Kaufmann's discussion of these chapters (*History of the Religion of Israel*, vol. 7 [Jerusalem 1955] 430), upon which Greenberg is strongly dependant.

[52] Morton Smith, in particular, makes no differentiation between the visionary report of Ezekiel and the more straightforward style of Jeremiah and Lamentations. Thus, with characteristic bluntness, he ascribes to Greenberg's position the view that Ezekiel is "lying" ("Veracity", 12). Greenberg is actually more circumspect: though he describes Ezekiel as an "untrusty [sic] witness to current temple practice" ("Prolegomenon", XXII), he later adds that Ezekiel is "visionary" (XXIII). Note also his comments on the possibility of a certain amount of incoherence within a vision in "The Vision of Jerusalem in Ezekiel 8-11: a Holistic Interpretation", *The Divine Helmsman: Studies on God's Control of Human Events, presented to L.H. Silberman*, J.L. Crenshaw and S. Sandmel, eds. (New York 1980) 158.

[53] J. Becker, "Ez 8-11 als einheitliche Komposition in einem pseudepigraphischen Ezechielbuch", *Ezekiel and His Book*, J. Lust, ed. (Leuven 1986) 142.

[54] U. Cassuto, "The Arrangement of the Book of Ezekiel", *Biblical and Oriental Studies* 1 (Jerusalem 1973) 231.

[55] E.W. Hengstenberg, *Die Weissagung des Propheten Ezechiel, für solche die in der Schrift forschen erläutert* (Berlin 1867/8) 82; cf. A.W. Blackwood, Jr., *Ezekiel, Prophecy of Hope* (Grand Rapids 1965) 73; Blenkinsopp, *Ezekiel*, 54.

[56] "Prolegomenon" XXXIII, n.47.

Ezekiel beheld.[57] Ezekiel's point is that the cultic defilement of the land (even if through private cults) is such that even the most sacred area, the Temple, has been thoroughly defiled—and that precisely by the entry of those practicing such cults into the Temple (cf. Ezek. 23:38f.). Appeal to the purity of Temple worship in the face of such private idolatry could provide no help in the day of disaster.[58] Avoidance of such defilement of the future Temple by the entry of the impure is, after all, a central emphasis of chapters 40-48. If, however, "private and clandestine pagan cults clearly existed" in Ezekiel's day,[59] then it is not at all clear how Ezekiel is being "unjust" to his generation in attributing these sins to them. By describing the Temple as totally defiled through the acts of people committed in the service of idolatrous cults, Ezekiel declares the people no better than Manasseh—in spite of the fact that they may have sinned in private, without benefit of official clergy.

To sum up then, the events described in chapters 8-11 are a vision, a stylized presentation of reality. They should not be thought of as descriptions of actual events taking place within the Temple in Ezekiel's day. This does not mean that Ezekiel is therefore an "untrustworthy witness" or a "liar"; his purpose was not to preserve historical data but to convict Judah of cultic sin and thus provide a theological rationale for the destruction of Jerusalem. He has done this in shocking fashion by proclaiming a vision in which the abominations of the "private" cults are depicted as having taken place within the Temple itself.[60]

The Vision of Ezekiel 8-11 and the Priesthood

It is often taken as axiomatic that because these chapters deal with cultic abuses within the Temple they must therefore be critical of the priesthood. In fact, nothing could be further from the truth. The priests are nowhere explicitly mentioned in these chapters.[61] Some have found the priests indicated in the twenty five sun worshippers of Ezekiel 8:16. There are two lines of evidence adduced for this identification, which is not explicit in the text. First, their location is described as "in the inner court of the house of

---

[57]   Note the comment of Messel: "Was Ezechiel im Tempel sieht, ist nicht was bei einem zufälligen Besuch dort zu sehen wäre" (Ezéchielfragen, 56).

[58]   There is apparently a comparable rejection of such a dichotomy between "public" and "private" religion in Ezekiel 14:1ff. For a similar outlook, cf. Jeremiah 7:9f.

[59]   For the evidence, see Greenberg, "Prolegomenon", XXIII and XXXIII n.47.

[60]   Ultimately however, for our analysis, the historicity of Ezekiel's observations is not of definitive importance: we are interested in establishing not who was *actually* responsible for the cultic abuses which terminated in the exile, but rather *upon whom* Ezekiel placed the blame for those abuses. It is this perception on the part of Ezekiel which is of decisive importance for our argument that there is a connection between those identified as responsible for the abuses in Ezekiel's oracles of judgement and those pushed to the margins of Ezekiel's vision of the future.

[61]   As is observed by McConville, "Priests and Levites", 17.

Yahweh, at the door of the Temple of Yahweh, between the porch and the altar". According to Joel 2:17, this is where the priests stand to make intercession on a day of fasting, so the conclusion has been drawn that these must therefore also be priests.[62]

The second line of reasoning is based on the number, twenty five, which has been interpreted as representing the twenty four courses of priests and the High Priest.[63] This latter argument will immediately be rejected by those who prefer the LXX reading *hōs eikosi* ("about twenty") to the MT *k^e'eśrîm wah^amiššâ*;[64] however, given the symbolic prominence of the number twenty five elsewhere in Ezekiel,[65] the Massoretic Text should not be too quickly abandoned.[66] It may also be pointed out, though, that this interpretation of the significance of the number twenty five as symbolizing the priesthood is purely conjectural — and that other (equally conjectural) explanations have been proposed for this number.[67] The idea of twenty four courses of priests is only found in Chronicles and may well reflect post-exilic rather than pre-exilic realities.[68] The first argument is also based on a number of false assumptions. For one thing, it is not at all clear that this area in the inner court was out of bounds to lay people in the pre-exilic era.[69] The presence in this area of priests during a festival does not auto-matically preclude access by lay people. However, even if it could be proven that entry to this area was forbidden to lay people at this time, in view of the enormities which Ezekiel sees committed in the rest of the chapter it seems perfectly possible that in his vision lay people could also

[62] So von Orelli, *Ezechiel*, 37; Taylor, *Ezekiel*, 100; H.L. Ellison, *Ezekiel: The Man and His Message* (London 1956) 43; H.F. Fuhs, *Ezechiel*, Die Neue Echter Bibel (Würzburg 1984) 53. More cautiously, Zimmerli speaks of "kein zwingender Gegenbeweis gegen die Deutung der Männer als Priester zu führen" (*Ezechiel*, 221). Against this identification, see Eichrodt, *Hesekiel*, 62; H. Lamparter, *Zum Wächter Bestellt: Der Prophet Hesekiel* (Stuttgart 1968) 73; J.A. Bewer, *Ezekiel*, Harper's Annotated Bible (London 1954) 1,30.
[63] Hitzig, *Ezechiel*, 61; A. van Hoonacker, "Les Prêtres et Les Lévites dans le livre d'Ezechiel", *RB* 8 (1899) 175-204; Keil, *Ezechiel*, 76; Brunner *Ezechiel*, 1, 108.
[64] E.g. Eichrodt, *Hesekiel*, 46; Fohrer & Galling, *Ezechiel*, 51; E. Tov cites it as an example of "a harmonizing plus" ("Recensional Differences between the MT and the LXX of Ezekiel", *EThL* 62 [1986] 97).
[65] Cf. Ezekiel 11:1; 40:1,13,21,25,29,30,33,36 and with "thousand" throughout Ezekiel 45 and 48. Cf. Zimmerli, *Ezechiel*, 1020; E.F. Davis, *Swallowing the Scroll. Textuality and the Dynamics of Discourse in Ezekiel's Prophecy*, JSOTS 78 (Sheffield 1989) 123. On the other hand, E. Vogt argues that it is 100 rather than 25 which is the dominant number (*Untersuchungen zur Buch Ezechiel* [Rome 1981] 140).
[66] This symbolic significance provides one answer to Eichrodt's assertion that the prophet is unlikely to have seen "about (*k^e*) twenty five men" since twenty five is not a round number (cf. also Greenberg, *Ezekiel 1-20*, 172). An alternative explanation is offered by Becker ("Ezechiel 8-11", 142) who interprets the *k^e* as a *kaph veritatis*: "exactly twenty five men".
[67] E.g. in Ezekiel 11:1ff., Keil interprets the twenty-five men seen there as the king, the twelve tribe-princes and the twelve royal officers (*Ezechiel*, 89).
[68] H.G.M. Williamson, "The Origins of the Twenty Four Priestly Courses", *SVT* 30 (1979) 251-68.
[69] Cooke, *Ezekiel*, 99; Fohrer, *Hauptprobleme*, 175.

have transgressed by impiously entering the realm of the sacred.[70] Arguments from what was normal and proper have very little value in a vision where everything is far from normal and proper. The point of their location is simply to make clear the extent to which the sanctuary has become polluted: from the outside to the inner courtyard, the Temple has been thoroughly defiled.

Having demonstrated that there is no evidence in the text of this passage in favour of identifying these men as priests, we may go on to point out that, in fact, in the next chapter these men are explicitly identified not as priests but as elders ($z^e q\bar{e}n\hat{i}m$). The verse in question is Ezekiel 9:6, which marks the conclusion of Yahweh's charge to the six destroyers to slaughter all who were not marked out by the seventh man for salvation:

> "Slay old men outright and[71] young men and maidens, little children and women, but touch no one upon whom is the mark. And begin at my sanctuary." So they began with the elders ($b\bar{a}$ $^{\prime a}n\bar{a}\check{s}\hat{i}m$ $hazz^e q\bar{e}n\hat{i}m$) who were before the [Temple] house.

Their task of destruction begins from the centre out, starting with the sanctuary. Their first targets are, as one might have expected, the chief idolaters of the previous chapter. The agents of judgement were standing beside Solomon's bronze altar (Ezek. 9:2), which was in the north east corner of the Temple court, so they would have been in close proximity to the sun-worshippers.[72] These sun-worshippers, whose location is described in Ezekiel 8:16 as "in the inner court of the house of Yahweh, at the door of the Temple of Yahweh", are the only *men*[73] whose position fits the description of Ezekiel 9:6: *lipnê habbayit*.[74] These men are described by Ezekiel as *[hā] $^{\prime a}n\bar{a}\check{s}\hat{i}m$ $hazz^e q\bar{e}n\hat{i}m$*, which could mean either "the old men" or "the men who held the office of elder". The former option has been preferred by a number of translations and commentators,[75] but the latter interpretation, in which $hazz^e q\bar{e}n\hat{i}m$ is understood as being a title in apposition to $h\bar{a}$ $^{\prime a}n\bar{a}\check{s}\hat{i}m$, is perfectly grammatical.[76] Moreover, the construction is

---

[70] J. Calvin, *Commentaries on the First Twenty Chapters of the Book of Ezekiel*, tr. T.R. Myers, (Edinburgh 1849) I, 295.

[71] Supply the copula with the versions. It has most likely fallen out due to haplography with the preceding *nûn*; see Zimmerli, *Ezechiel*, 197.

[72] Blenkinsopp, *Ezekiel*, 58. On sun worship, see J. Glen Taylor, *Yahweh and the Sun: Biblical and Archaeological Evidence for Sun Worship in Ancient Israel*, JSOTS 173 (Sheffield 1993).

[73] The location of the women of Ezekiel 8:14 might also be considered to fit this description.

[74] Eichrodt, *Hesekiel*, 132; Lamparter, *Wächter*, 74; Becker, "Ez 8-11", 143. Fisch connects this verse with the seventy elders of Ezekiel 8:11 (*Ezekiel*, 49), but these could hardly be said to have been before (*lipnê*) the house.

[75] AV; RV; Keil, *Ezechiel*, 81.

[76] Cf. Genesis 37:28 *$^{\prime a}n\bar{a}\check{s}\hat{i}m$ midyān\hat{i}m* "men who were Midianites"; Numbers 13:3 *$^{\prime a}n\bar{a}\check{s}\hat{i}m$ ro'šê b^enê yiśrā'ēl* "men who were heads of the children of Israel"; on this see

similar to that utilized in Ezekiel 14:1 and 20:1, *nāšîm mizziqnê yiśrā'ēl* "men of the elders of Israel", where it clearly has reference to office, not age.[77]

One further objection to this interpretation which is often posed is that the word *hazzᵉqēnîm* is merely an inaccurate gloss, since it is suggested that it is absent from the original text of the Septuagint.[78] On closer inspection, however, it turns out that it is only actually absent from one 6th century manuscript of the Septuagint, LXX[106], though it is also marked as an addition in LXX[Q]. LXX[B] (4th century) is in accord with the MT, and LXX[A] (5th century) reads simply *apo tōn presbuterōn*. It therefore seems most probable that the alternative greek readings simply represent free renderings of the present Hebrew text.

In view of these arguments, we understand this verse to be identifying the sun worshippers as elders (*zᵉqēnîm*).[79] At the very least there is no reason to identify them as priests, and we may therefore conclude that the priests of the Jerusalem Temple are not identified as to blame for the cultic abuses listed in these chapters. As Vawter & Hoppe put it:

> These rites are "lay" observances...The point to notice is that Ezekiel's Temple vision portrays the evils [as] committed not by Israel's priesthood.[80]

This may seem at first sight a surprising — even astonishing — state of affairs. However, several factors which we have noted already in our study make it less surprising. First, we noted above that the priesthood exercised little control in the running of the pre-exilic Temple.[81] Therefore, they are not held responsible for abuses which were introduced at the bidding of others. This perspective is not unique to Ezekiel: in 2 Kings 16 we find Uriah the priest introducing a variety of novelties into the Temple at the bidding of King Ahaz, yet the censure falls upon Ahaz, not upon Uriah. Second, and more importantly, we also noted that Ezekiel 8-11 is a *vision*, not a description of actual concurrent historical events which could have been observed by any bystander in the Temple.[82] In fact, we suggested above that Ezekiel

---

R. Mosis, "Ezechiel 14:1-11 - Ein Ruf für Umkehr", *Biblische Zeitschrift* NForsch 19 (1975) 188.

[77] The full phrase *[hā]*nāšîm hazzᵉqēnîm* is perhaps used to distinguish them from the class *zāqēn*, "old men", with which the verse opens.

[78] Cf. e.g. BHS; K. Carley, *Ezekiel among the Prophets*, SBT 31 (London 1975) 61; Vogt, *Untersuchungen*, 48.

[79] Becker notes: "Unleugbar ist jedoch daß 9:6b auf 8:16f. zurückgreift" ("Ez 8-11", 143). Kraetzschmar observes that Ezekiel "öfter bei seinen Visionen Einzelheiten hinterherbringt" (*Ezechiel*, 102).

[80] Vawter & Hoppe, *Ezekiel*, 66.

[81] See above, p.63.

[82] See above, p.65ff.

has in all likelihood taken practices found in the "private cults"[83] of his day
and combined them all together into a single scene set in the Temple.[84]
Therefore, we should be cautious in drawing wide conclusions from the
vision as to the actual state of Temple worship during this period. We will
discuss further in a later section the implications of these chapters for
identifying who Ezekiel felt was really to blame for the cultic defilement
of the land.[85]

3 Ezekiel 22:26

Thus far the texts we have considered have had nothing critical to say ,
regarding the priesthood. However, our third and final text from Ezekiel
1-39 does appraise the priesthood in a negative light.

> Her priests have done violence to my law and have profaned my holy things;
> they have made no distinction between the holy and the common, neither
> have they taught the difference between the unclean and the clean, and they
> have disregarded[86] my sabbaths, so that I am profaned among them.

This verse forms part of a description in Ezekiel 22:25-29 of the sins of
different leadership groups in the land ($n^e\acute{s}\hat{i}'\hat{i}m$,[87] $k\bar{o}h^a n\hat{i}m$, $\acute{s}\bar{a}r\hat{i}m$, $n^e b\hat{i}'\hat{i}m$
and $'am\ h\bar{a}'\bar{a}re\d{s}$). The connection of this passage with Zephaniah 3:3f. has
long been recognized,[88] and has usually been explained as due to dependence of Ezekiel upon Zephaniah.[89] Recently, however, Bettenzoli has attempted to argue that it is Zephaniah who is dependent upon Ezekiel.[90] He
sees the accusations of Ezekiel as being more concrete than those of
Zephaniah and argues that the designation of the different classes in
Zephaniah best fits a post-exilic setting. However, it seems to me that the
"concreteness" of the accusations in these verses is exactly the same as that
in Ezekiel 22:6-12, where Ezekiel has adapted citations from the Holiness
Code to his own purposes.[91] As for terminology, the choice of $n\bar{a}\acute{s}\hat{i}'$ rather
than $\acute{s}ar$ is not simply a matter of pre- and post-exilic usage but the choice
of a word particularly favoured by Ezekiel. Once the $\acute{s}\bar{a}r\hat{i}m$ had been
displaced from their position at the head of Zephaniah's list, it is an open

---

[83] I.e. precisely those operating without benefit of an official clergy! Cf. Greenberg,
"Prolegomenon", XXXIII, n.47.
[84] See above, p.67.
[85] See below, pp.111-118.
[86] Literally: "They hid their eyes from...".
[87] On the text, see p.19 n.61.
[88] D.H. Müller, "Der Prophet Ezechiel entlehnt eine Stelle des Propheten Zephanja und
glossiert sie", WZKM 19 (1905) 263-70.
[89] So e.g. Zimmerli, Ezechiel, 522; M. Fishbane, Biblical Interpretation in Ancient Israel
(Oxford 1985) 462f.; Garscha, Studien, 51.
[90] Bettenzoli, Geist der Heiligkeit, 113.
[91] Hölscher, Hesekiel, 117; Burrows, Literary Relations, 31-34; Reventlow, Wächter, 101-
106; Bettenzoli, Geist der Heiligkeit, 114-116.

question whether their appearance in Ezekiel in place of Zephaniah's *šōpᵉṭîm* implies that they are functional equivalents, as Bettenzoli assumes.[92] Perhaps the clinching argument in favour of the priority of Zephaniah, however, is the use of *bᵉqirbāh* in v.27 rather than *bᵉtôkāh*, which is found frequently throughout Ezekiel 22. It occurs in a phrase directly parallel to Zephaniah (*śārêha bᵉqirbāh*; cf. Zeph. 3:3) — indeed it is the opening phrase of the section cited, which may be why it is left unaltered. *bᵉqereb* with suffix is used six times in Zephaniah 3, but in Ezekiel it only appears otherwise in 11:19 and 36:26, where it has the specific sense of "inside".[93]

Even while Ezekiel has used the earlier material of Zephaniah, he has not taken it over unaltered. He has stamped it with his own vocabulary and shaped it to fit his own purposes, as the following comparison shows:[94]

Zephaniah 3:3-4	*Ezekiel 22:25-9*
3a. Her officials (*śārêha*) within her are roaring lions;	25. Her princes (*nᵉśî'êha*) in the midst of her are like a roaring lion, tearing the prey; they have devoured human lives; they have taken treasure and precious things; they have made many widows in the midst of her.
3b. Her judges (*šōpᵉṭehā*) are evening wolves that leave nothing till morning.	27. Her officers (*śārêhā*) in the midst of her are like wolves tearing the prey, shedding blood, destroying lives to get dishonest gain.
4a. Her prophets are wanton, faithless men.	28. Her prophets have daubed for them with whitewash, seeing false visions and divining lies for them, saying, "Thus says the Lord God," when the Lord has not spoken.

---

[92] *Geist der Heiligkeit*, 112.

[93] Zimmerli, *Ezechiel*, 525. Note that in both cases it forms part of the (fixed?) formula "And I will put a new spirit within you/them" (*bᵉqereb* + suffix).

[94] This presentation has rearranged the order in Ezekiel for the purposes of comparison. It shows how he has expanded the four classes of Zephaniah into five, changed their order, renamed some of the groups and expanded and further defined the scope of all the accusations with his own material.

4b. Her priests profane what is sacred (ḥillᵉlû qōdeš); they have done violence to the law (ḥāmᵉsû tôrâ).

26. Her priests have done violence to my law (ḥāmᵉsû tôrātî) and profaned my holy things (wayᵉḥallᵉlû qodāšay); they have made no distinction between the holy and the common, neither have they taught the difference between unclean and clean; and they have disregarded my sabbaths, so that I am profaned among them.

29. The people of the land have practised extortion and committed robbery; they have oppressed the poor and needy, and have extorted from the sojourner without redress.

As far as the charge against the priests is concerned, Zephaniah 3:4b is cited in inverted form, but it is also sharpened by the predicate "my" attached to "holy things" and "law". This addition connects the verse with Ezekiel 22:8, with its similar concern for "my holy things" and "my sabbaths", which is derived in turn from Leviticus 19:30.[95] The additional charge of failing to distinguish between sacred and profane, between clean and unclean, also takes us back into the world of Leviticus. The closest parallel is Leviticus 10:10, which reads: "...that you may distinguish between holy and common, and between clean and unclean" (ulᵉhabdîl bên haqqōdeš ûbên hahōl ûbên haṭṭāmē' ûbên haṭṭāhôr).[96] Thus the entire charge against the priests, like that against the people of Jerusalem in verses 6-12, is based on the laws of Leviticus. Even the unusual phrase "they have hidden their eyes from my Sabbaths" (ûmišabbᵉtôtay he'lîmû 'ênêhem), in which the idiom "to hide the eyes from" seems to mean the failure to prosecute transgressors, has a parallel in Leviticus 20:4. There the possibility is considered that the people of the land might "hide their eyes from" (ya'lîmû 'am-hā'āreṣ 'et-'ênêhem min) a man offering his children to Molech; to commit such an act would be "to profane my holy name" (lᵉhallᵉl

---

⁹⁵ Cf. also Leviticus 26:2.

⁹⁶ This could explain the anomalous article on haṭṭāmē' in Ezekiel 22:26 as being an unconscious assimilation of the quotation with the source on the part of Ezekiel or a later scribe. However the same feature (article with the first term, none with the second) occurs also in Ezekiel 42:20 (bên haqqōdeš lᵉhōl) which suggests rather that this was an idiom accepted to Ezekiel (J. Barr, "Some Notes on bên "Between" in Classical Hebrew", JSS 23 [1978] 5). The replacement of the idiom bên...bên with bên...lᵉ may be due to assimilation to the very similar command in Leviticus 20:25, though it may alternatively be due to Ezekiel's preference for the latter phrase (Cf. Barr, 10; M. Rooker, Biblical Hebrew in Transition. The Language of the Book of Ezekiel, JSOTS 90 (Sheffield 1990)117; A. Hurvitz, A Linguistic Study of the Relationship between the Priestly Source and the Book of Ezekiel, Cahiers de le Revue Biblique 20 [Paris 1982] 113f.).

'et-šēm qodší; Lev. 20:3) just as in Ezekiel closing the eyes to the sabbaths leads to the Lord "being profaned among you" (*wā'ēhal bᵉtôkām*).[97]

This background of the accusations in Leviticus carries with it the implicit threat of the curses laid out in Leviticus 26, a passage having other links with the book of Ezekiel.[98] Yet alongside the threats lies also a promise: that those who confess their iniquity and humble their hearts and accept their guilt may be restored (Lev. 26:40ff.). While the accusations are schematized, we have no reason to doubt their basic validity, any more than that of the accusations against the other social classes. Though a priest, Ezekiel is not blind to the sins of his own class. They are indicted for neglect of their duties, which included giving direction (*tôrâ*) and protecting Yahweh's sacred things by ensuring the proper distinction between holy and unholy, clean and unclean.[99] Included in the latter task was ensuring that the sabbath was kept holy. Their failures and sins had resulted in the profaning of Yahweh in their midst. These are serious offences—yet even in these offences the priesthood is not *singled out* for blame. Not only the priests but the whole city of Jerusalem is guilty of having "despised my holy things and profaned my sabbaths" (Ezek. 22:8). Overall then, the priests must be adjudged to escape the condemnations of chapters 1-33 with remarkably little blame, certainly in comparison to every other stratum of society.

4 Ezekiel 44: The "Downgrading" of the Levites

This chapter has been used since the time of Wellhausen as part of the basis for arguing that prior to the time of Ezekiel all Levites had served as priests. Many had been deprived of their livelihood and forced to come to Jerusalem with the closing of the High Places during the reign of Josiah where, however, the Jerusalemite (Zadokite) priesthood was unwilling to allow them a share in the perquisites of the Temple. They were only permitted to fulfil the tasks of a lower order of minor clergy. This is then said to be the situation Ezekiel inherited and which he sought to justify on moral grounds. Notwithstanding the popularity which this interpretation has enjoyed down through the years, it rests on a misreading of the passages concerned.

The first point to notice about this chapter is that the object of critique

---

[97] Apart from these passages, the idiom "to hide one's eyes" only occurs in Proverbs 28:27; Isaiah 1:15 and 1 Samuel 12:3.

[98] Reventlow, *Wächter*, 42.

[99] Cooke, *Ezekiel*, 244f.

is not simply the Levites but the entire house of Israel (v.6).[100] In a similar way to Ezekiel 43:7ff., where the polemic is first aimed at the whole house of Israel, and only secondarily at the former kings who bore a specific responsibility for the area affected by the sin,[101] so here also the attack focuses first on the whole house of Israel and only subsequently on the Levites as those who should have prevented the sin.

What was the sin with which this chapter is concerned? The people of Israel, under the form of address characteristic of Ezekiel: "[House of] rebelliousness",[102] are accused of having "brought foreigners uncircumcised in heart and flesh into my sanctuary, desecrating my Temple".[103] This offence has been variously evaluated: reference has often been made to Joshua 9:27, where the Gibeonites are made hewers of wood and drawers of water for the sanctuary.[104] On the other hand, Hengstenberg thought that the word "foreigners" was used in a purely metaphorical sense, the actual referent being the unfaithful priests.[105] More likely, however, it referred to the well attested practice of employing foreign Temple guards (cf 2 Ki. 11:14-19).[106] J. Milgrom has argued that in the Old Testament *šāmar mišmeret* is cultic terminology which refers to guard duty.[107] Such a technical sense would seem to fit well in this context: the people are accused of not having "kept charge of my holy things" (*š^emartem mišmeret qodāšāy*; v.8).[108] Instead they have assigned others "to keep my charge in my sanctuary" (*l^ešōm^erê mišmartî b^emiqdāšî*; v.8). Further, the Levites are envisaged as replacements for these foreigners: v.10 is a dependent clause which is subordinate to what has preceded it in v.9, and which picks up its verbal

---

[100]   Ebach, *Kritik und Utopie*, 239.In view of the fact that the prophet blames the laity for the transgressions observed in Ezekiel 8 (see below, p.111ff.), it is perhaps significant that it is while the prophet is entering the Temple complex through the North Gate, as he had in the vision of chapter 8, that he is reminded of the sins of the people.

[101]   See above, p.41.

[102]   S.R. Driver, *An Introduction to the Literature of the Old Testament* (Edinburgh and New York ⁹1913) 296. MT has simply *'el-merî*, LXX reads *pros ton oikon ton parapik-rainonta*; it is hard to tell whether *bêt* has actually dropped out of the Hebrew text or whether it was originally left unexpressed in view of the immediately following *'el-bêt yiśrā'ēl*.

[103]   The term used for foreigners, *b^enê-nēkār*, is otherwise unattested in Ezekiel (Zimmerli, *Ezechiel*, 1124). It is however also used in Genesis 17 in a context where the ideas of circumcision and breaking covenant are prominent, and it may be that the latter ideas dictated the choice of the term. Alternatively *zārîm* could have been avoided here because of its technical usage in P of a person unauthorized to perform a cultic act, a layperson (L. Allen, *Ezekiel 20-48*, 245).

[104]   E.g. by E. König, "The Priests and Levites in Ez 44:7-15", *ET* 12 (1901) 300.

[105]   Hengstenberg, *Ezechiel*, 268. In this he is following the earlier rabbinic interpretation; see S. Fisch, *Ezekiel*, Soncino Books of the Bible (London 1950) 303.

[106]   Carley, *Ezekiel*, 318; Skinner, *Ezekiel*, 427f.

[107]   *Studies in Levitical Terminology, I: The Encroacher and the Levite; The Term 'Aboda* (Berkeley 1970) 8-11.

[108]   A similar accusation is levelled against the city of Jerusalem in Ezekiel 22:8: "You (sing.) have despised my holy things" (*qodāšāy bāzît*).

idea from that verse.[109] The thought is "No foreigner will enter...*but rather* the Levites [will enter]". the specific role assigned to the Levites is that of "armed guards (*p^{e}quddôt*)[110] to the house" (Ezek. 44:11), a term which also describes the royal bodyguard in 2 Kings 11:18.[111] The replacement of this royal bodyguard with a group of higher cultic sanctity would then correspond to the distancing of the Temple from the royal palace found in the previous chapter.[112] The concern in both sections is to protect the sanctity of the Temple better than in the past, paying particular attention to entrances and exits (compare Ezek. 43:11 with 44:5). This focus would naturally draw attention to the role of those controlling these entrances. The replacement of the foreign guards with Levites is not regarded by Ezekiel as an innovation, however. The description of the offence of using foreigners as Temple guards as a breach of covenant (Ezek. 44:7) would seem to imply the existence of legislation for a class of lawful keepers of the charge of the sanctuary, such as is found in Numbers 18:3f.[113] It would appear then that Ezekiel had in mind a similar arrangement to that described by P.

Having addressed the whole house of Israel and rebuked them for their failure to employ proper (i.e. Levitical) gatekeepers, the prophet moves on to deal with the specific sins of the Levites. The assertion in v.10 that the Levites, and not the foreigners, are the appropriate gatekeepers of the restored Temple immediately raises a possible objection: "Have the Levites not disqualified themselves from this position by their own sinful behaviour?". In response to this objection, the prophet recognizes a certain validity to the charge. The Levites have indeed strayed far away from Yahweh, serving the House of Israel before their idols and leading them astray. They have failed in their responsibility to guard the house, instead allowing others to take over their proper roles. For this offence they shall "bear their iniquity" (*nāś^e'û ^{a}wōnām*; Ezek. 44:10,12) — that is, receive the divine punishment that this kind of sin brings upon the person who commits it.[114] Because of the guilt that they bear, they may not undertake the most holy tasks of ministering before Yahweh as a priest or approaching the

---

[109] Duke, "Punishment or Restoration", 65. For a fuller discussion of the syntactical connections of this passage, see below, p.84.

[110] For this translation compare also Ezekiel 9:1; cf. Milgrom, *Levitical Terminology*, 84; Ahlstrom, *Royal Administration*, 47f.

[111] Duke, "Punishment or Restoration", 65.

[112] Note that the Chronicler in his version of the events recounted in 2 Kings 11 also replaces the royal bodyguard with Levites for reasons of cultic sanctity (L. Allen, *Ezekiel 20-48*, 261).

[113] Abba, "Priests and Levites", 6; van Hoonacker, "Prêtres et Lévites", 183.

[114] R. Whybray, *Thanksgiving for a Liberated Prophet. An Interpretation of Isaiah 53*, JSOTS 4 (Sheffield 1978) 31-57. *Contra* Duke ("Punishment or Restoration", 66) and Milgrom (*Levitical Terminology*, 27) the phrase never has the sense "They (the Levites) will be responsible for their (the people's) guilt (of encroachment)". The Levites do act to shield the people - but if they fail in this it is their own ^{a}wōn which they incur (cf. Whybray, 45).

most holy place.

This restriction does not in itself indicate that they had such a right in immediately prior times which is now being removed from them through a process of "downgrading". An interesting parallel is found in Leviticus 21:17-23, which lays down the regulations for a blemished descendant of Aaron. Many of the handicaps listed are birth defects, so that the people affected would never have served as priests — and are not called priests. Yet it would not be appropriate to describe their situation as a "downgrading". They share important privileges with the priests (v.22) — but they are not permitted to serve at the altar. Notice how the phrases "he has a defect" in Leviticus and "they shall bear their sin" in Ezekiel serve as functionally equivalent motive clauses for the exclusion. Exclusion from the altar is thus not necessarily in itself "downgrading". In fact, for the Levites rather the opposite is the case: in spite of their past sin they are still graciously to be restored to the position of privilege and honour which they once held as gatekeepers in the Temple. [115] In a society in which prestige is indicated by one's relationship to the Temple this is no small privilege. [116]

In parallel with the idea of the Levites "bearing their sin", they will also "bear their shame and the abominations which they have committed" (nāśᵉ'û kᵉlimmātām wᵉtô ᶜᵃbôtam ᵃšer 'āśû; Ezek. 44:13). The most striking parallel to this is found in Ezekiel 16:44-63. There Jerusalem is called upon to "bear her own shame" (Ezek. 16:52,54) because of the abominations she has committed. That is, she is to recognize the justice of the divine judgement which has overtaken her. Yet this recognition occurs within the framework of restoration. It is when Yahweh brings back the captives that Jerusalem will "bear her shame" (Ezek. 16:54). Zimmerli has noted that the idea of shame over transgressions is characteristic in Ezekiel "nicht im Rahmen der Gerichtspredigt sondern in der Heilsankündigung". [117] As Duke puts it:

> To receive God's forgiveness and gracious acts of restoration, after having sinned against God, resulted in one bearing shame and humiliation. [118]

For the Levites, restoration to their former position in the second rank of Temple clergy acts as a reminder of their former sins in two ways. First, the wall of separation between the clerical ranks is raised higher than ever before in the new Temple, with its strong stress on separation and gradation. Second, in Ezekiel's Temple this separation is founded in the past

---

[115] We shall demonstrate later in more detail that this passage is indeed a restoration. See below, p.84ff.

[116] Niditch, "Ezekiel 40-48", 219.

[117] Zimmerli, *Ezechiel*, 1085.

[118] Duke, "Punishment or Restoration", 70.

behaviour of the two groups. Not only are the Levites not priests more clearly than ever before, but now they are not priests because of their own past sins.

Many attempts have been made to identify the exact sin of the Levites to which Ezekiel refers. The most frequent explanation since the time of Wellhausen has been that they were the priests of the High Places prior to Josiah's reform.[119] But Ezekiel describes their error as serving "before the idols" (gillûlîm), a term which is never applied to the High Places; rather it has reference to foreign gods and images.[120] Further, it is hard to see why they should be so harshly judged when ex hypothesi this group gave up their condemnable practices many years ago and have been serving, presumably faithfully, in the Temple ever since. Why should the (righteous) descendants suffer for the sins of their fathers? Such an interpretation would be in apparent conflict with the doctrine of Ezekiel 18:20:[121]

> The person who sins shall die. The son shall not bear the guilt of the father, nor the father bear the guilt of the son. The righteousness of the righteous shall be upon himself and the wickedness of the wicked shall be upon himself.

To be sure, Ezekiel recognizes also the sins of past generations (ch. 16, 20), but the force of his condemnation falls always upon the present sinful generation, who are seen as sharing the sins of the past and who therefore stand justly condemned.[122]

In an attempt to find a sin which the Levites could have committed which would not have implicated the Zadokites, Abba identifies the sin of the Levites with the idolatrous calf worship of the Northern Kingdom.[123] This "national apostasy", however, likewise ceased many years before, with the end of the Northern Kingdom in 722 BC, and so the same criticism may be levelled that the punishment does not fall on those committing the sin. A further objection which can be raised against the interpretations given above is that there is no indication in the text that the Levites previously functioned as priests. Certainly they served (šrt) Israel in front of their idols, but this is not exclusively a priestly function (cf. Num. 1:50;

---

[119] E.g. Carley, Ezekiel, 294; Kaufmann, Religion, 444; Hals, Ezekiel, 319.

[120] M. Haran, Temples and Temple Service in Ancient Israel (Oxford 1978) 104f.

[121] H.S. Warleigh, Ezekiel's Temple: its Design Unfolded, its Architecture Displayed, and the Subjects Connected with it Discussed (London 1856) 179.

[122] For this principle, see Sedlmeier: "die Strafe für die Greuel immer den trifft, der sie verübt" (Studien zu Komposition und Theologie von Ezechiel 20, Stuttgarter Biblische Beiträge 21 [Stuttgart 1990] 210). A similar objection applies to Haran's idea (Temples and Temple Service, 106) that the sin of the Levites and the righteousness of the Zadokites are both to be located in the time of Manasseh. Berry's suggestion, that the priests of the Samaritan Temple destroyed in 130 BC are indicated ("Priests and Levites", JBL 42 [1923] 237), obviously depends on his theory of a very late date for Ezekiel 40-48!

[123] Abba, "Priests and Levites", 5; similarly Douglas, "Ezekiel's Temple", 516.

3:31; 1 Chr. 16:37).[124] Indeed, in the context an exact parallel is drawn between their former ministry on behalf of the people before idols and their future ministry on behalf of the people before the Lord (v.11b, 12). Since the latter ministry is expressly non-priestly, it seems likely that the former was also non-priestly. Thus we must understand the Levites to be a pre-existing (lower) class of cultic personnel who went astray with the mass of the people after idols (cf. Ezek. 20:30ff.; 23:37ff.), and performed cultic duties in the service of idolatrous cults. This may have been the worship offered to those cults which were revived during the last years of Judah's existence (cf. Jer. 7:16-18; 11:9-13).[125] Alternatively, it might refer to the continuing exercise of cultic worship in Jerusalem after its destruction in 587 BC.[126] That such existed is evidenced by the account of the fate of eighty men on their way to Jerusalem bringing offerings to be presented in the "house of the Lord" (Jer. 41:5ff.). As noted above, if this is the sin in question, Levitical involvement in this cult may have been limited to non-sacrificial work,[127] but even such might have been unacceptable to a purist such as Ezekiel. Without fuller knowledge of the events of this period, however, a conclusive identification of the sin of the Levites is unlikely to be possible.

C. The Future Of Priestly Leadership In The Book Of Ezekiel

1 The Priests

The future for the (Zadokite)[128] priesthood is rosy indeed. Their privileges are expressed in a variety of ways: their land surrounds the territory of the Temple within the sacred area (t⁽ᵉ⁾rûmat haqqōdeš; Ezek. 45:4; 48:10). They are the ones who may enter the inner court to approach Yahweh and offer sacrifices and to keep his charge (Ezek. 44:15). They acquire the sole right to stand as judges over the people (Ezek. 44:24), a task previously shared with the z⁽ᵉ⁾qēnîm.[129] What is more, all this privilege is described as a reward

---

[124] Duke, "Punishment or Restoration", 64f.

[125] The "private cults" discussed above, p.67.

[126] This is suggested by N. Allan, "Jerusalem Priesthood", 262ff. So also E. Achtemeier, The Community and Message of Isaiah 56-66 (Minneapolis 1982) 23.

[127] Thus favouring the view of D.R. Jones that animal sacrifices were not offered ("The Cessation of Sacrifice after the Destruction of the Temple in 586 B.C.", JTS n.s. 14 (1963) 12-31) against that of N. Allan, "Jerusalem Priesthood", 263. There is no conclusive evidence one way or the other, however; see Cody, Priesthood, 144.

[128] The priests are specifically identified as Zadokites in Ezekiel 40:46, 43:19, 44:15 and 48:11. Some commentators have sought to separate these references out into a separate "Zadokite" stratum (on which, see below p.87). For the appropriateness of the identification priests = Zadokites at the time of Ezekiel see McConville, "Priests and Levites", 8-13.

[129] On this see further above, p.54, and below p.131.

for their faithfulness in a time of error (Ezek. 44:15; 48:11).[130] But this very righteousness of the Zadokites has caused even more difficulties for commentators than the sin of the Levites. It is not so much the inclusion of the Levites in a movement of grievous error that is found unthinkable as the exoneration of the Zadokites.[131] This is chiefly because of the failure to observe what was noted above,[132] that the outrages in chapters 8-11 are a visionary compilation rather than a historical report and the blame for them is nowhere attributed to the priests. In fact, much of the force of Ezekiel 23:38f. would be lost if the state of the Temple had literally been as bad as chapters 8-11 suggest. There the people are accused of committing abominable practices outside the Temple and then defiling the Temple by entering it. But if the Temple were completely defiled to begin with in the manner described in Ezekiel 8, this would hardly matter.[133]

The "righteousness" of the Zadokites is also found incompatible with the criticisms levelled against the priests in chapter 22.[134] The writer of Ezekiel 44 is certainly not unaware of the faults of the priesthood listed in chapter 22. In fact, he specifically insists that these particular sins be done away with. In the past, the priests failed to distinguish between the holy and the common and taught that there was no difference between clean and unclean (Ezek. 22:26); the future priests *will* teach the difference between holy and common and how to distinguish between unclean and clean (Ezek. 44:23). Whereas in the past they did violence to Yahweh's law and shut their eyes to the keeping of his sabbaths (Ezek. 22:26), in future they will keep his laws and keep his sabbaths holy (Ezek. 44:24).[135] This awareness of the past sin of the priests suggests that the reference to their past faithfulness should not be pressed as an absolute statement. Rather, even while on the one hand he affirms the comparative righteousness of the Zadokite priests, on the other he insists that their past sins shall not be repeated.[136] The faithfulness of the past is not to be a source of pride in which the Zadokites may rest, but rather it brings them greater responsibilities which require of them a higher standard of commitment (Ezek. 44:17-31).

Thus from the perspective of Ezekiel 40-48 the Zadokite priests are not

---

[130] Thus Hals is surely wrong when he states "The only 'reward' or 'salvation' given to the Zadokites is that they are not deposed" (*Ezekiel*, 319). The privilege of offering sacrifices and occupying the land around the Temple is indeed a great reward.

[131] Cf. e.g. Zimmerli, "Planungen", 251f.; Gunneweg, *Leviten und Priester*, 203; Procksch, *Fürst und Priester*, 107; Abba, "Levites", 5; Klein, *Ezekiel*, 178; Hölscher, *Hesekiel*, 197; Carley, *Ezekiel among the Prophets*, 61.

[132] See above, p.67.

[133] Hengstenberg, *Ezechiel*, 73.

[134] Zimmerli, *Ezechiel*, 1140.

[135] Zimmerli, *Ezechiel*, 1135. Ebach comments: "Was dort als typische Verfehlung der Priester galt, soll für die Zukunft ausgeschlossen sein" (*Kritik und Utopie*, 241).

[136] We noted a similar insistence on the non-repetition of the sins of the past in the case of the *nāśî'*. See above, p.56.

in a separate category from everyone else—the "righteous" as opposed to all the "unrighteous". It is rather a question of degree: more or less righteous. Just as there are gradations of holiness in his apportionment of the land, ranging from the Most Holy Place, through the inner and outer courts of the Temple, to the *t^erûmâ* and the land apportioned to the tribes, so also there are exactly corresponding gradations in access based on Ezekiel's evaluation of the past righteousness of the people concerned. No one is permitted access to the Most Holy Place: that is for Yahweh alone. In his guided tour of the new Temple precincts, it is striking that while Ezekiel himself is allowed to go all the way to the doors of the Most Holy Place, it is only the accompanying angel who enters the Most Holy Place to measure it; Ezekiel remains outside (Ezek. 41:1-4).[137] It is particularly notable that a ritual to cleanse the Holy of Holies, such as the one prominent in Leviticus 16,[138] is absent from Ezekiel's atonement ceremony. Just as the east gate was closed to human access after the glory of Yahweh passed through it (Ezek. 44:2), so the Most Holy Place is likewise out of bounds now that the glory has once again taken up residence in his Temple.[139] When the land is distributed, there is an ascending scale of sanctity as one approaches the Temple (people, *nāśî'*, Levites, priests), but the highest level is reached with the priesthood who have access to the inner court: there is no higher level of sanctity permitted access to the Most Holy Place.

If, however, the righteousness of the Zadokites was only relative, how then are we to explain the strength of the positive language applied to them? A solution to this problem is suggested by M. Weinfeld's study of the "Covenant of Grant".[140] In this type of covenant, in which the faithfulness of an ancestor secures the rights of his progeny, there is a distinctive terminology, which extends across Hittite and Akkadian documents of the Late Bronze Age, Neo-Assyrian documents and several biblical covenants. In these the ancestor is described as having "kept my charge" (Akkadian *issur massartī* ; Hebrew *šāmar mišmartî*), having "walked before me" (*ina maḫrīya ittalak, izziz*; *hithallēk l^epānay*) and as having "a perfect heart" (*libbašu gummuru*; *lēb šālēm*).[141] This suggests that the proper background against which to evaluate the "righteousness" of the Zadokites is the righteousness of someone like Abraham (Gen. 26:5) or David (1 Ki. 3:6; 9:4)

---

[137] L. Allen, *Ezekiel 20-48*, 232.

[138] Cf. Leviticus 16:11-17.

[139] Chary, *Prophètes et Culte*, 18. The absence of a ritual for this area may well contribute to the lack of prominence given to the Chief Priest in Ezekiel's design (so Haran, *Law Code*, 61 n.29).

[140] M. Weinfeld, "The Covenant of Grant in the Old Testament and in the Ancient Near East", *JAOS* 90 (1970) 184-205. Cf. also Levenson, *Theology*, 145ff.

[141] Weinfeld, "Covenant of Grant", 186f.

—neither of whom was entirely free from blemish. During a time when such fidelity to Yahweh was rare, the Zadokites—at least according to Ezekiel—were marked out as a class by such fidelity.[142]

This picture should make it clear that even to Ezekiel the Zadokite, the faithfulness of the Zadokites was a relative characteristic and not absolute perfection. Thus they too can be criticized—though in less severe terms than the other groups—for their past failings and urged on to greater faithfulness in the future. Nor do the Zadokite priests have unlimited power. They are certainly not conceived as ruling over the people in a hierocracy, nor do they even claim all the limelight within the cult. As we noted in our discussion of the $n\bar{a}\acute{s}\hat{\imath}$', his is the dominant single figure within the cult. He is given the task of preparing the offerings "to make atonement ($l^ekapp\bar{e}r$) for the house of Israel" (Ezek. 45:17), a notable privilege given the central place of atonement in the plan of Ezekiel.[143] It seems that there is a harmony of the offices in the restored kingdom envisaged here.[144] It is not simply a matter of the $n\bar{a}\acute{s}\hat{\imath}$' assisting the priests,[145] nor of the priests being simply the officials of the $n\bar{a}\acute{s}\hat{\imath}$';[146] rather the $n\bar{a}\acute{s}\hat{\imath}$' has chief public prominence at the official offerings, yet the Zadokite priests have the privilege of operating in a realm where only they can, because of their greater sanctity.[147]

2 The Levites

Most discussions of the future role of the Levites in Ezekiel 40-48 have, since the time of Wellhausen, been phrased in terms of their "downgrading". In view of the honourable role which they are assigned in the cult of Ezekiel 40-48, it is questionable whether this is an adequate perspective on their position.[148] Certainly they are not permitted to enter the inner court of the Temple and perform the acts assigned to the Zadokite priests there. However, it is not at all clear that such a right was actually theirs before the exile either. Certainly the Levites are criticized for their past misdeeds, but so also are all the other classes of personnel as well, even the Zadok-

---

[142] Levenson, *Theology*, 146.
[143] See above, p.52.
[144] Levenson speaks in a different context of the priesthood as a "counterbalance" to the monarchy (*Theology*, 115). Is a similar harmony - though perhaps with a different slant, more in favour of the Davidic Ruler - envisaged in Zechariah? Cf. P. Hanson, "Israelite Religion in the Early Postexilic Period", *Ancient Israelite Religion. Essays in Honor of F.M. Cross*, P.D. Miller, Jr., —— and S.D. McBride, eds. (Philadelphia 1987) 496; D.L. Petersen, *Haggai and Zechariah 1-8*, Old Testament Library (Philadelphia and London 1984) 278.
[145] So Procksch, "Fürst und Priester", 119; R. Smend, *Ezechiel*, 311.
[146] U. Kellermann, *Messias und Gesetz*, Biblische Studien 61 (Neukirchen-Vluyn 1971) 42.
[147] Ebach, *Kritik und Utopie*, 270.
[148] See above, p.78.

ites.[149] Instead of the Levites being simply "downgraded" to a lower cultic position, we shall seek to demonstrate that the Levites are actually being restored to an honourable cultic position, which had existed prior to the exile, as well as being assigned additional tasks as a consequence of their sin and the people's sin. To do this, we need to take a closer look at Ezekiel 44:9-12:

> Thus says the Sovereign Lord: No foreigner uncircumcised of heart and uncircumcised of flesh shall enter my sanctuary, out of[150] all the foreigners who are in the midst of the children of Israel, [10]but rather the Levites who went far from me when Israel strayed, who strayed from me after their idols. They shall bear their iniquity [11]but they shall be in my sanctuary, serving [as][151] armed guards at the gates of the house and serving in the house. They shall slay the burnt offering and the sacrifice for the people, and they shall stand before them [the people] to serve them. [12]Because they served[152] them before their idols and were a stumbling block of iniquity to the House of Israel, therefore I have raised my hand against them, declares the Sovereign Lord, and they shall bear their iniquity. [13]They shall not approach me, to act as my priest, nor to approach any of my sacred things, to the most sacred things.[153] They shall bear their shame, because of the abominations which they have committed. [14]Yet I will appoint them keepers of the charge of the Temple, to do all its work and all that is to be done in it.[154]

Because of the versification of this passage, the force of some of the contrasts which it brings out are commonly overlooked. Notably, the connection between v.9 and v.10 is often severed[155] and the sentence breaks which I have put in the middle of verses 10 and 11 are often placed at the end of those verses.[156] The result is to obscure completely the flow of the passage. There are several syntactical observations which support the division given above. The first is the fact that v.10 is a dependent clause which is subordinate to what has preceded it in v.9, and which picks up its

---

[149] See above, p.81.

[150] Hebrew *l*. Cf. GKC § 143 e; G.R. Driver, "Ezekiel: Linguistic and Textual Problems", *Biblica* 35 (1954) 301.

[151] The clause "armed guards at the gates of the house" defines more closely the nature of the Levites' service. Compare 1 Samuel 2:18, where Samuel is described as serving [*šrt*] as a *na'ar* in the Temple at Shiloh. Cf. Cody "Priesthood", 74ff. On the construction cf. GKC § 116 q.

[152] There is no need to replace *y'šār'tû* by *šēr'tû* (so BHS; Zimmerli, *Ezechiel*, 1120) since the imperfect can have the sense of an action in the past which continued throughout a shorter or longer period; cf. e.g. Jeremiah 36:18; GKC § 107 b. Cooke explains it as a frequentative action (*Ezekiel*, 491). The imperfect is also supported by the following *wāw* consecutive + perfect (*w'hāyû*).

[153] On *qodšê haqqodāšîm* see Haran, *Temples and Temple Service*, 172 n.50.

[154] My translation.

[155] So RSV; NKJV; REB; Fohrer & Galling, *Ezechiel*, 247. In favour of a connection see Duke, "Punishment or Restoration", 65.

[156] So RSV; NKJV; Zimmerli, *Ezechiel*, 1118. In favour of the division I have proposed in verse 10 see L. Allen, *Ezekiel 20-48*, 239.

verbal idea from that verse.[157] The thought is "No foreigner will enter...*but rather* the Levites [will enter]". This emphasis is supported by the word order of v.11: instead of "They will be serving in my sanctuary...", where the focus would be on their service, it reads "They will be in my sanctuary, serving...". This puts the focus on the *location* of their service, namely "in my sanctuary". In contrast to those not permitted to enter the sanctuary, the Levites will enter it.

The phrase "They will bear their guilt" is clearly related to the description of the Levites as those who have gone astray, but in the context it serves as a preparatory statement for what follows, rather than as a conclusion for what precedes it. A comparison with Ezekiel 14:10f. is instructive. There too the phrase "They will bear their guilt" (*w⁽ᵉ⁾nāś⁽ᵉ⁾'û ⁽ᵃ⁾wōnām*) is used in a context of judgement upon those who have sinned —yet a judgement which is combined with a promise of restoration for the future, introduced (as in Ezek. 44:11) with *w⁽ᵉ⁾hāyû*.[158] In Ezekiel 14, the guilty parties are excluded from the covenant people (v.8f.). Yet the Levites of Ezekiel 44, in spite of bearing their sin, will still be found "in my sanctuary" (*b⁽ᵉ⁾miqdāšî*). Verse 11 is divided into two halves by the contrast between the participles in the first half (*m⁽ᵉ⁾šār⁽ᵉ⁾tîm*, twice) and the finite verbs (*yišh⁽ᵃ⁾tû, ya'am⁽ᵉ⁾dû*) in the second part, introduced by the emphatic pronoun *hēmmâ*.[159] The participles refer here to the resumption of their former duties, while the imperfect introduces the new element. This new element, slaying the burnt offering and the sacrifice for the people and standing before them [the people] to serve them, is then explained as a judgement appropriate to their sin in v.12:

> Because they served them before their idols and were a stumbling block of iniquity to the House of Israel, therefore I have raised my hand against them, declares the Sovereign Lord, and they shall bear their iniquity.

Just as they served the House of Israel before idols, now they will serve them before Yahweh.

The train of thought of the passage may thus be paraphrased as follows: The foreigners who were previously employed to do the Temple guard duty[160] are no longer to fulfil that role; rather that responsibility is to be returned to the Levites, even though they joined in Israel's sin. The Levites past is not forgotten—they *will* bear their sin—but still they are to be

---

[157] Duke, "Punishment or Restoration", 65.
[158] This similarity, as well as the use of *'āwōn* in v.12, militates against Duke's opinion that the phrase "they shall bear their guilt" is used in a technical sense in Ezekiel 44:10 ("Punishment or Restoration", 66f.).
[159] Duke, "Punishment or Restoration", 68.
[160] See above, p.76.

restored to their former tasks in the Temple: guard duty and service of the
house. As a consequence of their past involvement with abominations, they
cannot share in the privileges of the Zadokite priesthood (v.13). The extent
to which this involves an element of "downgrading" depends on what
privileges the Levites exercised before. The possibility has been suggested
that after the destruction of 587 BC the Levites exercised a more significant — and from a Zadokite perspective illegitimate — ministry in Jerusalem
in the absence of the Zadokites.[161] If this is the case, Ezekiel's demand for
a return to the former *status quo* would have been a downgrading. On the
other hand, as we noted above, there is nothing in the passage which
requires them to have acted as priests in the past.[162] The focus of the
passage itself is not judgement but restoration. Even though the Levites may
not have the privilege of priestly ministry, yet they still have a ministry of
their own.[163] This ministry is not, in fact, restricted in comparison to their
pre-exilic role but rather *extended*: now they are to have the additional tasks
of slaughtering the burnt offerings and sacrifices on behalf of the people
(Ezek. 44:11). This is a clear departure from the former custom[164] and
represents a "downgrading" of the people in relation to the Levites.[165]

This privileged position of the Levites compared to the people becomes
even clearer when their place in the restored land is considered. They are
alotted a portion of the land which is within the sacred portion, second
only to the priests in terms of nearness to the Temple (Ezek. 48:13). As
with their ministry in the cult, they do not receive the full privilege granted
to the Zadokite priesthood, yet their status is clearly higher than that of the
remaining lay tribes.[166] In view of these privileges, therefore, it would be
better to speak of a clarification of the distinctive position of the Levites
rather than a downgrading.[167]

---

[161] See above, p.80.

[162] See above, p.79. Note also that in a closely related passage, Numbers 18, the laity
are prohibited from approaching (*hiqrîb*) the tabernacle (v.22), a proscription which hardly
implies that they earlier held a priestly office. Cf. Fishbane, *Biblical Interpretation*, 140.

[163] Ezekiel's propositions do not represent the end of discussion of the relationship between
priesthood and Levites by any means. The Temple Scroll grants a higher status to Levites than
any biblical record, including some priestly privileges. Cf. J. Milgrom, "Studies in the Temple
Scroll", *JBL* 97 (1978) 503.

[164] Cooke, *Ezekiel*, 481.

[165] L. Allen, *Ezekiel 20-48*, 261; Milgrom, *Levitical Terminology*, 84.

[166] However, note that in Ezekiel 40-48 the Levites are the servants of the people, not of
the priests, as they are in the Priestly stratum.

[167] Condemnation and restoration co-exist in other places in Ezekiel also, as with "the
mountains of Israel" which are condemned in Ezekiel 6 and promised a restoration in Ezekiel 36 (L. Boadt, "Rhetorical Strategies in Ezekiel's Oracles of Judgement", *Ezekiel and His
Book*, J. Lust, ed. (Leuven 1986) 190).

D. Conclusions

This examination of the texts in Ezekiel which concern priests or Levites has shown that there is no disharmony among them. Rather, there is a consistent pattern, as we found also for the *nāśî'*, that future standing in the restored kingdom depends on past faithfulness. From Ezekiel's perspective, the Zadokite priesthood represented the most faithful stratum of society. Therefore, they are the ones qualified to exercise a priestly role in the new Temple. They do not have a perfect record, however, so even their access is limited. Only Yahweh can enter the Most Holy Place. In comparison to the Zadokites, the Levites have a flawed record and so take a lower place in the new Temple. Yet it is an honourable place, a restoration to their former functions of guarding the house and serving in it. Indeed, they receive additional responsibilities which extend their duties further at the expense of the laity. All this is in harmony with the picture given in the judgement oracles of Ezekiel.

Excursus: The So-Called Zadokite Stratum In Ezekiel 40-48

Gese's influential literary-critical discussion of Ezekiel 40-48 designates the following sections as belonging to what he terms "die Sadoqiden-schicht": Ezekiel 44:6-16, with the appendices 44:17-30 (especially 28-30a) and 45:13-15. Its distinctives are said to be the "you (pl.)" style of address to Israel, the confining of the priestly rights to Zadokites and the degradation of other priests to Temple servants. To express this distinction a terminology is developed connecting *šrt* or *mšmrt* with the object *hbyt* or *hmqdš*.[168] According to Gese, this stratum has influenced the rest of chapters 40-48 through a row of striking glosses (Ezek. 40:46b; 43:19; 48:11).[169]

More recent studies have been less confident about the connection of Ezekiel 45:13-15 with the Zadokite stratum, effectively reducing this stratum to the block 44:6-16, 28-30a.[170] Since the "you (pl.)" address to Israel is by no means confined to this block,[171] all that is now distinctive of the "Zadokite stratum" when compared with the "earlier material" is a supposedly different view of the priesthood. The earlier material (such as

---

[168] Gese, *Verfassungsentwurf*, 111.
[169] *Verfassungsentwurf*, 112.
[170] E.g. Zimmerli suggests that Ezekiel 45:13-15 could "möglicherweise" belong with 44:6-16, 28-30a. Cf. Gunneweg, *Leviten und Priester*, 188; L. Allen, *Ezekiel 20-48*, 253.
[171] Cf. e.g. Ezekiel 43:27; 45:1,6,13,20b,21; 47:13,14,21; 48:8.

Ezek. 40:45,46a) is said to distinguish two levels of priestly service, but with both groups still termed priests, while later material (the Zadokite stratum) terms the lower group Levites and denies them priestly status, while it defines the upper group explicitly as Zadokites.[172] Is such a stratification actually in evidence in the text?

Turning first to Ezekiel 40:45f., this passage describes two rooms for the priests:

> And he said to me, This chamber which faces south is for the priests who have charge of the Temple (*hakkōhᵃnîm šōmrê mišmeret habbayit*), ⁴⁶and the chamber which faces north is for the priests who have charge of the altar (*hakkōhᵃnîm šōmrê mišmeret hammizbēaḥ*); these are the sons of Zadok, who alone among the sons of Levi may come near to the Lord to minister to him.

In the reconstruction described above, the last sentence is viewed as a gloss identifying the priests who have charge of the altar with the Zadokites, while the priests who have charge of the Temple are identified as the Levites on the basis of the identical language of Ezekiel 44:14. But in the first place it must be questioned whether the terminology will bear the weight placed upon it. McConville has argued that the terminology for the priesthood is actually quite flexible in the Old Testament, especially where the primary concern is other than the inner relations of the clergy.[173] It is a methodological error to equate the group assigned "to guard the house" in Ezekiel 40:45 with the group similarly assigned in Ezekiel 44:14, as a cursory comparison with the book of Numbers will show. In Numbers 18:1-7, the Aaronides (in two groups?) were assigned the duty of guarding the sanctuary and the altar (*'ēt mišmeret haqqōdeš wᵉ'ēt mišmeret hammizbēaḥ*; v.5) while the lower duty given to the Levites is guarding the Tent of meeting (*mišmeret kol-hā'ōhel*; v.3). Elsewhere in Numbers, however, guarding the sanctuary (*mišmeret haqqōdeš*) can equally be defined as the duty of the Levites (Num. 3:32). *This points to a fluidity in the terminology which precludes immediate identification of groups charged with the same responsibilities.* This is true not simply because the words used (*bayit, qōdeš*) have a wider and a narrower sense,[174] but also even more fundamentally because the lower clergy carried out their tasks under the supervision of the higher clergy. Thus the Aaronides were ultimately responsible for guarding the sanctuary (Num. 3:38) because they supervised the execution of this task by the Levites (Num. 3:32). Regardless of terminology, both rooms are located within the inner court and thus the two

---

[172] A clear statement of this position is found in Zimmerli, *Ezechiel*, 1131; cf. also Gunneweg, *Leviten und Priester*, 190ff.

[173] McConville, "Priests and Levites", 24.

[174] Duke, "Punishment or Restoration", 75; Milgrom, *Levitical Terminology*, 14 n.47.

groups are not subject to any discernible gradation with regard to sanctity.[175] As perhaps also in Ezekiel 42:13, the talk is of two groups of *priests*, equal in status but separate in duties: the first group are responsible for the oversight of the Temple, the second group for the oversight of the altar. That oversight of the Levites who kept charge of the sanctuary is assigned to no less significant a personage than Eleazar the son of Aaron in Numbers 3:32 underlines clearly the point that there is no sacerdotal hierarchy in view here.[176]

Since then both groups in Ezekiel 40:45f. can be identified as priests of equal sanctity, attempts to discern any gradation are fruitless and the identification of the former group with the Levites should be abandoned. Rather, the designation "These are the sons of Zadok", whether original or a later gloss, should be seen as covering both groups, not simply the latter.[177] Its inclusion was perhaps stimulated by the fact that this is the first reference to priests in Ezekiel 40-48. It has no polemic intent and gives us no further insight into the relationship intended for the priests and Levites.

Once the misconception of fixed terminology is removed there is no further obstacle to viewing the perspective of these chapters on this matter as a unity, since the other verses clearly distinguish between an upper clergy (the priesthood) who are usually further defined as related to Zadok, and the lower clergy, usually called "Levites". The exact terminology can vary according to the needs of the situation, however.[178]

Ezekiel 43:19 does not mention the lower clergy explicitly, but defines the upper clergy as "The levitical priests who are of the seed of Zadok" (*hakkōhⁿnîm halⁱwiyyim ⁿšer hēm mizzera' ṣādôq*). For a distinction between upper and lower clergy expressed in similar terms, compare Numbers 17:5[16:40]. Ezekiel 45:4f. describes the land assigned to the priests and the Levites, using language similar to chapter 44 to describe their tasks: the priests are denoted as those "who minister in the sanctuary" (*mⁱšārⁱtê hammiqdāš*) and the Levites described as "those who minister in the Temple" (*mⁱšārⁱtê habbayit*). Ezekiel 46:20-24 describes the locations for cooking the guilt, sin and grain offerings and the offerings of the people. Since the former task is carried out inside the inner court, those performing it are necessarily identified as priests. Those performing the latter task are identified as "the ministers of the house" (*mⁱšārⁱtê habbayit*).

---

[175] Zimmerli, *Ezechiel*, 1028.

[176] *Contra* L. Allen, *Ezekiel 20-48*, 253.

[177] Duke, "Punishment or Restoration", 75. This idea was actually tentatively suggested much earlier by G.R. Berry ("Priests and Levites", 237); however, his contribution seems to have been overlooked.

[178] This flexibility argues against P. Hanson's view that the duties of the Zadokites are broadened from charge of the altar in Ezekiel 40:46 to charge of the entire sanctuary in Ezekiel 44:16 (*The Dawn of Apocalyptic* [Philadelphia 1975] 267).

These are presumably the Levites in their role as servants of the people.[179] Finally, Ezekiel 48:11 contrasts the Zadokite priests with the Levites in terms identical to Ezekiel 44:10, describing the Zadokites as: "the consecrated priests from the sons of Zadok, who kept my charge, who did not go astray when the people of Israel went astray, as the Levites did".[180] The terminology may be flexible but the relationship between upper and lower clergy is consistent throughout. There is thus no reason to distinguish Ezekiel 44:6-16, 28-30a as a separate "section" or "stratum". The so-called "Zadokite stratum" is, like the so-called "nāśî' stratum",[181] a myth.[182]

---

[179] Cf. Ezekiel 44:11.
[180] The reference to Yahweh in the first person in Ezekiel 48:11 is not exactly "aberrant" (L. Allen, *Ezekiel 20-48*, 254) since the whole section from Ezekiel 47:13 on is characterized as divine speech.
[181] See above, p.27ff.
[182] This does not in itself require that the diverse materials of Ezekiel 40-48 all come from a common source. Much has undoubtedly been taken up from pre-existing material (cf. e.g. S. Talmon and M. Fishbane, "The Structuring of Biblical Books: Studies in the Book of Ezekiel", *ASTI* 10 [1976] 139; Ebach, *Kritik und Utopie*, 32), which may in turn help to explain some of the diversity of terminology. What is argued for here is rather the basic consistency of outlook throughout this section.

CHAPTER FOUR

PROPHETS

A. INTRODUCTION

The conflict between "true" and "false" prophets[1] became of increasing importance in the years leading up to the exile. The battle lines were drawn between on the one hand those who believed that the first exile of 597 BC was sufficient punishment and that Yahweh would soon reverse that captivity, bringing back the exiles, and on the other hand those who saw that Israel's future held further doom and punishment. Both camps could appeal to the old covenant traditions for support; the question, however, was which side had received the call and commission of Yahweh and was thus able correctly to discern the word of Yahweh to this particular situation.[2] Ezekiel encountered the problem of prophetic opposition, just as his fellow prophet Jeremiah had, and struggled in the face of it to validate his message.[3] In some ways the struggle was of greater importance than ever, for in the exilic situation, with the institutions of the monarchy and the Temple broken down, only prophecy remained to act as mediator between God and man.[4] In what ways then does Ezekiel criticize the activities of his fellow prophets? What future does he foresee for prophets and prophecy? What

---

[1] The difficulties involved in the differentiation of 'true' and 'false' prophets have been extensively discussed in recent literature. Cf. e.g. J.L. Crenshaw, *Prophetic Conflict*, BZAW 124 (Berlin 1971); F.L. Hossfeld & I. Meyer, *Prophet gegen Prophet* (Fribourg 1973); J.A. Sanders, "Hermeneutics in True and False Prophecy", *Canon and Authority*, G.W. Coats and B.O. Long, eds. (Philadelphia 1977); B.O. Long, "Social Dimensions of Prophetic Conflict", *Semeia* 21 (1982) between the two, and it is likely that charges and counter-charges of falsity were common (cf. 1 Ki. 22:23f.). In this section, however, it should be remembered that we are interested more in Ezekiel's own assessment than in attempting to uncover "objective reality". Ezekiel seems to have had no difficulty – at least in his own mind – in distinguishing between true and false prophecy.

[2] T. Overholt, *The Threat of Falsehood* 43ff.

[3] Hossfeld & Meyer deny that Ezekiel himself came into real opposition with other prophets in his position in exile (*Prophet*, 115). However, in order to hold their position, they are forced to attribute large portions of Ezekiel 12:21-14:11 to Ezekiel's disciples. The evidence of Jeremiah 29 points clearly to the activity of prophets among the exiles, and there seems little reason to deny that Ezekiel himself would have come into conflict with these men, just as Jeremiah did with those who remained in Judah. If Hossfeld & Meyer are willing to concede, as they do, that the core of Ezekiel 13 can be traced back to a concern on the part of the prophet himself with the phenomenon of false prophecy (143), then it is hard to see why this concern should have been purely theoretical. In favour of a real encounter see Fishbane ("Sin and Judgement", 136) and Hals, who comments with reference to Ezekiel 13:17-23: "The colorful vividness of the language suggests that we do have here the record of a direct confrontation" (*Ezekiel*, 90).

[4] Hossfeld, *Untersuchungen*, 514f.

role does he himself play as a prophet in bringing the future into being?

B. THE CRITIQUE OF PROPHETIC LEADERSHIP IN THE BOOK OF EZEKIEL

Along with the royal rulers and the priesthood, the prophets were a major force in pre-exilic Israelite culture. Unlike the other two groups, however, very little work has been done thus far to determine Ezekiel's attitude towards the prophets.[5] This is not because the book of Ezekiel lacks interest in their activities: as we shall see, there is a considerable discussion of their past actions and their future prospects. It is to the sections of the book relevant to this discussion to which we now turn.

1 *Ezekiel 13*

The major critique of prophets in the book of Ezekiel is contained in this chapter. It divides readily into two halves, vv. 1-16 and 17-23, which concern themselves respectively with "the prophets of Israel"[6] and "the daughters of your people who prophesy out of their heart". These two sections betray a high degree of parallelism in their structure.[7] The first part is as follows:

> Son of man, prophesy against the prophets of Israel, prophesy[8] and say to those who prophesy out of their own minds: 'Hear the word of the Lord!' [3]Thus says the Lord God, "Woe to the foolish prophets who follow their own spirit, and have seen nothing![9] [4]Your prophets have been like foxes among ruins, O Israel. [5]You have not gone up into the breaches, or built up a wall for the house of Israel, that it might stand in battle in the day of the Lord. [6]They have spoken falsehood and divined a lie; they say, 'Says the Lord,' when the Lord has not sent them, and yet they expect him to fulfil their word. [7]Have you not seen a delusive vision, and uttered a lying divination, whenever you have said, 'Says the Lord,' although I have not spoken?" [8]Therefore thus

---

[5] Many of the general studies of false prophecy have virtually ignored the contribution of Ezekiel, focussing rather on the extensive material in Jeremiah. Note, however, the discussion of Hossfeld & Meyer (*Prophet*, 113-43).

[6] The very form of address raises a paradox. In spite of the existence of a body of men who could be addressed thus, their ineffectiveness to accomplish Yahweh's purpose is such that he must still raise up someone like Ezekiel so that "the people may know that there has been a prophet among them" (Ezek. 2:5). Cf. Vawter & Hoppe, *Ezekiel*, 82.

[7] Hossfeld-Meyer, *Prophet*, 127ff.; Greenberg, *Ezekiel 1-20*, 242; Hals, *Ezekiel*, 87.

[8] MT has *hannibbā'îm*, "who are prophesying", which is unlikely in the absolute form. RSV is following LXX (*kai prophēteuseis*) in its translation, giving the construction "prophesy [and say...]" (*hinnābē'*) which is not without parallels elsewhere in the book of Ezekiel. Brownlee suggests that MT originated as a marginal gloss *hann'bî'îm*, intended to qualify *millibbām* (*Ezekiel 1-19*, 185). It is also possible that such a marginal gloss, describing the contents of this chapter, could have found its way into the text without any original textual warrant.

[9] This is the only place in the Old Testament where *l'biltî* is construed with the perfect. GKC § 152 x suggests that *l'biltî rā'û* is a relative clause governed by *l'* ("according to things which they have not seen").

says the Lord God: "Because you have uttered delusions and seen lies, therefore behold, I am against you, says the Lord God. [9]My hand will be against the prophets who see delusive visions and who give lying divinations; they shall not be in the council of my people, nor be enrolled in the register of the house of Israel, nor shall they enter the land of Israel; and you shall know that I am the Lord God. [10]Because, yea, because they have misled my people, saying, 'Peace,' when there is no peace; and because, when the people build a wall, these prophets daub it with whitewash; [11]say to those who daub it with whitewash that it shall fall! There will be a deluge of rain, great hailstones will fall, and a stormy wind break out; [12]and when the wall falls, will it not be said to you, 'Where is the daubing with which you daubed it?' [13]Therefore thus says the Lord God: I will make a stormy wind break out in my wrath; and there shall be a deluge of rain in my anger, and great hailstones in wrath to destroy it. [14]And I will break down the wall that you have daubed with whitewash, and bring it down to the ground, so that its foundation will be laid bare; when it falls, you shall perish in the midst of it; and you shall know that I am the Lord. [15]Thus will I spend my wrath upon the wall, and upon those who have daubed it with whitewash; and I will say to you, The wall is no more, nor those who daubed it, [16]the prophets of Israel who prophesied concerning Jerusalem and saw visions of peace for her, when there was no peace", says the Lord God.

The first fault attributed to the prophets of Israel is the *origin* of their prophecy: they "prophesy from their own heart" ($n^e b\hat{i}$'$\hat{e}$ $millibb\bar{a}m$; v.2).[10] Ezekiel calls them "foolish prophets[11] who follow their own spirit, and have seen nothing" (v.3). They confidently proclaim the divine origin of their words, saying "Hear the word of Yahweh" ($\check{s}im^e$'$\hat{u}$ $d^e bar$-$yhwh$; v.2) and using the oracle formula "Oracle of Yahweh" (n^e'um $yhwh$; v.6f.). They even hope to see what they have prophesied established (v.6), though in actuality they have no calling from Yahweh (v.7).

The second fault which Ezekiel finds with these prophets is the *content* — or rather lack of content — of their messages. They have "seen vanity and a lying divination" ($h\bar{a}z\hat{u}$ $\check{s}\bar{a}w$' $w^e qesem$ $k\bar{a}z\bar{a}b$); this phrase, and variations upon it, are a constant refrain in verses 6-9. What this content consists of is revealed in verse 10: they have been prophesying "Peace, peace" when in fact there was no peace to be expected. [12]

Finally, Ezekiel criticizes the *result* of their prophesying. In speaking according to their own hopes, rather than the word of Yahweh, they have

---

[10] According to Greenberg (*Ezekiel 1-20*, 235), *millibbām* is treated as a unit in which the *m-* is fused to the noun, representing the authority on whose behalf the prophets speak. Cf. the standard phrases *n^{e}bî'ê yhwh* (e.g. 1 Ki. 18:4) and *n^{e}bî'ê habba'al* (e.g. 1 Ki. 18:19). Compare *"lōhê mērāhōq* in Jeremiah 23:23. On the wider use of the construct state in general, see GKC § 130 a.

[11] LXX reads simply "Woe to those who prophesy out of their hearts", the latter part of the phrase being absent from its rendition of v.2. This simpler text may be correct, but alternatively a pun on the similar sounding words *n^{e}bî'îm* and *n^{e}bālîm* may be intended.

[12] Cf. also v.16 and Jeremiah 6:14; 8:11.

seduced God's people into a false security which will be devastatingly exposed on the coming day of judgement. This criticism of the prophets is expressed in a series of pictures. They have acted "like foxes among the ruins" (*kᵉšu'ālîm bāhᵒrābôt*; v.4). Foxes were not simply of no positive use, but were actually thought of as agents of destruction, as may be seen from Nehemiah 4:3: "Whatever they have built, if even a fox went up on it he would break it down".[13] What is more, these prophets have failed to take on the dangerous, but necessary, task of standing in the gaps to build up a solid protection for Israel on the Day of Yahweh (v.5). Here the picture is of a besieged city, whose walls have been breached. The downfall of the city is certain unless the breaches can be repaired.[14] The third picture Ezekiel uses also involves a wall. In verse 11-15 the image is of a poorly constructed wall,[15] built by another[16] but covered with whitewash (*tāpēl*) by the prophets, thus giving it a misleadingly solid appearance. Its true nature will be exposed by the coming of the storm, to the destruction of all concerned in the venture.

There is little help given in this passage to anyone seeking a criterion to distinguish between true and false prophecy.[17] Ezekiel is able to characterize the message of his opponents as false prophecy on the basis of a word from Yahweh to him (v.1).[18] There is no hint here of moral inadequacy on the part of the prophets, as in Jeremiah 23:14. Nor are they charged with using inferior means: the problem is not that they see visions—so also does Ezekiel[19]—nor that they engage in divination, for that too can be an accurate means of guidance.[20] The problem is not simply that they prophesied peace,

---

[13]   Ellison, *Ezekiel*, 56.

[14]   This metaphor has been vividly illuminated by the excavations of siege ramps and counter-ramps at Lachish. On these see I. Eph'al, "The Assyrian Siege Ramp at Lachish", *Tel Aviv* 11 (1984) 60-70; D. Ussishkin, "The Assyrian Attack on Lachish: The Archaeological Evidence from the Southwest Corner of the Site", *Tel Aviv* 17 (1990) 53-86.

[15]   *hayis* is a hapax legomenon in the Old Testament. In *Šebî'ît* 3:8 a *hayyîs* is a rough stone wall not filled in with earth.

[16]   Hebrew has an indefinite "one" (*hû'*).

[17]   Hals, *Ezekiel*, 87.

[18]   Cf. Jeremiah 28:12ff.

[19]   Though it is striking that he himself never uses the root *hzh* to describe his own visions, preferring to call them *mar'ôt* (Ezek. 1:1; 8:3f.;11:24; 40:2; 43:3). Outside chapter 13, the root *hzh* is only found in Ezekiel 12:27, where the people describe Ezekiel's activity as *hōzeh hehāzôn*, and in Ezekiel 21:34[29] and 22:28, where it is used in conjunction with *šāw'* to denote worthless visions, as in chapter 13.

[20]   Cf. Ezekiel 21:26[21]ff., especially v.28[23] which clearly implies that not all divination is vain divination. Divination is sometimes mentioned in a negative light in the Old Testament (cf. Deut. 18:10,14), but this is not universally the case. In Micah 3:11 the problem was not that the prophets divined (*yiqsōmû*)—any more than it was a problem that the priests taught or the chiefs judged. It was rather that they were performing their legitimate functions for money. On divination, see L. Ruppert, "*qesem*", *Theologische Wörterbuch des Alten Testament*, in G.J. Botterweck, H. Ringgren and H.-J. Fabry, eds. (Stuttgart 1990) VII, 78-84.

for Ezekiel himself has words of hope and peace for the future.[21] No, the problem was that, however confident they were of the validity of their words, they preached the wrong message at the wrong time because Yahweh had not sent them. As a result they have misled the people, who turned to them for guidance (v.10).

The charge against the women who prophesy in the second part of Ezekiel 13 has both similarities to and differences from that against the prophets of Israel:

> [17]And you, son of man, set your face against the daughters of your people, who prophesy[22] out of their own minds; prophesy against them [18]and say, Thus says the Lord God: Woe to the women who sew magic bands upon all wrists,[23] and make veils for the heads of persons of every stature, in the hunt for souls! Will you hunt down souls belonging to my people, and keep your own souls alive?[24] [19]You have profaned me among my people for handfuls of barley and for pieces of bread, putting to death persons who should not die and keeping alive persons who should not live, by your lies to my people, who listen to lies. [20]Wherefore thus says the Lord God: Behold, I am against your magic bands with which you hunt the souls, and I will tear them from your arms; and I will let the souls that you hunt go free like birds. [21]Your veils also I will tear off, and deliver my people out of your hand, and they shall be no more in your hand as prey; and you shall know that I am the Lord. [22]Because you have disheartened the righteous falsely, although I have not disheartened him, and you have encouraged the wicked, that he should not turn from his wicked way to save his life; [23]therefore you shall no more see delusive visions nor practice divination; I will deliver my people out of your hand. Then you will know that I am the Lord.

In common with the critique of the prophets of Israel, the source of the women's prophecy is identified as "from their own heart" (*millibb^ehen*;

---

[21] E.g. chapters 33-48 which are hardly all the pure product of a later redactor's imagination (*pace* S. Herrmann).

[22] According to Greenberg, the Hitpael of *nb'* denotes the external behaviour peculiar to prophecy while the nifal tends to be used for verbal prophesying (*Ezekiel 1-20*, 239). The suggestion that the use of the hitpael here implies a note of contempt for what the women are doing (so Cooke, *Ezekiel*, 145; Ellison, *Ezekiel*, 56), while superficially attractive, cannot be conclusively demonstrated from the usage elsewhere in the Old Testament: the hitpael is also used of Ezekiel himself in 37:10, and of Micaiah in 1 Kings 22:8,18 (where both stems are used of the false prophets! Cf. vv. 10,12). On the Hitpael of *nb'*, see R.R. Wilson ("Prophecy and Ecstasy: A Reexamination", *JBL* 98 [1979] 329ff.) who examines both positive and negative usages. Note the cautious statement of J. Jeremias: "Eine sichere Abgrenzung der Grundbedeutung des Ni. gegenüber der des Hitp. gelingt nicht" ("*nābî*'", *Theologisches Handwörterbuch zum Alten Testament*, E. Jenni, C. Westermann, eds. (Zürich 1976) II, 16). Hossfeld's view (*Untersuchungen*, 382) that the Hitpael describes a "fast zauberische" activity cannot be supported by the usage outside Ezekiel. However, a note of contempt *may* be implied by the refusal to term these women "prophetesses".

[23] MT *yāday* "my hands" seems likely to be a textual error. Read either *yādayim* with some Hebrew mss, Targum, Peshitta, or *yād* following LXX (*cheiros*).

[24] RSV translates "and keep other souls alive for your profit?". For the translation given here, see below, p.97.

v.17). However, there does seem to be a greater degree of condemnation for the practices used by the women. Whereas the prophets of Israel were apparently prophesying in forms indistinguishable from those used by Ezekiel, there is general consent that the practices described in v.18ff. had magical overtones.[25] Exactly what those practices were has been, and will continue to be, a matter for some debate due to the obscure terminology employed.[26] It seems clear that they were involved in tying magic bands (*kᵉsātôt*, v.18),[27] though whether the object being tied up was the medium herself,[28] the enquirer[29] or an image of the victim[30] is not completely clear. Further, they are charged with making "*mispāḥôt* for heads of every stature to catch *nᵉpāšôt*". *mispāḥôt* occurs only here and in v.21 and the translation "veils"[31] is at best a tentative suggestion on the basis of the following clause "for heads of every stature".[32] Saggs suggests that *mispāḥôt* has come about through metathesis of an underlying *mshpwt*, which he links with the Akkadian *musaḫḫiptu*, "a net".[33] This fits very neatly with the image of hunting in the passage, but it is not immediately clear how it makes sense as part of the whole clause: "They make nets for heads of every stature to catch *nᵉpāšôt*". Overall, it seems better to see a contrasting parallelism of function between the *kᵉsātôt* (from Akkadian *kasû*, "to bind") and the *mispāḥôt* (from Akkadian *sapaḫu*, "to scatter, disperse, and (in magical contexts) to thwart spells"),[34] even if we cannot identify their exact nature. Whatever the precise form of their actions, they are not those of a true prophet (or prophetess) of Yahweh.

The central concern of their activities is also different from that of the prophets castigated in verses 1-16. Whereas the "prophets of Israel" were concerned with the great questions of the future of the nation, the "prophesying women" were concerned with the future of individuals. They mediated

[25] Zimmerli comments: "Es ist unverkennbar der Bereich einer niederen Kleinmantik und des Zaubers, in den das Doppelwort 17ff. hineinführt" (*Ezechiel*, 296).
[26] In addition to the commentaries, see the discussion in F. Dumermuth, "Zu Ez xiii:18-21", *VT* 13 (1963) 228-9, and H.W. Saggs, "'External Souls' in the Old Testament", *JSS* 19 (1974) 1-12.
[27] For the meaning of this hapax legomenon compare the usage of the Akkadian cognate *kasû*, "to bind", often in a magical context (Saggs, "External Souls", 5).
[28] As apparently v.20 would suggest. For this opinion see Dumermuth, "Ez 13:18-21", 228.
[29] So Cooke, *Ezekiel*, 145f. Both this explanation and the following one require the emending of MT *zᵉrô'ōtêkem* in v.20 to *zᵉrô'ōtêhem*, for which there is no manuscript evidence.
[30] So Saggs, "External Souls", 5.
[31] RSV; cf. LXX *epibolaia*, "kerchiefs".
[32] Even if the Akkadian *sapaḫu*, ("to disperse, scatter") does indeed lie behind this Hebrew word (so G.R. Driver, "Linguistic and Textual Problems: Ezekiel", *Biblica* 19 [1938] 63f.; see further below) it seems a very long jump from there to his proposed meaning "a loose-fitting shawl, veil"!
[33] "External Souls", 6.
[34] Cf. *sapaḫu* 5c, *CAD* 15, 154.

"life" and "death" to "the righteous" and "the wicked". There is certainly nothing wrong in such concerns: they were part of Ezekiel's own calling to prophetic ministry.[35] The women are not criticized for dealing with the wrong questions but for giving the wrong answers. They were motivated not by divine calling but by pursuit of personal profit in the form of small payments of barley and bread.[36] The result of their activities was deadly, "putting to death persons who should not die and keeping alive persons who should not live" (v.19). They were, in a graphic image, "hunting the people like birds" (v.20). These statements should be read against the background of Ezekiel's own call to be a watchman, warning the wicked to turn from his way and encouraging the righteous to remain steadfast (Ezek. 3:17-21; 33:1-9). Fulfilment of this role is a possible means of turning the wicked from death to life, and releases the prophet from responsibility for him: "you have delivered your soul" (*wᵉ'attâ 'et-napšᵉkā hiṣṣaltā*; Ezek. 3:19,21; 33:9). Failure to do this confirms the evildoer in his wicked way, and the responsibility for his fate is upon the prophet: "his blood I will require at your hand" (*wᵉdāmô miyyādᵉkā ᵃbaqqēš*; Ezek. 3:18, 20; 33:6). This perhaps illuminates the difficult phrase of Ezekiel 13:18b: *hanᵉpāšôt[37] tᵉsôdēdnâ lᵉ'ammî ûnᵉpāšôt lākenâ tᵉhayyênâ* ("Will you hunt down souls belonging to my people, and keep your own souls alive?"). The last part is sometimes translated: "and keep other souls alive for your profit",[38] but in view of the strong warnings given to Ezekiel about the consequences of disobedience on his part, a threat to the prophesying women seems more likely.

As with the condemnation of the prophets of Israel, there is a focus on the negative results of the activities of the prophesying women. They have lied to the people, who in turn have listened to lies (v.19; cf. v.10a: "They have seduced my people"). Out of concern for the people of Israel, referred to as "my people" five times in this chapter (Ezek. 13:9,10,19,21,23), Yahweh will act to break the power of the prophesying women over the people, destroying their equipment so that the people will no longer be their victims (v.20f.).

We may conclude our discussion of the critique of the prophets and prophesying women in this chapter by underlining once again the strong parallel-

---

[35] Cf. Ezekiel 3:17-21; 33:1-9.

[36] On the analogy of 1 Samuel 9:7, where the seer gives his oracle in return for a small payment of bread, this interpretation of the significance of the barley and bread is to be preferred to that which sees these as the materials for the magical practices. For the latter interpretation, see Kimhi; Cooke, *Ezekiel*, 147; Greenberg, *Ezekiel 1-20*, 240; for the former, see Zimmerli, *Ezechiel*, 296; Brownlee, *Ezekiel 1-19*, 196.

[37] Vocalizing as an interrogative *hē*, as opposed to MT *hannᵉpāšôt*.

[38] RSV; see the similar translation in Zimmerli, *Ezechiel*, 282.

ism between the two parts. This is particularly evident in structural terms,[39] and it also accounts for the fact that the closing verses (Ezek. 13:22f.), while still grammatically addressed to the women, pick up themes from the first section to round off the whole. The chapter gains a sense of overall unity from the fact that the "prophets of Israel" and the "women who prophesy" both oppose in different ways the ministry to which God has called Ezekiel.[40] The "prophets of Israel" are a stumbling block to the reception of Ezekiel's message of national judgement by the people, while the "women who prophesy" undermine his calling to proclaim life to the righteous and to warn the wicked to turn from their ways. To be opposed to the prophet God has sent is to be a false prophet(ess), and while Ezekiel gives no simple tests by which the people may validate the truth-claims of competing prophets, he asserts that the future fate of his opponents will show him to have been the true prophet of Yahweh. When Yahweh acts to destroy the works of his opponents, then the people "will know that I am Yahweh" (Ezek. 13:14,21,23) and (by implication) that Ezekiel has acted as his true prophet.[41]

2 *Ezekiel 22:28*

Ezekiel's oracles against the prophets have been gathered together to form a comprehensive picture in chapter 13, as we saw above. The only other verse critical of the prophets is Ezekiel 22:28,[42] which is itself entirely dependent upon Ezekiel 13:1-10. It accuses the prophets of "daubing for them with whitewash" (*ṭāḥû lāhem tāpēl*, cf. 13:10), of "seeing false visions and divining lies for them" (*ḥōzîm šāw' weqōsemîm lāhem kāzāb*, cf. 13:6-9) and of "saying 'Thus says the sovereign Lord' when the Lord had not spoken" (*'omerîm kōh 'āmar "dōnāy yhwh wayhwh lō' dibbēr*, cf. 13:7). It has nothing new to add to Ezekiel's condemnation of the prophets, except to link their sin together with that of the other leading members of society (*nesî'îm*, priests, *śārîm*, and *'am hā'āreṣ*).

C. THE FUTURE OF PROPHETIC LEADERSHIP IN EZEKIEL

We saw in our discussion of Ezekiel 13 that a contrast is being drawn between Ezekiel's own ministry and that of the "prophets of Israel" and the

---

[39] See Hossfeld & Meyer, *Prophet*, 127ff., where the two sections are laid out side by side.
[40] Greenberg, *Ezekiel 1-20*, 245.
[41] Cf. Ezekiel 2:5.
[42] In the MT Ezekiel 22:25 also refers to the prophets, but this is almost certainly a textual corruption. See above, p.19 n.61.

"prophesying women".[43] In different ways these two groups are opposed to Ezekiel's prophetic ministry. The same dichotomy between Ezekiel and his opponents can be seen in his views on the future of prophetic leadership in Israel; in brief, he sees quite different prospects for himself from those he expects for those who have opposed him. We shall divide our discussion into two sections accordingly.

1 The Future of Ezekiel's Prophetic Opponents

Ezekiel 12:24

The problem of prophetic conflict, without clear means of validating the competing claims, meant that it was difficult for the people to distinguish between the true and false prophets. This led to a cynicism among the population as to the reliability of the prophets:[44] their words were seen as only applying to the distant future, if at all (cf. Ezek. 12:22,27), or as an interesting curiousity, not a vital message (Ezek. 33:30-33). It is this cynicism which is addressed in Ezekiel 12:21-28.

Yahweh's response to this situation is two-fold. The people are certainly culpable for their attitude in refusing to listen to true prophecy, which attitude is but a symptom of their rebelliousness (Ezek. 12:25; cf. 2:4ff.). Yet at the same time there is a pastoral concern for a people who have been deceived.[45] In the days to come, the situation which brought about the state of cynicism will be repaired. This is the promise of Ezekiel 12:24:

> For there shall be no more any false vision or flattering divination within the house of Israel.

The mention of the "false vision" ($h^a z \hat{o} n$ $\check{s} \bar{a} w$') points forward to the worthless activities of the "prophets of Israel", which are criticized in the next chapter.[46] There is not yet in this verse an explicit mention of the future of those who have been false prophets themselves, but there is an assertion that things will no longer be as they have been. With the expression "no more" ($l\bar{o}$'.... '$\hat{o} d$), we encounter again a characteristic idiom of the proph-

---

[43] According to R.P. Carroll, a similar distinction between a single prophet and all of his opponents is evident in the book of Jeremiah. He comments: "Jeremiah excepted....no prophet is presented in a positive light" (*Jeremiah*, Old Testament Guides [Sheffield 1989] 101).

[44] W. McKane notes that Ezekiel 12:21-28 counters "a frame of mind induced by the activities of false prophets, by the proven unreliability of prophecy and its inability to shed light on the course of events" (*Proverbs*, Old Testament Library [London 1970] 30). Cf. Eichrodt, *Hesekiel*, 84.

[45] Note the repeated use of the phrase "my people" in chapter 13 (Ezek. 13:9,10,18,19, 21,23). Cf. Greenberg, *Ezekiel 1-20*, 245.

[46] J. Herrmann suggests that it has been introduced here specifically in order to provide a link with what follows (*Ezechielstudien*, 19). The connection is certainly not coincidental. Cf. S. Talmon & M. Fishbane, "The Structuring of Biblical Books: Studies in the Book of Ezekiel", *ASTI* 10 (1976) 137.

et's contrast between the way things were in the past and the way they will be in the future.[47] False prophecy will be silenced, so that the people may no longer be led astray by it.[48]

Ezekiel 13

As well as criticizing the "prophets of Israel" and the "prophesying women" for their actions, this chapter also indicates the fate of those who have opposed Ezekiel. Regarding the "prophets of Israel", the divine hand is raised in judgement upon them[49] and it is decreed that they "will not be in the assembly of my people, nor be written in the record of the House of Israel, nor enter into the land of Israel" (Ezek. 13:9b). To be excluded from "the council of my people" (sôd 'ammî) was to be cut off from their place in the assembly[50] of the righteous, the true Israel.[51] It was surely a fitting fate that those who had falsely claimed to be prophets, and thus to have access to the council of Yahweh (sôd yhwh),[52] should ultimately be excluded even from the council of his people. Further, their names will not "be written in the record (bik'tāb) of the House of Israel". To be left off the roll of the people would be to be excluded from full participation in the community.[53] The importance of such a list may be seen from Nehemiah 7, where the finding of a register purporting to list those who first returned from exile becomes the basis on which certain families were excluded from the priesthood (cf. vv. 61-64 = Ezra 2:62f.). Third, they will not "enter into the land of Israel". This already presupposes an exile and an expected return, in which return the false prophets will not participate. Like rebellious Israel in the wilderness, they will not [re-]enter the promised land.[54] In Jeremiah 29:32, that prophet threatened his opponent, Shemaiah, with

---

[47] Cf. Ezekiel 12:23-28; 13:21,23; 14:11; 16:41,42,63; 18:3; 23:27; 34:10,22,28,29; 36:12,14,15,30; 37:22,23; 39:7,28; 43:7; 45:8.

[48] Graffy, A Prophet Confronts, 55.

[49] This expression normally occurs with nth (Ezek. 6:14; 14:9,13; 16:27; 25:7,13,16; 35:3) while here in Ezekiel 13:9 it occurs with hyh: "my hand will be upon them". Greenberg suggests that this construction, which elsewhere indicates ecstatic possession, is here used as a pun: "those upon whom God's hand never came in prophetic seizure will experience his punishment" (Ezekiel 1-20, 237).

[50] For this more general meaning of sôd see Genesis 49:6 (parallel to qāhāl) and Psalm 111:1 (parallel to 'ēdâ). Cf. M. Saebø, "sôd", Theologisches Handwörterbuch zum Alten Testament, E. Jenni and C. Westermann, eds. (Zürich 1976) II, 146.

[51] Cooke, Ezekiel, 140.

[52] Cf. Jeremiah 23:18ff.

[53] Zimmerli, Ezechiel, 293.

[54] Cf. Numbers 14:23. Strictly speaking, the addition in square brackets is unnecessary. According to J. Lust one of the basic themes in the book of Ezekiel is that Israel was sent into exile before it reached the Promised Land. The geographic Israel of pre-exilic times was not yet the Promised Land Israel. In Ezekiel, God does not make his people return (hēšîb) to the land, he brings (hēbî') them there ("Gathering and Return in Jeremiah and Ezekiel", Le livre de Jérémie. Le prophète et son milieu; les oracles et leur transmission, P.M. Bogaert, ed. [Leuven 1981] 137).

a comparable fate.

A similar judgement on the "prophets of Israel" is expressed pictorially in Ezekiel 13:14-16: when the wall they have whitewashed falls down under the divine onslaught, those who whitewashed it will be consumed in its fall, and those looking on will say: "The wall is no longer in existence, nor those who whitewashed it". In other words, those who have prophesied peace for Jerusalem will be destroyed in its downfall.

The judgement against the women is often thought to be less severe, focussed on the breaking of their power rather than their own destruction.[55] Their *k'sātôt* and *mispāhôt* will be torn off and the people will be set free from their power (Ezek. 13:19f.). Yet their own ultimate fate is far from secure, since the answer to the question of v. 18b ("Will you hunt down souls belonging to my people, and keep your own souls alive?")[56] must surely be negative. Though their destruction is not explicitly stated, the emphasis of the passage being rather on the freeing of the people, it is not excluded and may be implied. If the prophet Ezekiel is warned that, in the event of unfaithfulness to his commission, the blood of the wicked will be required at his hand, how much more so is this true of these self-appointed declarers of "life" and "death"?

Ezekiel 14:9-11

Ezekiel 14:1-8 deals with the approach of certain elders of Israel to Ezekiel, seeking an oracle. In return Ezekiel accuses them of inward idolatry and refuses to give them any answer — except an answer which states in general terms the principle that the secret idolater will receive no answer from Yahweh but his own destruction.[57] Verses 9-11 presuppose, however, that there were other prophets who might be quite willing to give an oracle to the elders, notwithstanding Ezekiel's refusal.[58] An atmosphere of prophetic conflict that is far from theoretical seems evident.[59]

> [9]And if the prophet be deceived and speak a word, I, the Lord, have deceived that prophet, and I will stretch out my hand against him, and will destroy him from the midst of my people Israel. [10]And they shall bear their punishment — the punishment of the prophet and the punishment of the inquirer shall be alike — [11]that the house of Israel may go no more astray from me, nor defile themselves any more with all their transgressions, but that they may

---

[55] So Greenberg, *Ezekiel 1-20*, 245; Taylor, *Ezekiel*, 125.

[56] For this translation, see above p.97.

[57] The critique of the lay leadership implied in this section will be discussed in more detail in chapter 5. See below, p.116.

[58] Note the comment of Brownlee (*Ezekiel 1-19*, 203): "It may well be that Israel's elders were 'shopping around', inquiring of several prophets and accepting the messages of the prophets who pleased them".

[59] *Contra* Hossfeld & Meyer, *Prophet*, 121.

be my people and I may be their God, says the Lord God.

Unlike chapter 13, there is no *explicit* accusation that the oracle given under such circumstances is self-manufactured. Ezekiel traces its origin back to its primary cause: the will of Yahweh. The prophet will give the oracle because Yahweh has deceived him (*pth*, piel; v.9).[60] Yet this in no way exempts the prophet, as secondary cause, from responsibility for his own words. In Deuteronomy 13:2-6[1-5] primary and secondary causes are brought together, the will of Yahweh to test the people (v.4[3]) and the will of the prophet to lead the people astray from the way of Yahweh (v.6[5]). Here in Ezekiel the emphasis is on the primary cause, the divine actions of Yahweh bringing judgement upon the people by giving them lying prophets who will tell them what they want to hear. The people are placed in a similar position to that of Ahab in 1 Kings 22: as a judgement for their refusal to listen to prophetic truth, Yahweh will send them a deceitful oracle through another prophet. Ezekiel also underlines the fact that the prophet remains responsible for his own actions, however.[61] Prophet and idolater alike shall "bear their iniquity" (*nāś^e'û ^{ʿa}wōnām*):[62] the guilt of each is equal (v.10) and so they are destined for an similar fate, that of being "cut off" (hifil of *krt*; v.8)[63] or "destroyed" (hifil of *šmd*; v.9)[64] from the covenant people. The punishment Ezekiel has in mind has often been interpreted as excommunication.[65] This fate is entirely in line with that predicted for the "prophets of Israel" in Ezekiel 13:9.[66] According to this understanding, the similarly severe language of Ezekiel 13:14-16,18[67] should also be interpreted metaphorically as referring to excommunication. However, as we also noted in our discussion of Ezekiel 13:18, in view of the warnings to Ezekiel himself of the consequences of failure to take his prophetic mission sufficiently seriously (cf. Ezek. 3:18-21; 33:7-9), the expectation of a literal destruction of the false prophets and the prophesying women cannot be ruled out.[68] Both are consonant with the expectation of a future absence of false prophecies within the house of Israel expressed in Ezekiel

---

[60]   Mosis ("Ez 14", 166ff.) prefers to translate the verb as having the sense "to make a fool of" rather than "to deceive", seeing it as part of the punishment rather than as part of the state of affairs leading up to the punishment.

[61]   Cooke, *Ezekiel*, 152.

[62]   On this phrase, see above, p.77.

[63]   This is priestly language; cf. Leviticus 20:3,5,6 (Brownlee, *Ezekiel 1-19*, 203).

[64]   For these two verbs together, see Leviticus 26:30; Deuteronomy 12:29f.; Ezekiel 25:7.

[65]   So Joyce, *Divine Initiative*, 67; A. Phillips, *Ancient Israel's Criminal Law* (Oxford 1970) 29ff.; Hals, *Ezekiel*, 93; W. Zimmerli, "Die Eigenart der prophetischen Rede des Ezechiel", *ZAW* 67 (1955) 1-26 = *Gottes Offenbarung* (Munich 1963) 13ff.

[66]   Note that in both cases the hand of Yahweh is the agent of destruction (Zimmerli, *Ezechiel*, 292, 312).

[67]   On Ezekiel 13:14-16,18 see above, p.101.

[68]   See above, p.101.

12:24.[69] In fact, a definitive choice between the alternatives is not easy since the two practices were actually linked, with excommunication often acting as a preparation for the covenantal death penalty.[70] On balance, the literal interpretation is probably to be preferred here, especially since the expectation of divine destruction is indubitably present in the immediately following passage.[71]

Against a background of prophetic conflict, the assertion that in the days to come Ezekiel's opponents will be silenced so that the people may no longer be led astray by them, is entirely understandable.[72] The present cacophony will, it seems, give way to silence. Thus in his plan for the future there is at first sight no continuing role given to prophecy by Ezekiel.[73] In contrast to the Chronicler, who makes prophesying the activity of an order of cultic officials, the cult singers (cf. 1 Chronicles 25),[74] Ezekiel apparently sees no continuation of the office of prophet. The words for "to prophesy" (nb' in Niphal and Hithpael) and "prophet" (nābî') do not occur in chapters 40-48. Yet one important feature should not be overlooked in this regard, and this is Ezekiel's own role in bringing into being the new order.[75] It is to an examination of this role that we now turn.

2 Ezekiel's Role in Constituting the Future

In contrast to the unfaithful prophets, who have been a stumbling block to the people with their prophecies and will thus have no part in the reconstituted Israel, Ezekiel has been faithful to the ministry to which he has been called.[76] His reward is a key role in symbolically bringing the future people into being. In many respects, as we shall see, he is portrayed as a new Moses, standing with the people on the brink of the Promised Land and preparing them for entry. He is given a glimpse in visionary form of the

---

[69] Note, however, the comment of Krüger on the implications of this verse: "Die 'falschen' Prophet(inn)en sind nicht nur von der Restitution ausgeschlossen; ihre Beseitigung ist... Voraussetzungen der Restitution" (Geschichtskonzepte, 459).

[70] W. Horbury, "Extirpation and Excommunication", VT 35 (1985) 34.

[71] Cf. Ezekiel 14:13,17,19,21. In comparison, the "downgrading" experienced by the Levites, who are also said to "bear their iniquity" in chapter 44, is lenient indeed. See above, p.85.

[72] Skinner, Ezekiel, 125.

[73] According to Krüger (Geschichtskonzepte, 460): "[Es] fällt auf, daß der Komplex 12:21-14:11 keine Einsetzung "neuer Propheten" nach dem Gerichtshandeln Jahwes erwartet".

[74] D.L. Petersen, Late Israelite Prophecy: Studies in Deutero-Prophetic Literature and in Chronicles, SBLMS 23 (Missoula 1977) 55-96. For a different interpretation, see A.R. Johnson, The Cultic Prophet in Ancient Israel (Cardiff ²1962) 69-74. Whether they were seen as inheriting the traditions of classical prophecy or cultic prophecy is less important than the fact that the Chronicler finds a continuing place for an activity designated "prophesying".

[75] Krüger, Geschichtskonzepte, 460

[76] See, for example, Ellen Davis' comments on Ezekiel as a model of the human creature who hears the divine word and responds fully (Swallowing the Scroll, 83f.).

New Canaan, which will be the home of the Renewed Israel, though like Moses he would never set foot physically on the land he surveyed.

Ezekiel 37

The prophetic aspect of Ezekiel's role in bringing into being the future is readily apparent in chapter 37, the vision of the valley of dry bones. In this vision the prophet acts as the authorized messenger of Yahweh,[77] bringing the prophetic word to bear upon the bones, which results in their restoration to life.[78] He is not simply a casual observer of the scene but the means through which the powerful word is actualized.[79] The same pattern may be observed as in chapter 11:[80] the prophet observes a scene and is commanded to prophesy to (*'al*)[81] those involved (the twenty five men, 11:4 and the dry bones, 37:4). He is instructed in the form of words which he is to use (Ezek. 11:5-12; 37:5f.) and there follows a report that while he was prophesying (*kᵉhinnābᵉ'î*; Ezek. 11:13; 37:7) the words of the prophecy began to have an effect (the death of Pelatiah, 11:13, the coming together of the bones, 37:7f.).[82]

This same pattern is repeated in the second stage of the vision, the coming of *rûah* to the re-created bodies (Ezek. 37:9f.), although in simplified form. These two chapters are the only places in Ezekiel in which we find the prophetic word having such immediate effect, a link which serves to underline their differences as well as what they have in common. For the result which stems from the proclaiming of the prophetic word in chapter 11 is death, with the immediate death of Pelatiah serving as a graphic demonstration of the certainty of the promised judgement upon the twenty five men.[83] In contrast, the result of the proclamation of the prophetic word in chapter 37 is life from the dead.[84] The re-creation and restoration of the bones serves as a guarantee of the promised ultimate restoration of Israel as a nation. Thus, in a very real sense, the vision of chapter 37 provides the ultimate answer to the prophet's question in 11:13: "Ah, Lord God!

---

[77] Note the use of the messenger formula. Cf. Zimmerli, *Ezechiel*, 894.

[78] *Contra* M.V. Fox who argues that Ezekiel's role is as a spectator rather than the more usual prophetic role of messenger ("The Rhetoric of Ezekiel's Vision of the Valley of the Bones", *HUCA* 51 [1980] 9).

[79] According to Zimmerli (*Ezechiel*, 889) the prophet "participates" (wird beteiligt) in the divine activity. Cf. Baltzer, *Ezechiel und Deutero-Jesaja*, 112.

[80] L. Allen, *Ezekiel 20-48*, 124. These chapters are further linked by the fact that in both 11:5 and 37:1 the visionary process is attributed to the influence of the spirit of Yahweh (*rûah yhwh*) This is the only occurrence of this exact phrase in Ezekiel, though references to the activity of "The Spirit" are common.

[81] The tendency in the book of Ezekiel for *'al* and *'el* to be used interchangeably is well-known. See Rooker, *Biblical Hebrew in Transition*, 127ff.; Zimmerli, *Ezechiel*, 6.

[82] For a similar immediate effect of the prophetic word, compare 1 Kings 13:1-6.

[83] On this see below, p.124.

[84] Baltzer, *Ezechiel und Deutero-Jesaja*, 113.

Wilt thou make a full end of the remnant of Israel?" In another sense, however, both passages function together as a reply to the proverb of the sceptic: "The days grow long and every vision comes to naught" (Ezek. 12:22). Both claim a present fulfilment, at least in visionary form, which validates both the future aspect of the vision and, at least in theory, the credentials of the prophet, in accord with Deuteronomy 18.[85]

Before we leave Ezekiel 37, we should note further a contrast between it and another passage which bears superficial resemblance to it, namely Joel 3:1f. [2:28f.]. In the latter passage, a great future pouring-out of Yahweh's *rûaḥ* is promised, the result of which will be an extension of the gift of prophecy to all. This is reminiscent of the story in Numbers 11 in which the gift of Yahweh's *rûaḥ* is extended from Moses to the seventy elders of Israel (vv. 25-29). Indeed it is the fulfilment of Moses' wish on that occasion: "Would that all the Lord's people were prophets, that the Lord would put his *rûaḥ* upon them!". In contrast, for Ezekiel the result of Yahweh placing his *rûaḥ* upon his people was to be life in the land, not prophecy (Ezek. 37:14). The endowment with the *rûaḥ* of Yahweh will result not in charismatic gifts but power for right living, which is itself the prerequisite for life in the land (Ezek. 36:27f.). In the book of Ezekiel's depiction of the future there remains only one prophet, Ezekiel himself.

Ezekiel 40-48

Ezekiel's role in bringing into being the new order is not limited to chapter 37. In fact, he is portrayed in many respects in chapters 40-48 as the new Moses, leading the people through a new exodus and wilderness experience to the brink of the promised land.[86] Ezekiel 40-48 is the only corpus of legislation of the Hebrew Bible which is not placed in the mouth of Moses.[87] It begins with the prophet being transported to a very high mountain (Ezek. 40:2), which according to Levenson is "typologically identical to Sinai", reflecting Sinai's significance as the place of the giving of Torah.[88]

---

[85] L. Allen, *Ezekiel 20-48*, 188.

[86] McKeating, *Ezekiel*, 102. This portrayal may possibly extend more widely: J.-L. Ska ("La Sortie d'Egypte (Ex 7-14) dans le Recit Sacerdotal (Pg) et la Tradition Prophetique", *Biblica* 60 (1979) 203f.) has noted some similarities between Ezekiel's call (Ezek. 2:1-3:11) and the commissioning of Moses (Ex. 7:1-5). Briefly, they are as follows: in both God entrusts a mission to his envoy and before it begins announces the failure of that mission; the roots *hzq* and *qšh* are found side by side, in both cases connected with *lēb*; hardening of heart is a common theme, an attitude which is catastrophic, even perhaps fatal; the recognition formula appears in both, though in very different contexts. As Ska also notes, however, there are significant differences between the two texts which make literary dependence improbable. The connections between the call of Ezekiel and other Old Testament call narratives are thoroughly discussed by Zimmerli (*Ezechiel*, 16ff.).

[87] Levenson, *Theology*, 39.

[88] *Theology*, 41.

Ezekiel's vision of the "Promised Land" on this "very high mountain", a land which he sees but is not permitted to dwell in, is also analogous to Moses experience on Mt. Nebo (Deut. 32:49,52).[89] Ezekiel hears Yahweh speaking directly to him from the Temple (Ezek. 43:6), just as he had spoken to Moses in Numbers 7:89.[90] Further, Ezekiel plays a central role in the consecration of the new altar in Ezekiel 43:18-27; he is involved in both the sacrificial ritual and the blood rites associated with the cleansing of the altar, assisted by the (Zadokite)[91] priests, just as Moses did for the altar of the Tabernacle (Ex. 29:36ff.; Lev. 8:14ff.).[92] The prophet's role in this connection is properly described as that of "Kultanfänger".[93] McConville sums up the similarities between Moses and Ezekiel in Ezekiel 40-48 as follows:

> As in the case of Moses, God speaks directly to him. Like Moses, he has priestly status (cf. Exodus 24:6ff.). Like him he is to preside over the instit-
> ution of the cult, including the setting apart of the priests for their duty, and even continues in the priestly role in 43:20ff. having presented the Zadokites as priests.[94]

Kaufmann argued that the very idea of the Temple vision itself is drawn from Exodus 25:9,40 where Moses is shown the "blueprint" (*tabnît*) for the Tabernacle.[95] The similarity between these passages is underlined by the fact that many manuscripts read *tabnît* for the (probably corrupt) *toknît* in Ezekiel 43:10.[96] A similar motif is evident in the writings of the Chronicler in 1 Chronicles 28:11-19, where David is depicted as giving to Solomon a blueprint (*tabnît*; v.11) of the Temple—a blueprint which ultimately comes from God (v.19).[97] The concept of a deity revealing the design for his sanctuary is an old one in the ancient Near East,[98] and traces

---

[89] Levenson, *Theology*, 42f. W. Zimmerli notes that: "Le thème de la montagne du Temple remplace ici l'entrée en possession du pays" ("Le nouvel 'exode' dans le message de des deux grands prophets de l'exil" in *Hommage à Wilhelm Vischer* (Montpellier 1960) 216-27 [= "Der 'neue Exodus' in der Verkündigung der beiden grossen Exilspropheten" in *Gottes Offenbarung* (Munich 1963) 221].

[90] Douglas, "Ezekiel's Temple", 421.

[91] According to Ezekiel 43:19, though this is often seen as a late gloss. On this see Zimmerli, *Ezechiel*, 1102.

[92] Levenson, *Theology*, 38. Cf. Zimmerli, *Ezechiel*, 1106; McConville, "Priests and Levites", 28; Procksch, "Fürst und Priester", 125.

[93] Zimmerli, *Ezechiel*, 1102.

[94] "Priests and Levites", 28. More cautiously, Hals says that "there is a certain approp-riateness to the idea of Ezekiel as a new Moses" (*Ezekiel*, 311).

[95] Kaufmann, *History*, 524; Levenson, *Theology*, 40.

[96] Cf. the Targum and Vulgate. This correction is not accepted by most modern scholars, who prefer to emend to *t'kunâtô* on the basis of the LXX. However, it does serve at least to suggest a connection in the mind of the ancient scribes (Cooke, *Ezekiel*, 474).

[97] More probably due to the influence of P than to that of Ezekiel in the opinion of Levenson (*Theology*, 40).

[98] For the classic case of Gudea of Lagash, see A. Kapelrud, "Temple building: a Task for Gods and Kings", *Or* 32 (1963) 57f.

of it have been found elsewhere in the Old Testament.[99]

This patterning of prophetic experience after that of Moses is not unique to Ezekiel: W.L. Holladay has traced a similar patterning in the case of his older contemporary, Jeremiah.[100] In both cases it is likely to be due to the expectation of a coming "prophet like Moses" (Deut. 18:15,18). The claim to be such a prophet was a claim to a powerful authority.[101]

The task assigned to Ezekiel of ordering the renewed cult is seen as a distinctly prophetic task, as may be seen by the repeated use of the messenger formula *kōh 'āmar ˀªdōnāy yhwh* (Ezek. 43:18; 44:6,9; 45:9,18; 46:1,16; 47:13). Just as chapter 37 serves as the positive counterpart to chapter 11,[102] so chapters 40-48 have formal and thematic links which indicate them to be a positive counterpart to chapters 8-11. The formal theme of a conducted tour of the Temple grounds in which the prophet is "brought" (hifil of *bw'*)[103] from place to place to see certain things is common,[104] and the theme of the defiled Temple deserted by the glory of Yahweh is reversed when the glory returns to the restored Temple.[105] Whereas in the vision of chapters 8-11 the theological foundation was laid for the destruction of Jerusalem and the exile of the people, these chapters provide the theological basis for the return and re-establishment of life in the land. Since a corrupted cult led to exile, a purified cult will be necessary for life in the land, a theme already adumbrated in the earlier prophecies of Ezekiel (cf. Ezek. 20:40; 37:24b-28).[106]

As well as providing positive regulations for the establishment of the cult, these chapters also involve active rebuke upon various classes, in classically prophetic style.[107] Singled out for particular rebuke, as we have seen elsewhere, are the house of Israel and their kings (Ezek. 43:7ff.), the house of Israel and the Levites (44:6ff.), and the *nˀśî'îm* (45:8ff.). The

---

[99] E.g. the nocturnal revelation prior to the building of Solomon's Temple (1 Ki. 3:5,14). On this, see M. Weinfeld, *Deuteronomy and the Deuteronomic School* (Oxford 1972) 246-50.

[100] W.L. Holladay, "The Background of Jeremiah's Self-understanding: Moses, Samuel and Ps 22", *JBL* 83 (1964) 153-64; "Jeremiah and Moses: Further Observations", *JBL* 85 (1966) 17-27.

[101] Note the motif of the placing of Yahweh's words in the prophet's mouth through the touch of his hand (Jer. 1:9) or eating the scroll (Ezek. 3:3f.; cf. Deut. 18:18). This underscores the divine origin of the proclamation (K.P. Darr, "Write or True? A Response to Ellen Frances Davis", *Signs and Wonders. Biblical Texts in Literary Focus*, J.C. Exum, ed. [Atlanta 1989] 244).

[102] See above, p.104.

[103] Either *wayyābē' 'ōtî* (Ezek. 8:7,14,16; 40:1,3) or *wayˀbî'ēnî* (Ezek. 40:17,28,32, 35,48; 41:1; 42:1; 44:4; 46:19). Also *wattābē' 'ōtî* (with *rûaḥ* as subject) in Ezekiel 8:3 and 11:1 and *watˀbî'ēnî* in 11:24.

[104] Greenberg, "Design", 184.

[105] Note the comment of L. Allen: "The vision of chaps. 8-11 in which Temple and city are destroyed in reprisal for cultic aberrations finds here [in chapters 40-48] a positive counterpart" (*Ezekiel 20-48*, 213).

[106] Greenberg, "Design", 182.

[107] Levenson dubs it "outright preaching" (*Theology*, 46; cf. also 113).

common theme of these rebukes is the idea "no longer", whether expressed in the form *lō'....'ôd* (Ezek. 43:7; 45:8; cf. 34:10; 37:23; 39:7)[108] or *rab lākem* (44:6; 45:9). Although they are projected into the future their point of reference is at least partially the present and the past, when these activities have been very real problems. As well as acting as an injunction against present abuses, they also serve as a promise, looking forward to a time when such injustices will be done away with.[109] In fact, the whole of chapters 40-48, while future in form, actually also has a present purpose: that when the vision is described to the house of Israel they may be ashamed of their iniquities and may keep its whole design and all its ordinances, and perform them (Ezek. 43:10f.). As is typical of the prophets, the vision of the future hope is intended to have a present effect on behaviour.[110]

D. CONCLUSIONS

There are two classes of prophet described in the book of Ezekiel: the faithful prophets, and the unfaithful prophets. The former group seems at times to be represented only by Ezekiel himself (cf. Ezek. 22:30). Elsewhere, however, there does seem to be at least an awareness of the work of a history of faithful prophets in the past (Ezek. 38:17), and the prophet's dependence in many places on other canonical prophets, such as Jeremiah and Zephaniah, suggests that he recognized the existence of other legitimate prophets, even though he does not mention them by name.[111] The two groups, faithful and unfaithful prophets, are inevitably drawn into conflict over what Yahweh's word to the people is in the present situation. Ezekiel believed that history would vindicate him as the faithful one (Ezek. 2:5). The present cacophony of conflicting prophetic voices will die away to silence, as the two groups of prophets go to different fates. The unfaithful prophets will be cut off from the reconstituted people (Ezek. 13:9). But the true prophet Ezekiel plays a vital role in the cosmogonic process of creating and ordering the new world.[112] The re-creative all-powerful word must be spoken by the prophet in order for that process to begin, but once it has

---

[108] According to Fishbane (*Biblical Interpretation*, 374 n.141.) this expression, which recurs repeatedly in the eschatological-restoration prophecies of Jeremiah and Ezekiel, underscores a strong theological-psychological concern of the times.

[109] L. Allen, *Ezekiel 20-48*, 164.

[110] This past-present-future tension is well expressed by Zimmerli (*Ezechiel*, 1019): "Das Neue, das gezeigt wird, [wird] zum Gericht über Geschehenes und zum Aufruf, alle Sinne und auch allen eigenen Entschluß auf ein Neues hinzuwenden".

[111] On the reason for the lack of such a mention see Greenberg, "What are Valid Criteria for Determining Inauthentic Matter in Ezekiel?", *Ezekiel and His Book*, J. Lust, ed. (Leuven 1986) 127f. Cf. also D.I. Block, "Gog in Prophetic Tradition", *VT* 42 (1992) 163ff.

[112] Niditch, "Ezekiel 40-48", 216.

been spoken his task is essentially complete. He does not personally enter the land, though like Moses he is permitted to survey it from a high mountain. Having laid eyes upon it, he is content. In the words of a man who came by the Spirit into the Temple on another occasion, he may say:

> Lord, now you are letting your servant depart in peace, according to your word; for my eyes have seen your salvation which you have prepared before the face of all peoples.[113]

---

[113] Luke 2:19-21.

CHAPTER FIVE

LAY LEADERSHIP

A. INTRODUCTION

By lay leadership, we mean those individuals not of royal or priestly descent who nonetheless held positions of authority in the community. This is not a single group of people with a clearly identifiable title, but a stratum of society with several intersecting sub-strata. In terms of the book of Ezekiel, his primary interest is in the *śārîm* and the *z⁽ᵉ⁾qēnîm*, though there are other passages which address the lay leadership in more general terms.

The *śar* was originally simply "one who commands", especially in a military sense.[1] From at least the time of Solomon on, those commonly referred to as *śārîm* were a small council of high officials of the king, who wielded considerable power in Judah.[2] During the reign of Zedekiah, they apparently extended their powers in the face of his weakness and were even able to act independently of the king to some degree (cf. Jer. 38:25).[3] This weakness on the part of the king may have been due to his status as a puppet installed by the Babylonians in place of his exiled nephew Jehoiachin. There is evidence that many continued to regard Jehoiachin as the true king,[4] providing a fertile context for such power-politics.[5] Not every *śar* in Judah would have been a member of this inner circle of powerful men: some were merely minor military commanders (cf. 2 Ki. 11:4).[6] But in the book of Ezekiel it seems likely that the former group is indicated, as seems normally to be the case also in the book of Jeremiah.[7]

The *z⁽ᵉ⁾qēnîm*, on the other hand, were the heads of families who assumed overall leadership of the tribe.[8] As the tribes became sedentary these men

---

[1] Van der Ploeg, "Chefs", 40.
[2] Cf. Van der Ploeg, "Chefs", 42; Rüterswörden, *Beamten*, 64; Mettinger, *State Officials*, 3.
[3] Cf. Overholt, *Threat of Falsehood*, 32; Long, "Social Dimensions", 47; P. Dutcher-Walls, "The Social Location of the Deuteronomists: A Sociological Study of Factional Politics in Late Pre-Exilic Judah", *JSOT* 52 (1991) 90.
[4] Note the Babylonian texts (summarized in Zimmerli, *Ezechiel*, 44) which refer to the exiled Jehoiachin as "king of the land of Judah".
[5] Lang, *Kein Aufstand*, 142.
[6] Rüterswörden, *Beamten*, 65.
[7] Note how they are often bracketed with the king, as e.g. in Jeremiah 17:25 and 24:8. A similar linking of king and *śārîm* is perhaps to be found in Lachish letter 6, line 4, though the text is not completely certain. Along with this, G.I. Davies lists another 14 definite or uncertain readings of *śr* in *Ancient Hebrew Inscriptions. Corpus and Concordance* (Cambridge 1991) 505f.
[8] H. Reviv, *The Elders in Ancient Israel* (Jerusalem 1989) 11; J. van der Ploeg, "Les Anciens dans l'A.T.", *Lex Tua Veritas. Festschrift für H. Junker*, H. Gross, ed. (Trier 1961)

formed the "village council".[9] They were the representatives of the people in political and religious matters and held at this time authority to govern and to judge.[10] In rural areas their influence was gradually reduced with the transition—at their behest![11]—from collective leadership to a strong central monarchy, with its associated officials.[12] However, in Jerusalem and Samaria they became an influential part of the upper stratum of society (1 Ki. 12:6; 2 Ki. 10:1).[13] Thus, both *śārîm* and *zᵉqēnîm* held a significant amount of power in Jerusalem in the days leading up to the exile. If Ezra 10:8,14 give an accurate picture of the post-exilic community, this power was maintained and perhaps even extended in the return from the exile.[14] Further, though the Bible in general differentiates clearly between the two groups,[15] there would in practice have been considerable overlap between them because many of the *śārîm* would doubtless themselves have been heads of families.[16]

B. The Critique Of Lay Leadership In The Book Of Ezekiel

1 *Ezekiel 8-11*

In our discussion of these chapters above, we have shown the essentially visionary nature of the material[17] and that its thrust is not, as is commonly supposed, critical of the priesthood.[18] These chapters are indeed of central importance to Ezekiel's critique of the past, forming as they do a counterpoint in many respects to the final vision of chapters 40-48.[19] It remains for us to examine more closely exactly who receives the blame in Ezekiel's vision for the cultic defilement of the land, which defilement is so great that in the vision it can be depicted as filling even the Temple itself.

185.

[9] de Vaux, *Les Institutions*, 69; Reviv, *Elders*, 52ff.

[10] McKenzie, "Elders", 523ff.

[11] Cf. 1 Samuel 8:4.

[12] Reviv, *Elders*, 88; J. Conrad, "*zāqēn*", *Theologische Wörterbuch des Alten Testament*, G. Botterweck, H. Ringgren and H.-J. Fabry, eds (Stuttgart 1977) II, 644f.; G. Bettenzoli, "Gli 'Anziani' in Giuda", *Biblica* 64 (1983) 224.

[13] Conrad, "*zāqēn*", 646.

[14] McKenzie, "Elders", 527. On the position of the elders during and after the exile see D.L. Smith, *Religion of the Landless* (Bloomington 1989) 94ff.

[15] Reviv, *Elders*, 32. However, Reviv notes an exception to this rule where necessary to clarify a situation unfamiliar to later generations, when royal functionaries had taken over tasks earlier undertaken by the elders (45).

[16] McKenzie, "Elders", 528.

[17] See above, p.65ff.

[18] See above, p.71.

[19] Most obviously in the departure from the Temple of the glory of Yahweh and its corresponding return. L. Allen notes: "The vision of chaps. 8-11 in which Temple and city are destroyed in reprisal for cultic aberrations finds here a positive counterpart" (*Ezekiel 20-48*, 213).

First, it should be noted that the vision contained in these chapters apparently forms the answer given to a delegation of $z^e q\bar{e}n\hat{i}m$, described as the $ziqn\hat{e}$ $y^e h\hat{u}d\hat{a}$ (Ezek. 8:1). The purpose of their visit is not stated here; in view of the similar situations described in Ezekiel 14:1, 20:1 and 33:31, it seems very likely that they were seeking to inquire of Yahweh.[20] It is not immediately clear whether the $ziqn\hat{e}$ $y^e h\hat{u}d\hat{a}$ are to be distinguished from the $ziqn\hat{e}$ $b\hat{e}t$ $yi\acute{s}r\bar{a}'\bar{e}l$ (8:11f.) or the $ziqn\hat{e}$ $yi\acute{s}r\bar{a}'\bar{e}l$ (Ezek. 14:1; 20:1,3). Zimmerli thinks not, but regards the reason for such alternation as "nicht durchsichtigen".[21] On the other hand, Brownlee sharply distinguishes between the two groups,[22] as does Hölscher.[23] However, since the summary statements of the charge alternate between "the house of Judah" (Ezek. 8:17)[24] and "the house of Israel" (Ezek. 9:9),[25] it seems unlikely that any distinction was being made.[26]

What these men receive, instead of an answer to their apparent inquiry, is a categorical denunciation of their sins and the sins of the community which they represent. Chapter 8 is an account of a guided tour in which the prophet is shown four scenes of increasing abomination, with the offence to God being greater as the scenes in which they take place move nearer to the centre of the Temple. It begins with a vision of an "image of jealousy" ($s\bar{e}mel$ $haqqin'\hat{a}$) at the North gate of the city[27] (Ezek. 8:3-6). Next, he is shown "seventy elders of the house of Israel" ($\check{s}ib'\hat{i}m$ $'\hat{i}\check{s}$ $mizziqn\hat{e}$ $b\hat{e}t$ $yi\acute{s}r\bar{a}'\bar{e}l$) offering incense to idols in a secret chamber (8:7-13). After that,

---

[20] Cf. 2 Kings 6:32, where the elders of Samaria are sitting with Elisha and receive an encouraging word from Yahweh (2 Ki. 7:1). So Zimmerli, *Ezechiel*, 209.

[21] Zimmerli, *Ezechiel*, 1259.

[22] Brownlee, *Ezekiel 1-19*, 128. He sees the "elders of Judah" as being loyal to Yahweh while the "elders of Israel" are apostate.

[23] Hölscher, *Hesekiel*, 69. Hölscher then omits as spurious any reference to the $ziqn\hat{e}$ $b\hat{e}t$ $yi\acute{s}r\bar{a}'\bar{e}l$. Cf. also E. Balla, "Ez 8:1-9:11; 11:24,25", *Festschrift R. Bultmann zum 65. Geburtstag Überreicht* E. Wolf, ed. (Stuttgart 1949) 8.

[24] Note that Ezekiel 8:17, which castigates the abominations of the House of Judah is itself connected with the abominations in vv. 5-16. In those verses it is the House of Israel which is singled out for criticism (Ezek. 8:6,10,11,12). According to W. Zimmerli, no distinction is intended between these two titles ("Israel im Buche Ezechiel", *VT* 8 [1958] 82).

[25] MT reads $b\hat{e}t$ $yi\acute{s}r\bar{a}'\bar{e}l$ $w\hat{i}h\hat{u}d\hat{a}$. The latter word is, however, almost certainly a gloss (cf. Zimmerli, "Israel", 82).

[26] For a somewhat similar alternation, compare Ezekiel 25, where there seems little substantive distinction intended between the "House of Judah" (v.12) and "my people Israel" (v.14). On "Israel" in the Book of Ezekiel, see Zimmerli, "Israel", 75-90, and "Exkurs 2: 'Israel im Buche Ezechiel'" in *Ezechiel*, 1258-61.

[27] MT has $'el$-$petah$ $\check{s}a'ar$ $happ^en\hat{i}m\hat{i}t$ $happ\hat{o}neh$ $s\bar{a}p\hat{o}n\hat{a}$ ("to the entrance of the gate of the inner courtyard which faces north"). However, $happ^en\hat{i}m\hat{i}t$ with its feminine ending sits oddly beside the masculine $\check{s}a'ar$ (note the gender of the participle) and is not attested by the LXX. It also disturbs the general flow of the chapter from outer parts inward (as in chapters 40-43) and should therefore be omitted, according to Zimmerli (*Ezechiel*, 191f.) and S. Ackerman ("A *Marzēah* in Ezekiel 8:7-13?", *HTR* 82 [1989] 269f.). Brownlee suggests the emendation $hass^ep\hat{o}n\hat{i}$ in place of $happ^en\hat{i}m\hat{i}t$ (*Ezekiel 1-19*, 130), but it may simply be an (incorrect) explanatory gloss (so F.S. Freedy, "The Glosses in Ezekiel i-xxiv", *VT* 20 [1970] 138).

he sees women weeping for Tammuz at the North gate of the House of Yahweh itself (8:14-15). Finally, he sees twenty five men turning their backs on the House of Yahweh within the Inner Court, prostrating themselves to the east in worship of the sun (8:16). The acts themselves are apparently more or less interchangeable acts of idolatry, with prostration to the sun being no worse in itself than mourning for Tammuz. Equally, there is no clear progression in terms of the people involved, since it seems unlikely that the unspecified women would have been regarded as more significant personages than the seventy $z^c q\bar{e}n\hat{i}m$. It seems probable that the aggravating factor lies solely in the *location* of the offence, not in the specific acts themselves, nor the people performing them.[28] The point is that the entire Temple has been defiled from its outer parts to the inner court[29] by the sins of the people as a whole.[30] Further, the sins of the people as a whole are summed up and typified in the sins of their representatives, the $z^c q\bar{e}n\hat{i}m$—who are, after all, the initial audience for the recounting of this vision. As we shall see, there are several implicit and explicit references to the $z^c q\bar{e}n\hat{i}m$ in these chapters.

It is seventy *'îš mizziqnê bêt-yiśrā'ēl* who are standing before a wall of idols each offering incense from an incense burner (*miqṭeret*; Ezek. 8:11).[31] The practice of offering incense to animal figures may well have an Egyptian provenance.[32] Their actions provide a shocking contrast to the JE stratum of the Pentateuch in which seventy of the *ziqnê yiśrā'ēl* received the unique privilege of seeing God (Ex. 24:1-11) and were endowed with the same spirit as Moses (Num. 11:16-30).[33] One of their number is named

---

[28] *Contra* e.g. M. Schmidt, *Prophet und Tempel* (Zurich 1948) 139f. See Brownlee, *Ezekiel 1-19*, 135; Vogt, *Untersuchungen*, 42.

[29] It is interesting to note in this connection that the defilement goes no further than the inner courtyard: it never enters the Temple building itself. Similarly in the vision of reconstruction the activities are all restricted to the inner and outer courts. Was the building itself too holy to be entered?

[30] A similar point is made more directly in Ezekiel 5:11: "you have defiled my sanctuary with all your detestable things and with all your abominations".

[31] Mosis argues that the construction *'îš mizziqnê - X* focusses attention on the *representative* function of these men. They were not simply men, who happened also to be elders; rather they were men who particularly represented the body of $z^c q\bar{e}n\hat{i}m$ ("Ez 14:1-11", 188f.). According to Mosis, were their belonging to the circle of elders accidental additional information, a relative clause or simple apposition would more likely have been used.

[32] Schmidt, *Prophet und Tempel*, 139. Cooke argues for a Babylonian origin of this cult (*Ezekiel*, 94).

[33] Van der Ploeg, "Anciens", 182. The antiquity of the tradition behind the passage in Exodus is strongly defended by E.W. Nicholson in "The Origin of the Tradition in Exodus xxiv 9-11", *VT* 26 (1976) 148-60. Cf. also the comments on the possible circumstances behind the Numbers passage in Reviv, *Elders*, 106ff. The contrast would be sharpened even further if what is described in Exodus 24:11 is a covenant meal before Yahweh (so J. Lindblom, "What is a Temple? A Preliminary Typology", *The Quest for the Kingdom of God. Essays in Honor of George E. Mendenhall*, H.B. Huffmon, F.A. Spina, A.R.W. Green, eds. [Winona Lake 1983] 216; *contra* Nicholson, "Tradition", 148-50; the question hinges largely on the relation of vv. 3-8 to vv. 9-11)—or was perhaps understood as such by the author of this chapter of Ezekiel—and if Ackerman's proposal is accepted that the activity of the $z^c q\bar{e}n\hat{i}m$

as Jaazanaiah, who is designated the son of Shaphan—and thus equally shockingly associated with a family which was prominent in the reforms of Josiah's days (2 Ki. 22:3-14).[34] The only other place in the Old Testament where *miqteret* ("incense burner") is found is in 2 Chronicles 26:19, where Uzziah is similarly convicted of cultic irregularities.[35] The identity of these secret transgressors as *ziqnê bêt-yiśrā'ēl* is repeated for emphasis in the next verse (Ezek. 8:12). The *z*e*qēnîm* are also identified in Ezekiel 9:6 as the group of men involved in the most horrendous blasphemy of all: sun worship between the porch and the altar, an area of special sanctity in the inner court (Ezek. 8:16).[36] For that reason, they are the first to suffer in the visionary destruction of Jerusalem. It is also striking that when the justification for the destruction of the city is given, it is a saying of the *z*e*qēnîm* ("Yahweh has forsaken the land and Yahweh does not see"; 8:12) which is cited as the prime example of its perversity (Ezek. 9:9).[37]

A second scene of judgement (Ezekiel 11:1-21) has been woven into the original vision.[38] It concerns a further twenty five men, located this time at the door of the east gate of the House of Yahweh. This group includes in their number Jaazanaiah ben Azzur and Pelataiah ben Benaiah, who are designated *śārê hā'ām* (Ezek. 11:1). The significance of this emphasis on the office of Jaazaniah and Pelatiah will be discussed more fully below.[39] For now, however, note that they form part of the larger group of twenty five men, who are presumably *not* all *śārîm* since that designation is limited to the named individuals. What this vision concerns then is a group, including some *śārîm* but not limited to them, whose primary function has been to give counsel (*'ēṣâ*, Ezek. 11:2). Clearly they are men of authority within the city.[40] Giving counsel is the primary task of the *z*e*qēnîm* (cf. Ezek. 7:26), among whom we might well expect to find some of the *śārîm*, as we noted above.[41] Thus the party singled out for blame in chapter 11 is

---

in Ezekiel 8:11 is a *marzēaḥ*, a feast as part of a cult of the dead in front of a wall of idols ("*Marzēaḥ*", 245-65). Given the uncertainty of both proposals, however, a simpler contrast between the former and the latter activity may be all that is intended.

[34] Schmidt, *Prophet und Tempel*, 139. This family was also closely associated with Jeremiah (Jer. 26:24; 29:3; 39:14); cf. Long, "Social Dimensions", 46.

[35] The connection is noted in Zimmerli, *Ezechiel*, 217.

[36] On the originality of this designation, see above, p.70. Even though *zāqēn* has the sense "old man" in the all-inclusive formula of Ezekiel 9:6a, the sense "elders" seems to fit better in Ezekiel 9:6b. See further above, p.70.

[37] See below, p.124.

[38] The question of whether it was ever a separate vision (so Fohrer & Galling, *Ezechiel*, 58; *contra* Zimmerli, *Ezechiel*, 241) need not concern us here.

[39] See pp.115, 118, 123.

[40] As well as noting the fact that their words carry weight, it may be pointed out that only such people would have to fear being singled out for the kind of judgement envisaged in Ezekiel 11:9f. Cf. the events described in 2 Kings 25:18ff., to which there may or may not be an implicit reference.

[41] See above, p.111. Cf. Sedlmeier, *Ezechiel 20*, 165 n.114.

very probably to be identified as a group of $z^e q\bar{e}n\hat{\imath}m$, even though the express designation is lacking.[42]

We may conclude our investigation of who receives the blame for the events of chapters 8-11 in the following terms: although in Ezekiel's mind the abuses described in these chapters are certainly the responsibility of the whole house of Judah (Ezek. 8:17),[43] nonetheless within that totality the lay leadership is singled out for particular blame. These lay leaders are designated in chapter 8 by the term $ziqn\hat{e}\ y^e h\hat{u}d\hat{a}/b\hat{e}t\ yi\acute{s}r\bar{a}'\bar{e}l$, while in chapter 11 the presence is specifically noted of two of the $\acute{s}\bar{a}r\hat{e}\ h\bar{a}'\bar{a}m$.[44]

With what specific offences are the lay leadership charged in these chapters? The focus of chapter 8 is a variety of cultic abuses, both private (the incense offerings) and, apparently, public (the worship of the sun).[45] The $z^e q\bar{e}n\hat{\imath}m$ are here charged with idolatry, associated with foreign cults. They have decided in their hearts that Yahweh does not see what is going on because he has abandoned the land (Ezek. 8:12). Yahweh's response is then to depict his glory actually departing from the land and to show the catastrophes which will follow, falling first on the $z^e q\bar{e}n\hat{\imath}m$ (chapters 9 and 10).

The critique in chapter 11 is a little different. There the group of lay leaders are charged with bloodshed as well as wicked counsel (Ezek. 11:2, 6). They have declared:

> We have plenty of time to build up the houses;[46] this [city] is the cauldron, and we are the flesh.

Graffy notes the wide variety of interpretations of the first phrase which are possible, depending on whether the infinitive construct phrase is construed as a statement,[47] a question[48] or a command[49] and whether $b^e n\hat{o}t\ b\bar{a}tt\hat{\imath}m$ speaks of constructing physical houses or is used figuratively of providing descendants.[50] The harsh response which the prophet gives to refute the

---

[42] For a suggestion as to why the designation is absent here, see below, p.123.

[43] Rather than being chiefly the responsibility of the Zadokite priests as many modern commentators assume.

[44] For a somewhat similar condemnation, which also groups the $\acute{s}\bar{a}r\hat{\imath}m$ and $z^e q\bar{e}n\hat{\imath}m$ together and charges them with oppression, cf. Isaiah 3:14f.

[45] Although we have noted above the caution which needs to be exercised in interpreting the location of these visionary events.

[46] $l\bar{o}'\ b^e q\bar{a}r\hat{o}b\ b^e n\hat{o}t\ b\bar{a}tt\hat{\imath}m$; a literal translation might be: "Houses will not be built up soon". For the translation given here see Graffy, A Prophet Confronts, 43.

[47] RSV: "The time is not near to build up houses".

[48] So e.g. LXX, Vulgate.

[49] So e.g. F. Horst, "Exilsgemeinde und Jerusalem in Ez viii-xi: Eine literarische Untersuchung", VT 3 (1953) 340.

[50] J. Steinmann wishes to read this as a desire to rebuild the High Places, presumably emending $b\bar{a}tt\hat{\imath}m$ to $b\bar{a}m\hat{o}t$ (Le prophète Ézéchiel, Lectio Divina 13 [Paris 1953] 64). There is no evidence to support such an emendation, however, and it does not fit Ezekiel's response.

quotation suggests that the statement is an expression of arrogance and complacency. These men believe that the city will provide continued protection for them, and in due course they will be able to establish new homes and form a new ruling dynasty.[51] To this end they have already begun establishing themselves through bloodshed and judicial murder,[52] filling the city with their victims (Ezek. 11:6).[53] In all this they have acted according to the laws of the nations round about them rather than those of Yahweh (Ezek. 11:12).

Thus the charges against the lay leaders of the people in chapters 8-11 fall into two principal categories: idolatrous cultic acts, which are particularly associated with the $z^e q\bar{e}n\hat{i}m$, and the use of violent means to further their power and wealth, which is associated with the $\acute{s}\bar{a}r\hat{i}m$.[54]

2 Ezekiel 14:1-8

We have already mentioned this passage in its application to the prophets above;[55] the primary thrust of the passage, however, is critical of the $z^e q\bar{e}n\hat{i}m$. Similarly to chapter 8, the occasion for this oracle is the approach of "certain of the elders of Israel" ($^{a}n\bar{a}\check{s}\hat{i}m\ mizziqn\hat{e}\ yi\acute{s}r\bar{a}'\bar{e}l$).[56] We suggested there that this construction focusses attention on their *representative* function as men who particularly represented the body of $z^e q\bar{e}n\hat{i}m$.[57] The approach of these men to the prophet is described in a schematic, almost ritual, manner.[58] We should therefore see in this oracle a rebuke aimed not simply at certain individuals but at the whole circle of the $ziqn\hat{e}\ yi\acute{s}r\bar{a}'\bar{e}l$, whom they represent. The charge against them is given in v.3: "these men have taken their idols into their hearts, and set the stumbling block of their iniquity before their faces". The accusation of having caused their idols ($gill\hat{u}l\hat{e}hem$) to come upon their hearts[59] is reminiscent of Ezekiel 8:10ff.,

---

[51] Graffy, *A Prophet Confronts*, 42f.

[52] On the meaning of $h\bar{a}lal$ in Ezekiel see O. Eissfeldt, "Schwerterschlagene bei Hesekiel", *Studies in Old Testament Prophecy presented to T.H. Robinson*, H.H. Rowley, ed. (Edinburgh 1950) 73-81.

[53] Bettenzoli, *Geist der Heiligkeit*, 110.

[54] These two categories are not restricted to chapter 11; Messel notes that "auch andere Stellen neben dem Götzendienst Gewalttat oder Blutvergießen als zweite Hauptsünde Jerusalems nennen". He mentions Ezekiel 7:20,23; 8:17; 9:9; 22:3f.; 16:38; 23:37,45; 33:25 (*Ezéchielfragen*, 17f.).

[55] See p.101.

[56] Ezekiel 8:1 terms them $ziqn\hat{e}\ y^e h\hat{u}d\hat{a}$. On the usage of $ziqn\hat{e}\ yi\acute{s}r\bar{a}'\bar{e}l$ and $ziqn\hat{e}\ y^e h\hat{u}d\hat{a}$ in Ezekiel, see above, p.112. and Mosis, "Ez 14:1-11", 189f.

[57] See above, p.113, n.31.

[58] Cf. Ezekiel 8:1; 20:1. So Mosis, "Ez 14:1-11", 191. W. Zimmerli notes the similarity to Elisha in 2 Kings 6:32 ("Eigenart", 3). Cf. W. Zimmerli, "The Special Form and Traditio-Historical Character of Ezekiel's Prophecy", *VT* 15 (1965) 517f.; Carley, "Prophets", 45. For a different opinion see H. Bardtke, "Der Prophet Ezechiel in der modernen Forschung", *ThLZ* 96 (1971) 724f.

[59] H. Schoneveld ("Ez 14:1-8", *OTS* 15 [1969] 193ff.) interprets the hifil of '$\bar{a}l\hat{a}$ in this phrase literally as referring to the wearing of amulets or tattoos on their chests.

where the *zᵉqēnîm* are likewise denounced for secret idolatry with "all the idols (*gillûlîm*) of the house of Israel" and in their own "image-chambers" (*ḥadrê maśkît*).[60] The phrase "stumbling block of iniquity" (*mikšôl ᵃwōn*) occurs six times in the book of Ezekiel and invariably seems to be linked together with idolatry, as it is here.[61] Thus both sides of the accusation point to the *zᵉqēnîm* as guilty of the sin of idolatry; because of their divided hearts it would be inappropriate for Yahweh to give the *zᵉqēnîm* any answer to their inquiry, except an answer of judgement. Even while the accusation is broadened out in v.4f. into a general principle applying to the whole people, it should be noted that it is such only insofar as the people have fallen into the same sins as the *zᵉqēnîm*.

3 Ezekiel 20

As in chapters 8 and 14, Ezekiel 20 portrays the approach to the prophet of "certain of the elders of Israel" (*ᵃnāšîm mizziqnê yiśrā'ēl*), seeking to inquire of Yahweh.[62] What they receive however, again as in chapters 8 and 14, is a categorical condemnation of the people in general and themselves in particular for the sin of idolatry. That these men are not in view merely as a representative group of Israelites—though they are certainly at least that—is clear from the inclusion of specific personal names in the first passage (Ezek. 8:11; 11:1), and from the way that in both the second and third passages the initial focus is on the sins of the elders themselves (Ezek. 14:3; 20:3f.), before the scope is broadened to apply to the whole community. Ezekiel is instructed to address his tirade to "the elders of Israel" (v.3). They are the individuals whom Yahweh will not answer, and they are the ones who Ezekiel is invited to join Yahweh in judging.[63] Again, as in both chapters 8 and 11, the charge is of idolatry,

---

[60] On the *ḥadrê maśkît* see Greenberg, *Ezekiel 1-20*, 170.

[61] Taylor, *Ezekiel*, 126. In addition to the three occurrences in this chapter (vv. 3,4,7), it appears in Ezekiel 7:19; 18:30 and 44:12. In 7:19 it refers to silver and gold from which were made "abominable images and detestable things" (v.20). In 18:30 it refers to the transgressions described in the earlier part of the chapter which include idolatry (vv. 6,12,15). In 44:12 it refers to the activity of the Levites in leading the people astray into idolatry. *mikšôl* occurs on its own in 3:20, a passage which seems dependant upon Ezekiel 18 (Zimmerli, *Ezechiel*, 91), while in 21:20 the Massoretic vocalization *hammikšōlîm* is probably wrong and the text should rather be read *hammukšālîm* ("the collapsing"); cf. LXX; Targum; Zimmerli, *Ezechiel*, 472.

[62] Again the description of the approach is somewhat stereotyped (Sedlmeier, *Ezechiel 20*, 159). This does not mean that there was no historical event lying behind the oracle, but it does accent the essentially *literary* nature of the present form of the text (Sedlmeier, 14).

[63] Just as Ezekiel plays an important part in the re-creation of Israel through his powerful prophetic message of hope (see pp.103-08 above), so also he has played an important part in the destruction of the old by his powerful prophetic words of doom (cf. Ezek. 11:13). A key element of that activity is his participation with Yahweh in the tasks of judgement and making known the abominations of the people. For both judging and making known abominations, cf. Ezekiel 20:4; 22:2; 23:36; for making known abominations only, cf. Ezekiel 16:2.

depicted as the besetting sin of Israel from the time of the exodus from Egypt (v.8) down to the present ('ad-hayyôm, v.31). According to Sedl-meier, the striking correspondence of vv.2-4 and vv. 30ff. shows that they are consciously intended as a frame for the reflection upon history.[64] This observation is supported by the fact that in v. 30ff. we return to the direct address which characterizes the opening section of the chapter. The ease with which this direct address can shift from the *ᵃnāšîm mizziqnê yiśrā'ēl* to the broader *bêt yiśrā'ēl* indicates the extent to which the sins of the "men from the elders of Israel" are seen as representative of the sins of the people as a whole.[65] The focus of the whole first part of the chapter (vv. 1-31) is the condemnation of these men, as particular representatives of the circle of *zᵉqēnîm*,[66] for the sin of idolatry. The result of such a fixation with idols on the part of Israel's lay leadership is—again as in chapter 14—that no inquiry of Yahweh is possible.

4 Ezekiel 22:27

Her officials[67] (śārêha) in the midst of her are like wolves tearing the prey, shedding blood, destroying lives to get dishonest gain.

This verse forms part of a rogues' gallery of sin, as chapter 22 provides a comprehensive picture of the sinfulness of Jerusalem.[68] The description of the *śārîm* as wolves (*zᵉ'ēbîm*) is part of a section directly dependent upon Zephaniah 3:3f., but which has been expanded and adapted by Ezekiel to suit his own purposes.[69] Interestingly, in the transfer from Zephaniah some changes have been made, in addition to the expansions. The *śārîm* have lost their position at the head of the list in Zephaniah 3, and with it the designation as "roaring lions" (*ᵃrāyôt šōᵃgîm*), in order to make room for the *nᵉśî'îm*.[70] They take over instead the place of the wolves (*zᵉ'ēbîm*) which Zephaniah had alotted to the *šōpᵉtîm*.[71] The ferocity with which they are charged is hardly reduced thereby, since Ezekiel has added the further description of them as "tearing the prey" (*tōrᵉpê terep*). This is a designation which links the activity of the *śārîm* together with that of the

---

[64] *Ezechiel 20*, 195f.; R. Mosis, *Das Buch Ezechiel*, Geistliche Schriftlesung 8/1 (Düsseldorf 1978) 231f.

[65] Sedlmeier, *Ezechiel 20*, 163-6. Note that they are termed the *ziqnê bêt yiśrā'ēl* in 8:11f.

[66] See above, p.113, 116.

[67] RSV: "princes" invites confusion with the *nᵉśî'îm* of 22:25 (corrected text; see above, p.19 n.61).

[68] This section of L. Allen's commentary is given the title: "Jerusalem: The Inside Story" (*Ezekiel 20-48*, 30).

[69] See above, p.72.

[70] For the *nᵉśî'îm* as fierce lions cf. Ezekiel 19:3,6.

[71] The *šōpᵉtîm* as a class are entirely absent from the Book of Ezekiel.

$n^e\acute{s}\hat{\imath}'\hat{\imath}m$,[72] and which also has its background in animal activity (cf. Gen.
37:33). This metaphorical image is combined with the concrete accusation
of readiness to shed blood (*lišpok-dām*) and to seek dishonest gain (*b*ʿ*sōa'
bāṣa'*).[73] In any event the point of the charges is clear: they, like the kings,
are charged with the misuse of power for the purpose of dishonest gain.[74]
This charge is very similar to that made against the twenty five men in
chapter 11, who include two of the *śārê hā'ām*.[75]

5 Ezekiel 22:29: The 'am hā'āreṣ

In our discussion so far we have been focussing on the passages which
utilize specific terminology for lay leadership (*śar*, *zāqēn*). There are,
however, further passages critical of the lay leaders of the people which do
not use this specific language. In Ezekiel 22:29 the *'am hā'āreṣ* are
attacked in the following terms:

> The *'am hā'āreṣ* have practised extortion and committed robbery; they have
> oppressed the poor and needy, and have extorted from the sojourner without
> redress[76].

Exactly who the *'am hā'āreṣ* were has been the subject of much debate,
with solutions ranging from the population of the country in its widest
sense[77] through the full members of the political and cultic community[78] to
a narrow stratum of society, whether a great national council,[79] the landed
gentry,[80] or the proletariat.[81] In view of these bewildering alternatives,
E.W. Nicholson came to the conclusion that there was no fixed meaning for
the term: in different contexts it had different meanings.[82] By means of a
more sophisticated analysis, however, S. Talmon has argued that the term
had two basic senses: as a general noun which refers to a variety of human
groups and as a technical term which can be applied only to a specific
entity in the Judean body politic.[83] The latter was applied to an *ad hoc*

---

[72] Cf. Ezekiel 22:25 (corrected text), which in turn seems to owe something to Ezekiel
19:3,6.
[73] Cf. the accusations against Shallum (= Jehoahaz) in Jeremiah 22:17.
[74] Krüger, *Geschichtskonzepte*, 412.
[75] See above, p.115.
[76] Or "justice" (*mišpāt*).
[77] E. Klamroth, *Die jüdischen Exulanten in Babylon* (Leipzig 1912) 99-101.
[78] E. Würthwein, *Der 'am ha'arez im Alten Testament* (Stuttgart 1936).
[79] E. Auerbach, "'am hā'āreṣ", *Proceedings of the First World Congress of Jewish
Studies, 1947* (Jerusalem 1952) 362-66.
[80] M. Weber, *Das Antike Judentum* (Tübingen 1921) 30ff.
[81] K. Galling, *Die israelitische Staatsverfassung in ihrer vordeorientalische Umwelt*, Der
Alte Orient 28 (Leipzig 1929) 23.
[82] "The Meaning of the Expression *'am hā'āreṣ* in the Old Testament", *JSS* 10 (1965) 66.
[83] "The Judean *'am hā'āreṣ* in Historical Perspective" in *Papers of the Fourth World
Congress of Jewish Studies* (Jerusalem 1967) 71-6 [= *King, Cult and Calendar* (Jerusalem
1986) 68-78].

power group of supporters of the Davidic monarchy whose activities are closely linked with Hebron and Jerusalem.

Although Talmon does not discuss the usage of the book of Ezekiel, it appears that both of these senses are present there. His association of the *'am hā'āreṣ* with the Davidic monarchy is interesting in view of the frequent occurrence of *'am hā'āreṣ* together with *nāśî'* in the book of Ezekiel: of the nine[84] uses of this phrase in Ezekiel, seven occur in passages which also relate in some way to the *nāśî'*, though a direct connection is not always certain.[85] In Ezekiel 7:27 and 22:29 in particular the connotation of a Jerusalem power group is attractive.[86] Further, in the two instances in Ezekiel where *'am hā'āreṣ* occurs in passages completely unrelated to the *nāśî'* (Ezek. 33:2; 39:13), the context does seem to indicate Talmon's more general sense: all the residents of a certain place, in this case Judah.[87] Thus the data in Ezekiel would seem at first sight to support Talmon's hypothesis. On the other hand, however, it should be noted that in Ezekiel 40-48 a different kind of distinction seems to be operative between *'am hā'āreṣ* and *'am*. Ebach has attempted to encapsulate the distinction in these chapters in the following terms:

> Vor allem aber ist *'am* dann benützt, wenn das Verhältnis von Volk und Herrscher in der Vergangenheit und im blick auf die alternative Zukunft thematisiert ist...Die Abschnitte, in denen das Gegenüber des *nāśî'* (sing.) der *'am hā'āreṣ* ist, betreffen nicht das politisch-soziale Verhaltnis von Herrscher und Volk. In diesen Abschnitten (45:22; 46:2f.,9) stehen sich *nāśî'* und *'am hā'āreṣ* als Aktuere im Kult gegenüber.[88]

The first part of his statement is inadequate, because it is clear that the *'am* occur frequently also in cultic contexts (cf. Ezek. 42:14; 44:11,19,23; 46:20,24). However, the stress on the *'am hā'āreṣ* as *actors* in the cult seems to me to be a very significant observation, and one which can be supported syntactically. In chapters 40-48 the *'am hā'āreṣ* normally appear as the *subject* of the verb (cf. Ezek. 45:16;[89] 46:3; 46:9); in only one occurrence are they not the subject (45:22). On the other hand, the *'am* never appear as the subject of the verb in chapters 40-48, but rather as a

---

[84] Including the disputed reference in Ezekiel 45:16, on which see above, p. 29 n.125, and further below, p.120.

[85] Ezekiel 7:27; 12:19 (cf. 12:10); 22:29 (cf. 22:27, corrected text); 45:16; 45:22; 46:3; 46:9. In terms of chapters 40-48 this connection was already noted by Gese, who made it a distinctive mark of his *nāśî'* stratum (*Verfassungsentwurf*, 110). For an assessment of Gese's thesis, see above, p.27ff.

[86] This sense also perhaps fits well in Ezekiel 12:19, where the *'am hā'āreṣ* seem to be particularly linked with the inhabitants of *Jerusalem*.

[87] Talmon, "*'am hā'āreṣ*", 73.

[88] Ebach, *Kritik und Utopie*, 196f.

[89] On the text, see above p.29 n.125.

direct or indirect object of the verb.[90] Thus we may say that in Ezekiel 40-48, *'am hā'āreṣ* appears to denote the congregation specifically in regard to their activity in the cult. A corollary of this observation is that if the present, apparently ungrammatical, MT of Ezekiel 45:16 (*kōl hā'ām hā'āreṣ*) is to be emended then the reading *kōl 'am hā'āreṣ* should probably be preferred to *kōl hā'ām*, since it is the subject of the verb in this verse.[91]

In Ezekiel 22:29, the *'am hā'āreṣ* would fit the description of Talmon's second group, a group of powerful men in Jerusalem, with close ties to the Davidic house.[92] In this verse they are condemned for extortion, robbery and oppression, specifically of those least able to defend themselves. The charge against them appears to have close ties with chapter 18, where there is a similar linkage of oppression and robbery with the same cognate phrases *'āšaq 'ōšeq gāzal gᵉzēlâ* (Ezek. 18:18),[93] and forbidding of violence against the poor and needy (*'ānî wᵉ'ebyôn hônâ;* 18:12). However, reflection on the similarities and differences between Ezekiel 18 and 22 suggests common influences rather than direct literary dependence of one upon the other. These common influences may stem ultimately from the Holiness Code,[94] but the similarities of Ezekiel 22:29 to the oracle against the kings of Judah in Jeremiah 22 are also worthy of notice. This latter chapter also connects robbery and oppression (Jer. 22:3), is concerned for the poor and needy (Jer. 22:16) forbids violence against the alien (Jer. 22:3),[95] and complains of the lack of justice (*bᵉlō' mišpāṭ;* Jer. 22:13).[96] Such a connection further underlines the links adduced by Talmon between the *'am hā'āreṣ* and the Davidic rulers of Judah by finding both guilty of the same sins.

6 Ezekiel 34:17-21

Another passage critical of the lay leaders which does not use the terminology of *śar* and *zāqēn* is Ezekiel 34. In this chapter the sins of the former shepherds and the "fat sheep" are condemned, and the promise of a different future given, in an oracle which seems to be based on Jeremiah

---

[90] Cf. Ezekiel 42:14; 44:11,19,23; 45:8f.; 46:18,20,24.
[91] This reading is found in seven Hebrew mss[ken]. So (for different reasons) Ebach, *Kritik und Utopie*, 197. In favour of *kōl hā'ām* (on the basis of the LXX), see most recent scholars, including Gese, *Verfassungsentwurf*, 72; Zimmerli, *Ezechiel*, 1151; L. Allen, *Ezekiel 20-48*, 247.
[92] Cf. Hals, *Ezekiel*, 161.
[93] The MT of Ezekiel 18:18 reads *gēzel 'āḥ;* compare however verses 7,16 and the versions.
[94] For extortion (*'šq*) and robbery (*gzl*), cf. Leviticus 19:13; for oppressing (hifil of *ynh*) the stranger (*gēr*) cf. Leviticus 19:33.
[95] The precise form of Ezekiel 22:29, with *'šq* rather than the hifil of *ynh*, may have been coloured by assimilation of Jeremiah 22:3 to the very similar prohibition in Jeremiah 7:6 (*gēr yātôm wᵉ'almānâ lō' ta"šōqû*).
[96] Elsewhere in the Old Testament this phrase is only found at Proverbs 13:23; 16:8.

23:1-4.[97] We have argued above that the shepherds should be understood as the last kings of Judah,[98] while the "rams and male goats " (v.17) and the "fat sheep" (v.20) are the rapacious and self-serving leaders of the community.[99] The accusation against them is of general social misconduct; of oppressing the weak with violence and grasping the limited resources to the detriment of those without influence or power. Even what they did not need for themselves they have spoiled, thus denying it to others. They had abandoned the traditional responsibility of the upper class for the social well-being of the other classes.[100] This misuse of their position of power is reminiscent of the accusations against the lay leadership in chapters 11 and 22, where they are charged in more concrete language with having used violence in pursuit of their own aggrandizement.[101]

7 Ezekiel 40-48

It may seem at first sight that these chapters have very little to say concerning the lay leadership of Israel. That silence is itself not insignificant, as we shall see.[102] But bearing in mind Greenberg's strictures on the dangers of the argument from silence in this section,[103] we shall be more concerned with what the text *does* say, directly and by implication, than with what it does not say.

As far as the critique of lay leadership is concerned, we note that the same attitude to the past history of the laity is exhibited in Ezekiel 43:7-9 and 44:6ff. as has been evident in chapters 1-39. The "house of Israel"[104] is again described as a rebellious house (44:6),[105] associated with harlotry (z⁻nûtām = idolatrous worship; 43:7,9),[106] with defiling Yahweh's holy

---

[97] L. Allen, *Ezekiel 20-48*, 160; Lust, "Gathering and Return", 139.
[98] See p.40.
[99] Messel, *Ezéchielfragen*, 28.
[100] Willmes, *Hirtenallegorie*, 511; Bettenzoli, *Geist der Heiligkeit*, 141.
[101] Cooke, *Ezekiel*, 376.
[102] See below, p.127.
[103] See "Design", 203.
[104] For *bêt-yiśrā'ēl* as a term denoting the laity, as distinct from the priesthood, note how in Ezekiel 44:12 the *bêt-yiśrā'ēl* is contrasted with the Levites, and in 44:15 the *b'nê yiśrā'ēl* (LXX *oikon israēl*) are contrasted with the Zadokites (cf. Ezek. 48:11). Compare Psalm 115:12 (also v.9 in many mss.; MT simply reads *yiśrā'ēl* there); Psalm 118:2f.; Psalm 135:19f. (on these see F. Delitzsch, *Die Psalmen* [Leipzig ⁵1894] 705; H. Gunkel, *Die Psalmen*, HK [Göttingen 1926] 497; L.C. Allen, *Psalms 101-50*, WBC [Waco 1983] 108). Ezra 9:1 uses *hā'ām yiśrā'ēl* to denote the laity in a somewhat similar context, (W. Rudolph, *Esra und Nehemia*, HAT [Tübingen 1949] 86). It is, however, also possible in the latter context to see these terms as comprehensive, including both priests and laity (Williamson, *Ezra-Nehemiah*, 125f. For this comprehensive sense in Ezekiel cf. 44:22, where the seed of the house of Israel (*zera' bêt-yiśrā'ēl*) would certainly include priestly and Levitical families.
[105] Following the LXX. MT reads simply *'el-merî*. On the text see Zimmerli, *Ezechiel*, 1119. For *bêt m'rî*, cf. Ezekiel 2:5,6; 3:9,26,27; 12:2,3; for *bêt hammerî*, cf. Ezekiel 2:8; 12:2,9,25; 17:12; 24:3; for *m'rî* cf. Ezekiel 2:7.
[106] Zimmerli, *Ezechiel*, 1083. Cf. Ezekiel 23:27, though generally Ezekiel prefers to use the word *taznût*.

name[107] and with abominations (43:8; 44:6), in particular the abomination of admitting foreigners to the sanctuary (44:7f.). In doing so they have "caused my covenant to be broken" (44:7).[108] However, nowhere is the blame particularly laid upon any group of lay leaders, perhaps because of the past-present-future dynamic of these sections.[109] If, as we shall argue below, the whole layer of lay leadership is swept away in Ezekiel's plan for the future, then there is no reason to single it out for mention in these passages.

8 Summary

As we draw to a close this section on the critique of lay leadership in the book of Ezekiel it will be useful to summarize the results. We have seen that there are two primary groups of lay leaders singled out of the mass of the people for particular criticism, namely the $z^e q\bar{e}n\hat{i}m$ and the $\acute{s}\bar{a}r\hat{i}m$. The former group are especially associated with the sin of idolatry (Ezek. 8; 14; 20) while the latter group are particularly associated with the sin of violent misuse of power for their own ends (Ezek. 11; 22:27). Also implicated in the latter sin were the '$am\ h\bar{a}$'$\bar{a}re\d{s}$ (Ezek. 22:29) and the broader mass of lay leadership, described in chapter 34 as rams, male goats and fat sheep. Of course, there would not have been a hard and fast distinction between these groups. Many of the $\acute{s}\bar{a}r\hat{i}m$ would also have been $z^e q\bar{e}n\hat{i}m$,[110] and members of both groups would have been found among the '$am\ h\bar{a}$'$\bar{a}re\d{s}$.[111] Nonetheless, it is striking that where the specific terminology is used it is associated with these particular sins.[112]

Equally, the sins described in these chapters are not unique to this class of people. Their sins, especially idolatry, are also those of the whole people: the charges are repeatedly drawn up against such inclusive designations as "Jerusalem" (Ezek. 5:5f.; 16:2ff.; 22:2ff.; 23:11ff.; 24:6ff.), "the people of Israel" (2:3; 6:5), "the house of Israel/Judah" (3:7; 4:4; 6:11; 8:6; 9:9; 11:5; 14:5; 18:6; 20:30; 36:17; 39:23) — which may simply be characterized as a "rebellious house" (Ezek. 2:5ff.; 3:9,26f.; 12:3,9,25; 24:3), and even "the land of Israel" (7:2ff.; 22:24). In chapters 8, 14 and 20 the sins of the $z^e q\bar{e}n\hat{i}m$ are linked with the sins of the people as a whole. However, whenever a specific group is identified out of this

---

[107] For defiling Yahweh's holy name, cf. Ezekiel 20:39; 36:20,23; (39:7). On Ezekiel 43:7-9, see above, p.40.

[108] This translation is suggested by G.R. Driver on the grounds that the $b^e n\hat{e}\ n\bar{e}k\bar{a}r$ cannot have broken God's covenant ("Ezekiel: Linguistic and Textual Problems", 309).

[109] See above, p.107.

[110] See above, p.111.

[111] Using the term in its narrower sense of a group of powerful men particularly associated with the Davidic dynasty. On this term in Ezekiel, see above, p.119.

[112] This may perhaps be why the group in Ezekiel 11 are not designated $z^e q\bar{e}n\hat{i}m$.

mass for blame in cultic matters it is invariably the $z^e q\bar{e}n\hat{i}m$. As befits their
position of leadership, they bear much of the responsibility for the
transgressions of the people as a whole.

C. THE FUTURE OF LAY LEADERSHIP IN THE BOOK OF EZEKIEL

1 Ezekiel 9-11

Ezekiel 9 details the vision of the judgement befalling the transgressors of
chapter 8. The whole city is given over into the hands of six armed angelic
figures so that it may be destroyed. The destruction is not to be indiscrim-
inate, however: those who sigh and cry over the abominations which are
carried out in the city are to be marked on their foreheads by a priestly
figure (Ezek. 9:2ff.)[113] and thus spared in the general slaughter. Further,
although the judgement is to be carried out on the rest of the people as a
whole (cf. 9:6), the $z^e q\bar{e}n\hat{i}m$ are prominent both in the programme of
punishment and in the motive clause. They are first to be punished (9:6),[114]
and in justifying his actions to the prophet Yahweh quotes the saying of the
$z^e q\bar{e}n\hat{i}m$: "Yahweh has forsaken the land, and Yahweh does not see"
(Ezek. 9:9; cf. 8:12).[115] This statement is taken as proof of the perversity
of the city, the capstone, as it were, of the iniquity of the house of Israel.
Thus, while hardly alone in their sin, the $z^e q\bar{e}n\hat{i}m$ are seen as being leaders
in the sin which culminates in the departure of the glory of Yahweh from
the Temple (chapter 10). They are, therefore, first to suffer the
consequences which that departure brings in its train.[116]

In Chapter 11 the words and actions of a group of men are again judged
in visionary form. We identified the overall composition of this group
above as probably made up of $z^e q\bar{e}n\hat{i}m$, though in the account prominence
is given rather to the fact that two of them bear the title of $\acute{s}\bar{a}r\hat{e}\ h\bar{a}'\bar{a}m$,[117]
a prominence which is underlined by the description of the fate of one of
these $\acute{s}\bar{a}r\hat{e}\ h\bar{a}'\bar{a}m$. These men are guilty of iniquity[118] and of bloodshed in
the city. The consequence of their actions is that they will meet a similar

---

[113] Steinmann, *Ézéchiel*, 65.

[114] See above, p.70.

[115] P.C. Beentjes, "Inverted Quotations in the Bible: a Neglected Stylistic Pattern", *Biblica*
63 (1982) 508f. Sedlmeier comments: "Daß an die *ziqnê bêt yiśrā'ēl* gedacht ist, zeigt die
Wiederaufnahme des Zitates von 8:12 in 9:9" (*Ezechiel* 20, 164f.). Cf. Greenberg,
"Citations", 274.

[116] How many people were found "who sigh and groan over all the abominations" of the
city and were marked out for salvation by the priestly figure–if indeed any such were
found–is not made clear in the text. There is no reason to believe that any of the idolatrous
$z^e q\bar{e}n\hat{i}m$ were saved out of the slaughter.

[117] See above, p.115.

[118] In Micah 2:1 *hšb 'āwen* is used in parallel with *rā'* in a context of usurpation of
property, which may well also be implied here. Cf. Graffy, *A Prophet Confronts*, 42.

fate themselves. The sword which they feared will come upon them and they will be judicially slain—a fate which is especially appropriate if, as Graffy believes, their victims suffered judicial murder.[119] As the first fruits of the coming judgement, Ezekiel sees the sentence of death executed by the divine hand on Pelatiah, one of the *śārê hā'ām*, while he is prophesying (Ezek. 11:13). This judgement is exactly analogous to the judgement of Jerusalem depicted in chapter 9.[120] This is clear from the correspondence of Ezekiel 9:8 and 11:13, the only occasions in the book where Ezekiel attempts to intercede for his people.[121] In both cases the prophet responds to the deaths by falling upon his face and asking if this means the end for the remnant of Israel.[122] The death of Pelatiah is thus a token of the certainty of the fate awaiting all of the *śārîm* remaining in Jerusalem. Just as in Ezekiel 9:6 the *z^eqēnîm* had been singled out as prime targets of the coming judgement, so here the *śārîm* are singled out for destruction.

2 Ezekiel 14:1-11

We have already dealt with the consequences of disobedience threatened to the unfaithful prophets in this passage.[123] The same remarks apply, *mutatis mutandis*, to the *z^eqēnîm* who have been charged with idolatry earlier in this passage.[124] V.10 makes explicit the fact that the judgement of Yahweh rests equally upon both: "The punishment of the prophet and the punishment of the inquirer shall be alike" (*ka^{'a}wōn haddōrēš ka^{'a}wōn hannābî'*). Thus the prospect with which the idolatrous inquirer in v.8 is threatened by Yahweh, of being made "a sign and a byword" (*wah^aśimōt- îhû l^e'ôt ûl^emāšāl*)[125] and of "being cut off from the midst of my people" (*w^ehikrattîw mittôk 'ammî*), should probably be seen as parallel to the threat uttered against the deceived prophet in v.9 of "being destroyed from the midst of my people Israel". We have argued above that both verses speak of the threat of excommunication, exclusion from the covenant people, probably also followed by death.[126] It is therefore striking to note that, just

---

[119] *A Prophet Confronts*, 44. Cf. Lang, *Kein Aufstand*, 181.

[120] The "reality" of this event is therefore equally a visionary reality, just as for the destruction of Jerusalem pictured in Ezekiel 9 (Greenberg, *Ezekiel 1-20*, 189; *contra* e.g. Horst, "Exilsgemeinde", 342; Hölscher, *Hesekiel*, 76).

[121] Greenberg, "Ezekiel 8-11", 162. Cf. Messel, *Ezéchielfragen*, 55.

[122] Ezekiel 9:8: *wā'epp^elâ 'al-pānay wā'ez'aq wā'ōmar ^{'a}hâ ^{'a}dōnāy yhwh h^amašhît 'attâ 'ēt kol-š^e'ērît yiśrā'ēl*; 11:13: *wā'eppōl 'al-pānay wā'ez'aq qôl-gādôl wā'ōmar ^{'a}hâ ^{'a}dōnāy yhwh kālâ 'attâ 'ōśeh 'ēt š^e'ērît yiśrā'ēl*.

[123] See above, p.101.

[124] Cf. v.3. See above, p.116.

[125] MT reads *ûlim^ešālîm* which is attested also by the Targum. The normal form of this expression has the singular, however. Cf. Deuteronomy 28:37; 1 Kings 9:7 = 2 Chronicles 7:20; Jeremiah 24:9; Psalm 69:12. Greenberg interprets the plural as one of generalization or amplification (*Ezekiel 1-20*, 250). On this, cf. GKC § 124 e.

[126] See above, p.102.

as the prophets (apart from Ezekiel himself) play no part in the reconstituted Israel, so also the $z^e q\bar{e}n\hat{\imath}m$ are entirely absent from Ezekiel's plan for the future.[127]

3 Ezekiel 20:33-38

Those criticized by Ezekiel for their idolatry in this chapter are once again the $z^e q\bar{e}n\hat{\imath}m$ of Israel, as in chapters 8 and 14.[128] The consequences of their idolatrous actions are described in verses 33-38. The $z^e q\bar{e}n\hat{\imath}m$, who had thought[129] to be idolaters like the nations (v.32), are here warned of a future face-to-face judgement before Yahweh in "the wilderness of the peoples" (midbar hā'ammîm; v.35). The result of that judgement will be a separation of the rebels (hammōr'dîm) and transgressors (happôš''îm) from their midst (Ezek. 20:38). What happens to them once they have been separated is not made clear in this passage, however, since the basic thrust of this section is one of promise, not judgement.[130] As Zimmerli comments:

> Das unmittelbare Schicksal der Widerspenstigen, das sich in der Wüste draußen erfüllt, wird nicht weiter beschrieben. Es genügt die Aussage, daß sie das Erlösungsziel nicht erreichen. Wieder wird deutlich, daß das Leben auch des Einzelnen in Israel ganz im Leben der Gemeinde hängt.[131]

To this we might add that exclusion from the promise of renewed life in the land is simply another aspect of the threat of excommunication (and subsequent death?) which we found confronting the idolatrous $z^e q\bar{e}n\hat{\imath}m$ and those who would prophesy for them in chapter 14.[132]

4 Ezekiel 34:17-24

The focus of this passage is not on the fate which the "rams and he-goats" (v.17) and the "fat sheep" (v.20) will suffer, but rather on Yahweh's intervention to ensure that the conditions which gave rise to such oppression do not occur again. A judgement between one sheep and another is promised (v.17,22), which is reminiscent of what we have just seen in Ezekiel 20:33ff.,[133] but the punishment which will be meted out to the guilty parties is not made explicit. It is clear, however, that the power of the lay

---

[127] On this, see further below, p.131.
[128] Cf. v.1,3. See above, p.117.
[129] The emphasis on the hidden nature of the idolatry of the $z^e q\bar{e}n\hat{\imath}m$ forms another link between chapters 8, 14 and 20 (cf. 8:7f.,12; 14:3f.; 20:32). Their idolatry was apparently an idolatry of heart and mind.
[130] Graffy, A Prophet Confronts, 70.
[131] Zimmerli, Ezechiel, 456.
[132] See above, p.102.
[133] See above, p.126. Note especially the shepherd imagery incorporated into the judgement scene in Ezekiel 20:37 (Graffy, A Prophet Confronts, 71).

leadership to repeat such sins in the future will be significantly reduced by the introduction of a single strong leader, the *one* shepherd described as "my servant, David" (v.23). Just as the solution to the problem of warring sheep is a strong, just shepherd, so the solution to the problem of oppressive lay leadership is a strong — yet just — single leader.[134] As we shall see in Ezekiel 40-48,[135] the ruling class has been abolished and Yahweh rules his people directly through his under-shepherd, the nāśî'.[136]

5 Ezekiel 40-48

We noted above the criticisms levelled at the laity — though not explicitly at the lay leadership — in these chapters.[137] We also noted there that, in fact, the lay leadership fades from view altogether in these chapters. It is this absence of any role for the lay leadership, along with what we may term a "downgrading" in the status of the laity as a whole, which we now wish to explore.

So much attention has been focussed on the "downgrading" of the Levites in Ezekiel 44:6ff. that a parallel, even primary, downgrading of the laity has often been missed.[138] They are to lose their right of slaughtering their own burnt offerings and sacrifices (Ezek. 44:11 — to the Levites!).[139] This is not surprising when it is recalled that Ezekiel 44 is fundamentally critical of the laity (cf. Ezek. 44:6) and only secondarily of the Levites.[140] Further, their participation in worship is limited to a contribution to the offering of the nāśî' (Ezek. 45:16), a procession through the outer court on major festivals (Ezek. 46:9-11) and a brief act of prostration at the outer entrance of the gateway to the inner courtyard on sabbaths and on the new moons (46:3).[141] As Zimmerli notes, with eight steps leading up to the gateway (Ezek. 40:31) and beyond it a corridor fifty cubits[142] long (40:29), their view of ceremonies taking place in the inner court would have been

---

[134] On this, see further above p.47.
[135] See below, p.130ff.
[136] Bettenzoli, *Geist der Heiligkeit*, 141.
[137] See above, chapter 5 section B.7.
[138] It has, however, been noted in passing by Milgrom, *Levitical Terminology*, 84. Cf. also L. Allen, *Ezekiel 20-48*, 261; Fishbane, *Biblical Interpretation*, 138. Bertholet comments: "Die *einzige* [emphasis original] Bestimmung, die es [das Volk] in Ezechiels Verfassungsentwurf im übrigen noch betrifft, ist die folgende: Wenn das gewöhnliche Volk an Festzeiten vor Jahwe kommt, so soll, wer durchs Nordtor eintritt, um anzubeten, durchs Südtor wieder hinausgehen und umgekehrt; niemand soll durch das Tor zurückkehren, durch das er gekommen ist. Daß sich in dieser Vorschrift erschöpft, was Ezechiel über die Laien zu sagen hat, braucht keinen Kommentar" (*Verfassungsentwurf*, 13).
[139] For the former custom, cf. e.g. Leviticus 1:5,11; 3:2,8. Cf. Haran, *Temples*, 61 n.4; Greenberg, "Design", 206.
[140] On this see above, p.75.
[141] This assumes that the sense of 'am hā'āreṣ here in chapter 45f. is the active cultic community. For this see above, p.120.
[142] About 87.5 feet.

decidedly limited. [143]

This keeping of the laity at a distance from the sacred space is further emphasized in the distribution of the land: in order of rank from the centre outward the distribution is Zadokite priests, Levites, *nāśî'*, lay tribes, as the following diagram makes clear:

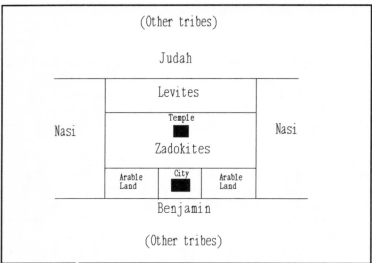

Figure 2. Distribution of land in the *t'rûmâ*.

Even within the lay tribes themselves there is a recognizable ranking relative to the Temple. [144] The sacred reservation (*t'rûmâ*) [145] acts as a further buffer zone, completely isolating the Temple from the dwelling places of the laity, except for those who inhabited the holy city (Ezek. 48:15-20). [146]

---

[143] Zimmerli, *Ezechiel*, 1171. One wonders if lay Israelites were really intended to feel that the open door constituted a "token of intimacy", as L. Allen suggests (*Ezekiel 20-48*, 267). Rather, it would seem that the whole process of keeping the laity at a distance was intended to cause them to feel shame (Ezek. 43:11).

[144] On the ordering of the tribes within the Promised Land in Ezekiel 48, see Levenson, *Theology*, 116ff.

[145] The use of the word *t'rûmâ*, which is elsewhere used of sacrificial gifts and offerings (cf. Ezek. 20:40; 44:30; 45:13,16), for this thirteenth strip of land shows clearly its status as a tribute from the twelve tribes to Yahweh (Ezek. 48:9). Cf. Zimmerli, *Ezechiel*, 1220; Ebach, *Kritik und Utopie*, 187. J.G. Snaith notes that the word *t'rûmâ* "used in a fairly general sense in the Bible, is employed in the Mishnah very frequently in the specific sense of the portions of offerings set apart for the priests" ("Ben Sira's Supposed Love of Liturgy", *VT* 25 [1975] 168).

[146] Chary, *Prophètes et Culte*, 21; Zimmerli, "Planungen", 248; Hals, *Ezekiel*, 345. The Temple area is also, of course, isolated from the land alotted to the *nāśî'* (for the motivation behind this, cf. Ezekiel 43:7-9) and from that alotted to the Levites (cf. 44:6ff.). Cf. Ebach, *Kritik und Utopie*, 188.

This "buffer zone" mentality finds concrete expression in Ezekiel 48:11, which states that the central portion of the land shall be:

> for the consecrated priests, the sons of Zadok, who kept my charge, who did not go astray when the people of Israel went astray, as the Levites did.[147]

In a world in which position is defined by one's role in the Temple and nearness to it,[148] the laity are clearly at the bottom of the heap — and the reason for that position is equally clearly stated as being their past transgressions. It is easy to see why the proper result of the house of Israel studying the reformed layout of the Temple is described as shame over their iniquities (Ezek. 43:10). These iniquities certainly include the abominations of chapters 8-11 for which, as we saw above, the laity and their leadership bear the brunt of the blame.[149] Now in these chapters their sentence is pronounced, a combination of gracious restoration to their former status as the covenant people of God (Ezek. 34:30; cf. "my people", 44:23; 45:8f.) with God dwelling in their midst (Ezek. 43:7) and new restrictions to prevent the repeat of past abuses.[150] The people who, following the example of their leaders, defiled the first Temple with their idolatry, are left with neither easy access to the restored Temple nor a clearly defined role in its worship. Yet this "downgrading" too should not be overstated. At least they are permitted a share in the promised land, with Yahweh dwelling in their midst forever (Ezek. 43:9).[151] Even to be the least in such a kingdom is unmistakably a mark of great privilege.[152]

This combination of gracious restoration and new restrictions also comes to expression in the special status of "the city". Positively, reflecting the status which Jerusalem once held, it finds a special place within the sacred reservation ($t^e r \hat{u} m \hat{a}$), the closest lay residence to the Temple.[153] Like the old Jerusalem, it is not part of any tribal area.[154] Negatively, however, it is nowhere named as "Jerusalem",[155] reflecting the criticisms which were

---

[147] This verse is often seen as a late gloss, part of the so-called "Zadokite Stratum". On this see above, p.87ff.

[148] Niditch, "Design", 219.

[149] See above, p.111ff.

[150] It may be recalled that a similar pattern was discerned in the treatment of the Levites (cf. Ezek. 44:13). See above, p.83.

[151] Cf. Ezekiel 11:17ff.; 20:40; 34:25ff.; 36:24ff.; 37:12ff.

[152] It is interesting to compare and contrast Ezekiel's system of gradations with that described in the Priestly stratum of the Pentateuch (for a clear description of the latter system see Jenson, *Graded Holiness*, esp. 115-148). Clearly both stem from a common world view. The fundamental difference, apart from the prominent place accorded to the *nāśî'* by Ezekiel and to the High Priest by P, is that Ezekiel roots the gradations on the basis of past merit, an element which seems to be lacking in P (Jenson, 133).

[153] This status must surely be more positively evaluated than as "einer gewissen Verlegenheitslösung" (so Zimmerli, "Planungen", 248).

[154] Macholz, "Planungen", 343.

[155] Macholz, "Planungen", 343; Baltzer, *Ezechiel und Deutero-Jesaja*, 29. A more positive outlook is expressed in the postscript, Ezekiel 48:30-5, where the city is given a new name:

levelled at that city and all who dwelt in her in the earlier part of the book.[156] More dramatically, in contrast to a theology which would link the election of David with the election of Zion/Jerusalem,[157] the new city is no longer the residence of the House of David nor the home of the Temple. Instead, it is a kind of federal district shared among the tribes, and welcoming members from all (Ezek. 48:19).[158]

In addition to a need to prevent a repetition of the sins of idolatry for which the lay leaders (especially the $z^e q\bar{e}n\hat{i}m$) are singled out in Ezekiel's condemnation of the past, there was also an evident need to prevent the sins of the strong, who had oppressed and dispossessed the weak.[159] These sins, which Ezekiel on two occasions particularly associates with the $\acute{s}\bar{a}r\hat{i}m$, are also to be dealt with in the new distribution of the land (Ezek. 47:13-48:29), for to regulate the land is at the same time to regulate the people.[160] Each of the tribes is alotted an identical portion of the land—identical not only in dimensions but in topography also.[161] The whole bureaucracy and structure of social classes which had built up over the course of the monarchy is swept away in what appears in many ways to be a return to the social conditions of the pre-monarchic era—albeit with the retention of the single, central, strong, yet servant figure of the $n\bar{a}\acute{s}\hat{i}'$.[162] Israel is reconstituted as a nation of free peasants occupying equal and inalienable portions of land.[163] That naturally suggests the absence of any upper class, and in particular the absence of a class of $\acute{s}\bar{a}r\hat{i}m$,[164] The $\acute{s}\bar{a}r\hat{i}m$ are those with most to lose from the strictures of Ezekiel 46:16-18, which legislates against the $n\bar{a}\acute{s}\hat{i}'$ dispossessing one of the people of their patrimony ($nah^a l\hat{a}$). Provision is made only for the continuance of the lower order of $^{a}b\bar{a}d\hat{i}m$, the personal servants of the $n\bar{a}\acute{s}\hat{i}'$ (Ezek. 46:17).[165] The latter can, however, never climb into a position of power through the acquiring of land since it may only be given to them as a lifetime grant (46:17).

Such a return to a (modified) earlier state of affairs does not automati-

---

no longer $y^e r\hat{u}\check{s}\bar{a}layim$ but now $yhwh$-$\check{s}\bar{a}mm\hat{a}$.

[156] Cf. Ezekiel 5:6; 11:15; 16:2ff.; 22:2ff.; 23:2ff.
[157] Macholz, "Planungen", 344.
[158] L. Allen, *Ezekiel 20-48*, 283.
[159] See the discussion of chapters 11, 22 and 34 above.
[160] Macholz, "Planungen", 326.
[161] Greenberg notes: "The scheme of Ezek. 48 adopts the only way the topography of Palestine allows to parcel the land into roughly similar shares" ("Idealism and Practicality", 65).
[162] See above, chapter 2. This fits very well also with the picture described in Ezekiel 34:17-24. On this, see p.126 above. For a contrasting hope for the future which still retains a place for the $\acute{s}\bar{a}r\hat{i}m$, cf. Isaiah 32:1.
[163] Macholz, "Planungen", 336; Ebach, *Kritik und Utopie*, 192.
[164] The absence of such a bureaucracy is also noted by Levenson (*Theology*, 113), who, however, ascribes it to a change in the theocracy with the introduction of the $n\bar{a}\acute{s}\hat{i}'$. According to Levenson, the latter figure was not an administrator but rather an "apolitical Messiah".
[165] See Rüterswörden, *Beamten*, 19.

cally spell the end for the *zᵉqēnîm* since that institution had deep roots in the history of Israel.[166] Precisely because it had such deep roots, we might have expected to find it playing a prominent part in Ezekiel's new constitution, if that programme had been simply a return to the life of Israel in the period before the monarchy. However, the *zᵉqēnîm* are entirely absent from these chapters and, what is more, one of their chief functions in earlier times, acting as judges,[167] is given now to the priests (Ezek. 44:24). It may be that on the local level Ezekiel would have envisaged the *zᵉqēnîm* continuing to exercise some minor leadership and representative functions, but their position of power and cultic prestige is entirely gone under his new schema.[168] In the new cultic order, only the *nāśî'* acts as representative of the people.

The *'am hā'āreṣ* too are no longer active as a significant independent power. In chapters 40-48 the term seems merely to indicate the cultic community as an actor in the cult; there are no overtones of a smaller group of powerful men with greater prerogatives than the populace at large, such as we saw in Ezekiel 7:27 and 22:29.[169]

D. CONCLUSIONS

We have seen then from our discussion of the position of the laity and their leaders in Ezekiel that, in his mind, it was they who were responsible for the departure of the Glory of Yahweh from his Temple (Ezekiel 10), as a result of the idolatrous practices of the people and their *zᵉqēnîm* which were depicted in visionary form in chapter 8. These events were no temporary aberration but are entirely consonant with the general depiction of the *zᵉqēnîm* wherever they occur in the book of Ezekiel. In consequence of this idolatry — and to prevent it occurring again — the laity are "downgraded" to the most circumscribed position in the new order. As did the Priestly writer, Ezekiel would have categorically opposed the viewpoint of Korah and his followers: "All the congregation is holy, every one of them" (Num. 16:3).

---

[166] See Reviv, *Elders*, 22f.

[167] Deuteronomy 21:18ff.; 22:15ff. Cf. McKenzie, "Elders", 526; Phillips, *Criminal Law*, 18-20.

[168] Contrast e.g. Exodus 12:21; 17:5; Numbers 11:25; 1 Kings 8:1. In McKenzie's summary of the *zᵉqēnîm* in the Old Testament the *first* function ascribed to the elders is to "represent the entire community in political or religious activity" ("Elders", 523).

[169] Würthwein suggested that this broadening of the concept of the *'am hā'āreṣ* was due to the fact that in the new order all would be property holders (*'am hā'āreṣ*, 48f.). However, it may simply be an example of the wider usage discussed by Talmon (see above, p.119). In the absence of any threat to the Davidic monarchy, there would certainly have been no role for the more narrowly defined group.

On the contrary, the holy things belonged in the Inner Court with the priests and were not to be brought out to the people for fear of contamination (Ezek. 42:14; 44:19). The laity were barely even to be allowed to glimpse these things from a distance (cf. Ezek. 46:3). Moreover, the $z^e q\bar{e}n\hat{i}m$, as their former leaders in idolatry,[170] are no longer to serve as their representatives in cultic matters. They stand under the judgement of Yahweh and will suffer excommunication and/or destruction.[171] They therefore have no share in the future. However, the people themselves, once the transgressors have been removed from their midst, *do* have a future in the land — albeit one which keeps them at a distance from the holy things. The purified people will be transformed by the gift of a new heart and a new spirit (Ezek. 11:17ff.; 20:40ff.; 36:24ff.) and thus fitted for their new life of obedience in the promised land.

In addition to his concern to prevent a recurrence of idolatry, Ezekiel was also concerned to prevent the lay leadership oppressing the weak.[172] In his description of the past, this sin is particularly associated with the $\acute{s}\bar{a}r\hat{i}m$ and the '*am hā'āre$\d s$* (in the narrower sense). Both groups are absent from his plan for the future, along with others who might fall under the categories of "fat sheep" and "rams and goats" in chapter 34. They too will face the judgement of Yahweh.[173] The restored community in its make-up and privileges reflects both reward for past faithfulness and punishment for past sin.

---

[170] See chapters 8, 14, 20 and the discussion above.
[171] Cf. Ezekiel 9:6; 14:8; 20:38. On the question of death or excommunication, see above, p.102.
[172] Cf. Ezekiel 11:2ff.; 22:27,29; 34:17ff. and the discussion above.
[173] The depiction of the power held by the $z^e q\bar{e}n\hat{i}m$ and $\acute{s}\bar{a}r\hat{i}m$ in the post-exilic community in Ezra 10:8,14, suggests that these prescriptions, like others proposed by Ezekiel, had no effect on the structure of the community.

CHAPTER SIX

SUMMARY AND CONCLUSIONS

A. Summary

We have sought to show in this study that what the prophet Ezekiel depicted in his plan for the future was not simply a tinkering with the status of one particular individual or group but a total re-ordering of society, with implications for every element of the community. For some members of society, there is the apportionment of positions of greater honour and increased power on the basis of an affirmed past righteousness. For others, their status is largely unchanged but their powers are restricted to prevent the repetition of the abuses of the past. For still others there is a clear downgrading in honour and privileges because of past unfaithfulness. Meanwhile, certain groups who are held peculiarly responsible for the abominations of the past are excluded from the community of the restoration altogether.

For the monarchy, the future will bring the replacement of the former *mᵉlākîm* by a *nāśî'*. The change in terminology does reflect a partial change in the nature of the office.[1] No longer will the *nāśî'* lord it over the people as a superior being with special privileges before Yahweh and the power to oppress the people.[2] There are safeguards built into the system to protect the rights and interests of both Temple and people from the interference which marked the monarchy, especially in its latter days. Yet what results is still an office of great prestige and even great power.[3] The *nāśî'* is no apolitical messiah. Such a figure would be inadequate to protect the people against oppression by other elements of society, especially the lay leadership, as the experience of the latter days of Zedekiah's reign certainly demonstrated. He retains a large measure of power—not absolute power, perhaps, but nonetheless significant power. Hence, he may still be said to be a shepherd or king (*melek*!) over (*'al*) the people, as well as being the *nāśî'* in their midst.[4] In chapters 40-48, he is depicted as a man who has lands and servants, prestige and influence. In the area of the cult, he

---

[1] See above, pp. 32, 55ff. Note, however, that the change in terminology does not *in itself* connote the change in the office, and there remains a degree of flexibility in the usage of the book of Ezekiel.

[2] Cf. Ezekiel 34:23f.; 45:8; 46:10. See above, pp. 49, 53.

[3] See above, pp. 45, 47, 50.

[4] Cf. Ezekiel 34:24; 37:24.

represents the people, presenting offerings on their behalf and approaching the Inner Court of the Temple more closely than any other lay figure.[5] He is, in fact, the most important single figure in the worship of the renewed people of God. Yet here too his power is limited, and safeguards are built into the system. He acts together with the Zadokite priesthood in the offering of sacrifices and neither is independent of the other.[6] He does not exercise control over the administration of the cult, as the former kings once had, and he has no power to appoint or dismiss priestly families.[7] Those who are priests in the new Temple are such by divine decree, not by the word of the king. He may not himself act as a priest, nor may he enter the Inner Court himself to offer sacrifices. Such tasks are protected by a stout wall of separation which keeps apart the offices of king and priest. This separation is further underlined by the physical separation of the Temple from the royal lands, the motivation for which is again presented as avoiding the recurrence of past sins.[8]

Not to be neglected in any discussion of the change of the office of monarch in Ezekiel's plan for the future — of which the terminological shift from *melek* to *nāśî'* is but one element — is the correlative change which is envisioned in the occupant of that office. Unlike the intervening kings, the new occupant of the office will be a return to the standard set by David,[9] the man who "walked before [Yahweh] in faithfulness, in righteousness, and in uprightness of heart".[10] Such a change does not mitigate the need for the modification in the office of monarch outlined above. Both changes operate alongside one another to ensure effectively that the future will indeed be different from the past.[11]

In the course of this study we have attempted to show that all of these changes in the rights and responsibilities of the monarchy reflect Ezekiel's perception of the failings of the past. We noted a consistent pattern of offences by the former monarchs stressed throughout the book of Ezekiel, especially violence, oppression, and injustice.[12] They were judged to have ruled harshly and out of self-interest, at the cost of the people.[13] Zedekiah is also accused of sacrilegious oath-breaking and pride.[14] The result of all

---

[5] Cf. Ezekiel 44:3; 45:17. See above pp. 53ff.

[6] See above, p.83.

[7] See above, p.54.

[8] Cf. Ezekiel 43:7-9; 48:21. See above, p.41, 50.

[9] See above, p.48.

[10] 1 Kings 3:6 (cf. 1 Sam. 13:14; 1 Ki. 9:4; Ezek. 34:24).

[11] Similarly the people will be given a new heart and a new spirit (Ezek. 36:26) but are still warned against future repetition of past transgressions (Ezek. 44:6) and kept at a distance from the Temple in the new division of the land.

[12] See above, p. 43.

[13] See above, pp. 38, 40.

[14] See above, pp. 34, 36.

of these offences has been the overthrow of the kingdom and the downfall
of the monarchy. The exalted have been brought down: things cannot
simply return to their former state.[15] We also noted, however, that the kings
are not generally accused of cultic sin[16] or idolatry. In particular, they are
not mentioned in the chapters where that accusation is centred.[17] The
changes which are made are thus indeed reflective of the areas in which
Ezekiel has apportioned blame upon the past monarchs, with most of the
new restrictions being directed against their ability to oppress the
people – note especially the appointment of the Zadokite priests to act as
judges[18] – and on their control of the cult, but comparatively little on their
actual access to the Temple.

A change in both office and occupants is also envisioned for the priesthood. Those who had been faithful in their exercise of the office in the
past – the Zadokites – are appropriately rewarded with the highest privileges
in the restored Temple and land.[19] They are the only ones who may approach the altar and offer sacrifices (Ezek. 44:15); they are the only ones
permitted access to the Inner Courtyard. They have the responsibility of
both teaching and judging the people (Ezek. 44:23f.). Yet they too do not
escape entirely free from any blame. For them too the future must be
different from the past – and different precisely in those areas in which they
failed in the past.[20] In the absence of conclusive knowledge of the restrictions upon the behaviour of the pre-exilic priesthood, it is not clear to what
extent the regulations of Ezekiel 44:17-31 reflect a tightening of the rules
which governed their lifestyles, but it seems quite possible that this was the
case. Further, even while the Zadokites are people of great privilege in the
restored Temple and land, their power too is not absolute. It would not be
correct to call the government which Ezekiel conceived a hierocracy. The
power of the priests is limited to the service of the Temple and to judging
the people. For the rest, they were dependent upon Yahweh and the good-
will of the people. They were to receive their food from the sacrifices and
offerings of the people.[21] They have neither inheritance (*naḥªlâ*) nor possession (*ªḥuzzâ*) in the promised land, only a strip of land for their houses
and for the new Temple, which is itself part of the sacred portion (*tªrûmâ*),
drawn from the possessions of every tribe.[22] Even with their great power

---

[15] See above, p.43f.
[16] Except in Ezekiel 43:7-9 where they are charged with sharing in the abominations of
the House of Israel. The charge is, however, primarily addressed to the House of Israel, and
only secondarily to the monarchy. See above, p.41.
[17] Cf. especially chapters 8-11, 14, 16, 20, 23.
[18] Ezekiel 44:24. See above, p.53.
[19] See above, p.80.
[20] Compare Ezekiel 44:23f. with Ezekiel 22:26.
[21] Cf. Ezekiel 44:28ff.
[22] Ebach, *Kritik und Utopie*, 245.

and prestige in the Temple, none of their members is permitted to enter the Most Holy Place,[23] which is now considered out of bounds to all because of the presence of the glory within.

If these restrictions fall upon even the most dedicated servants of Yahweh, those whose conduct has been most free of blame in Ezekiel's criticism of the past, then it comes as no surprise to find significant additional restrictions placed upon those who do not escape the taint of past sins. Thus the Levites, who are said to have gone astray with Israel after their idols, and to have served the people before their idols, will have to bear their shame and the abominations which they have committed (Ezek. 44:13).[24] Yet the element of grace which is operative in Ezekiel's plan for the future should not be overlooked. Though the Levites are to bear their iniquity, *in spite of that* they shall still retain an honoured position in the sanctuary as gatekeepers and ministers of the House (Ezek. 44:10f.).[25] Indeed, in one significant respect their responsibilities are extended so that it is now to be the Levites rather than the people who are responsible for slaughtering the burnt offerings and sacrifices of the people. In addition, in the distribution of the land, their portion falls within the sacred reservation (*tᵉrûmâ*), a position of great honour second only to that alotted to the Zadokites.

In contrast, "the prophets of Israel" and their female counterparts[26] have no future in the restored people. In different ways they have failed to live up to the prophet's commission to be a watchman: The "prophets of Israel" were a stumbling block to the reception by the people of Ezekiel's message of national judgement, while the "women who prophesy" undermined his calling to proclaim life to the righteous and to warn the wicked to turn from their ways.[27] The result of their activities has been to bring the judgement of Yahweh crashing down upon his people because they did not warn the people.[28] It is therefore an appropriate fate that they should also be destroyed in the fall to which they contributed, never to rise again. This is depicted in a variety of metaphors and expressions[29] which can either be interpreted as threatening them with excommunication or death or, quite possibly, with both.[30] If the prophet Ezekiel was warned that, in the event of unfaithfulness to his commission as a watchman, the blood of the wicked

---

[23] Unlike the High Priest in the ritual for the Day of Atonement in Leviticus 16.
[24] See above, p.77.
[25] See above, p.83.
[26] The "daughters of your people, who prophesy out of their own hearts" (Ezek. 13:17). See above, p.95.
[27] See above, p.98.
[28] Cf. Ezekiel 13:10,22; 22:30.
[29] Ezekiel 13:9,14,18 (on 13:18 see above, p.101); 14:9.
[30] See above, p.102.

would be required at his hand,[31] how much more so will this be true of
these men and women who through their activities have undermined the
impact of his message? In any event, as far as the restored people living in
the promised land are concerned, the result is the same. They have no part
or share in that people and are excluded from that state of bliss. It is
therefore no surprise to find them entirely absent from the depiction of
Restored Israel in chapters 40-48.[32]

Ezekiel himself, however, has been faithful to his commission as a
watchman and therefore receives the highest possible honour: a key role in
the re-constitution of God's people. This re-constitution takes place in
visionary form through the utterance of the prophetic word,[33] just as once
he had seen judgement take place in visionary form while he spoke.[34] He
is given the astonishing privilege of a guided tour of the new Temple,
which takes him to the very doors of the Most Holy Place (Ezek. 41:1-4).
He does not, however, enter the latter; that privilege is restricted to the
angel who accompanies him. In Ezekiel's plan for the future, there is no
figure of supreme cultic holiness, such as the High Priest of the Priestly
Code, who may enter even this sacred place.[35] In many respects in chapters
40-48, Ezekiel is portrayed as the new Moses, leading the people through
a new exodus and wilderness experience to the brink of the promised land.
Moses is the only other figure in the Old Testament who brings to Israel
new legislation, as Ezekiel does here. Moses too was transported to a very
high mountain from which he surveyed a Promised Land which he would
never enter. Like Moses, Ezekiel hears Yahweh speaking directly to him
from the sacred place. Both men act as "Kultanfänger", consecrating altars
and initiating the cult.[36] In the cosmogonic process of creating a new world
order, the true prophet, Ezekiel, is awarded a key role in recognition of his
past faithfulness.[37]

One area of Ezekiel's criticism of the past which has not previously
received the attention which it deserves is his criticism of the laity, and
their consequent "downgrading" in the depiction of the future state.[38] They
are pushed to the outer parts of the land, with the Temple protected against
any possibility of their defiling it by means of a "buffer zone".[39] In the
worship of the renewed Temple, they have no significant part to play. They

---

[31] Cf. Ezekiel 3:18-20; 33:2-5.
[32] See above, p.103.
[33] Cf. Ezekiel 37, where the events unfolded before Ezekiel "while I was prophesying..."
(k'hinnāb''î; v.7).
[34] Cf. the death of Pelataiah in Ezekiel 11:13. See above, p.104.
[35] See above, p.82.
[36] For all these parallels see above, p.105f.
[37] See above, p.108.
[38] See above, p.127.
[39] See above, p.128f.

may bring sacrifices but the sacrifices must be slaughtered by Levites and the blood offered by the priests. In the festivals, they march through the Temple in a procession with the *nāśî'* in their midst (Ezek. 46:9f.), but would barely get a glimpse of the rituals taking place in the Inner Court.[40] Here too, however, it must be recognized that there is an element of grace at work. Even to be the least in the restored kingdom is no small blessing.[41]

Linked with this downgrading of the laity is an attack on the lay leadership, which is especially focussed on the *z⁽e⁾qēnîm* (elders) and the *śārîm* (officials). We found that the *z⁽e⁾qēnîm* are particularly associated with the sin of idolatry in the book of Ezekiel — not that they were alone in that sin, but on several occasions the book of Ezekiel particularly picks out the *z⁽e⁾qēnîm* with reference to this sin.[42] The *śārîm*, on the other hand, are particularly associated with the sin of oppressing the people.[43] Ezekiel can also address his denunciation of the leading class to other groups, such as the *'am hā'āreṣ*,[44] or in more general terms to the "rams, male goats and fat sheep".[45] These attacks do not always indicate the fate which Ezekiel expected the guilty to suffer; nonetheless, in view of the symbolic death wreaked on the *z⁽e⁾qēnîm* (Ezek. 9:6) and on one of the *śārê hā'ām* (Ezek. 11:13), of the threats of "cutting off" (Ezek. 14:8) and of "purging" from the restored people (Ezek. 20:38), it is notable that there is no evidence of such an overclass in Ezekiel 40-48. Indeed, the land division plan, with its equal inalienable shares for all, would seem to undermine the possibility of such a class.[46] Since the *nāśî'* is to be prevented from making hereditary gifts of land to his followers, there is no possible provision made in the future for rewarding a class of *śārîm*; only the *⁽a⁾bādîm* survive, the personal servants of the monarch, who would presumably be expected to serve for the much more restricted reward of land gifts which may only be held until the year of liberty.[47] Nor is there any sign of the *z⁽e⁾qēnîm* in Ezekiel 40-48. The *nāśî'* acts directly as representative of the people in religious matters, leaving no room for any privilege for the *z⁽e⁾qēnîm* in this area.[48] Like the "prophets of Israel", it appears that the *z⁽e⁾qēnîm* and *śārîm* have been completely excluded from the renewed people in the restored land. This underlines the element of grace involved in the status of the people: even though they may

---

[40] See above, p.127.
[41] See above, p.129.
[42] Cf. Ezekiel 8,14,20. See above, pp.115-118.
[43] Cf. Ezekiel 11; 22:27. See above, pp.115, 118, 123.
[44] Ezekiel 22:29. See above, p.119ff.
[45] See above, p.121.
[46] See above, p.130. This is not, however, an ideological egalitarianism as the large estates alotted to the *nāśî'* attest.
[47] Ezekiel 46:16-18. See above, p.130.
[48] See above, p.131.

be the least in the promised land, at least entry to that promised land has not been barred to them.

B. CONCLUSIONS

1 *Implications for the Nature of Ezekiel 40-48*

Probably the most important result of this study has been to show the interconnected nature of the prophet's plan for the future with his assessment of the past — an interconnectedness that applies to each leadership group studied. Thus, it is inadequate to study simply "Ezekiel's attitude to the monarchy" or "The downgrading of the Levites" in isolation and draw sweeping conclusions from such a study. Ezekiel's vision encompasses the re-ordering of a whole society, not simply a tinkering with one or two elements of it. Setting the re-allocation of roles between the Zadokite priests and the Levites against the broader background of a re-ordering of society as a whole suggests that Ezekiel 44 should no longer be seen as the "Kampfprogramm" of the Zadokites, aimed at putting the Levites in their place. Indeed, as we have shown, the Levites come out of Ezekiel's plan for the future rather well in comparison to some other groups. Similarly the monarchy emerges with both limitations and a position of honour.

Such an antithetical interconnection between past and idealized future in Ezekiel's vision of the future may be properly described as "utopian". While he sketches out in detail certain elements of his plan, thus contrasting his utopian state with the past existence of Judah, he does not attempt to prescribe the means by which such a future is to be attained. As Ebach puts it:

> Es ist ein Merkmal des utopischen Denkens, den bestehenden Zustand so zu kritisieren, daß ihm eine bessere Möglichkeit für die Zukunft unvermittelt gegenübergestellt wird, ohne das strategische Frage, das Problem also der Abschaffung des schlechten Zustandes und der Realisierung des Besseren ausdrücklich thematisiert würde.[49]

This utopian contrasting of past and future, without attention to the means by which the future may be achieved, is also found in the Book of Ezekiel outside chapters 40-48, most notably in chapter 34. There too the depiction of the good shepherd is simply juxtaposed with that of the former bad shepherds. The direct intervention of Yahweh is the only means by which such a radical change may be brought about.[50] Indeed, it seems clear also

---

[49] Ebach, *Kritik und Utopie*, 2. Cf. similarly Lang, *Kein Aufstand*, 186.
[50] According to Lang, a similar dependence upon divine intervention is in evidence also in Ezekiel 17:22ff. (*Kein Aufstand*, 186).

in chapters 40-48 that without the intervention of Yahweh such a future cannot be achieved: even though Israel might through its own efforts construct a Temple which matched the blueprint given by Ezekiel, no man can bring about the return of Yahweh's glory to the Temple (Ezek. 43:1-11), nor will the fructifying river of Ezekiel 47:1-12 be the result of an impressive civil engineering project.[51]

In another sense, however, Ezekiel's plan is not strictly utopian. His promised land is not located "nowhere" or even "somewhere" but in the land of Israel, which Yahweh swore to the patriarchs.[52] The past history of Israel has not been ignored or abolished but rather reformed.[53] It is this history of promise and gracious fulfilment which provides the background for future hope. Indeed, encouraging that future hope seems to me to be one of the central concerns of Ezekiel 40-48. It is not incidental that Ezekiel describes in great detail the restored Temple, the relationships between the different offices and the land distribution. That level of detail serves the very concrete purpose of giving a solidity to the hope which Ezekiel envisaged. In much the same way as Jeremiah's action in buying a field served to underline the fact that there was a future for Judah, and that there would come again a time when houses and land would be bought and sold,[54] so also Ezekiel's action in providing a detailed description of the Restored Land and Temple serves to encourage hope in the reality of these things.

At the same time his description of the changes in the structure of society also serves to encourage hope by answering the potential counsel of despair: "What would it help to be returned to our land? Things would be no different to the way they were before". In response, he affirms that things will indeed be different, because the reformed land will be inhabited by a changed people living in a changed society. Safeguards against the abuses of the past will be introduced. In particular, as this study has sought to show, the entire structure of leadership in Israel will be reformed. No longer will power reside exclusively in the hands of the kings and the lay leadership, those who by their abominations brought about the exile. Instead there will be a sharing of responsibility between the Zadokite priests and the *nāśî'*. Neither will be independent of the other, and together they will make up the leadership of a renewed society.

Assessments of the impact of Ezekiel's vision of the future on the subseq-

---

[51] Zimmerli, "Planungen", 234.
[52] Macholz, "Planungen", 349.
[53] Levenson, *Theology*, 135.
[54] Jeremiah 32:6ff.

uent course of Israel's history vary immensely.[55] However, it appears that his Temple plan had little impact on that built under Zerubbabel.[56] Nor did his envisaged restructuring of society find much favour in the return from the exile. If anything, the power of the lay leadership increased in the returned community: we find the *śārîm* and the *zᵉqēnîm* with power to order property to be forfeited and people to be excommunicated.[57] The sharing of power between the priesthood and the civil authorities is perhaps envisaged by Zechariah 3,4 and 6, but it is power shared by two individuals, a High Priest and a Davidide, rather than a *nāśî'* and a class of priests. Other forces than Ezekiel's vision may equally well have led to this shift in the power balance.[58] The equal division of land among the tribes, and dedicated areas of land around the Temple for the priests, Levites and *nāśî'* which he depicted were never put into practice. In sum, Greenberg has perhaps not too greatly overstated the case when he says:

> Wherever Ezekiel's program can be checked against subsequent events it proves to have had no effect.[59]

Yet if what Ezekiel envisaged was a utopian design, such a lack of practical impact would not necessarily have been regarded as failure. The purpose of the document was rather to encourage repentance, faithfulness and hope among its immediate hearers in exile.[60] It was to encourage repentance by holding up a mirror to the House of Israel so that they might be ashamed of all their iniquities (Ezek. 43:11). It was to encourage faithfulness by depicting the rewards given to the faithful, most notably privileged access to God.[61] It was to encourage hope by depicting—in detail—a restored society living in a renewed land. It is impossible to measure the impact which Ezekiel's vision had on those qualities among the exiles. For a

---

[55] Compare R. Beaudet ("Le Sacerdoce et les Prophètes", *Laval Theologique et Philosophique* 15 (1959) 134), Chary (*Prophètes et Culte*, 46f., 66f.) and P. Herzog (*Die Ethischen Anschauungen des Propheten Ezechiel* [Münster 1923] 144ff.) for a positive assessment of the impact of Ezekiel 40-48 with the largely negative conclusions of Greenberg ("Design", 208), S. Tuell ("The Temple Vision of Ezekiel 40-48: a Program for Restoration?", *Proceedings of the Eastern Great Lakes Biblical Society* 2 [1982] 96) and L. Allen (*Ezekiel 20-48*, 214). Hanson adopts a more guarded variety of the first position in seeing certain streams of subsequent thought as strongly influenced by Ezekiel (*Dawn*, 238ff.).
[56] Fohrer, *Hauptprobleme*, 96; Zimmerli, *Ezechiel*, 1249.
[57] Cf. Ezra 10:8.
[58] See the discussion in C.L. & E.M. Meyers, *Haggai, Zechariah 1-8*, AB (Garden City, NY 1987) 220f.
[59] Greenberg, "Design", 208. Note the comment of L. Allen: "The post-exilic community, even when adoption of their rulings was within its power, found other models for its worship" (*Ezekiel 20-48*, 214).
[60] Compare these with the sociological functions which D.L. Smith ascribes to other exilic writings in his excellent study *Religion of the Landless*.
[61] Compare the similar promise of privileged access to a priest as a reward for faithfulness in Zechariah 3:7. On the syntax of this verse and its connection with Ezekiel 44 see Petersen, *Haggai and Zechariah 1-8*, 204.

people living in exile, cut off from their homeland, tempted to give up hope of any return, tempted to become like the other peoples around them, Ezekiel's vision had a vital message:

- God is just.
- God is gracious.
- God is not absent from us.
- God will return us to our own land.

If these messages were heeded by Ezekiel's hearers then his vision of a future with transformed leadership structures more than served its purpose.

2 Implications for the Unity and Date of the Book of Ezekiel

We noted in the introduction four quadrants of opinion on the unity and date of the book of Ezekiel, with none of these quadrants able to achieve the support of a clear majority in contemporary study of the book of Ezekiel. What implications does our study have for these important questions?

First it must be noted that a study of this kind by its very nature is not likely to impart a *definitive* conclusion on the unity of the whole book of Ezekiel. For one thing, large areas of the book have been entirely outside the purview of this inquiry.[62] A different weight might also be placed upon some of the data we have examined by those beginning from different presuppositions. Nonetheless, it seems to me that the central thrust of this study does provide further support for those quadrants which argue for a greater degree of unity within the present form of the book. The concern evident in several different areas of the book for a reordering of society, on the basis of the assessment of the past faithfulness of the group concerned, suggests a common background for at least these parts of the book. In particular, we have argued that the evidence in favour of a Zadokite stratum and a *nāśî'* stratum does not stand up to close examination. This is especially significant because Ezekiel 44:6ff., the heart of the so-called Zadokite stratum, is often cited as a prime example of a secondary addition to the book of Ezekiel.[63] Therefore, we believe that our study supports the view adopted at the outset, that the book of Ezekiel in its present form is substantially a unity.

With respect to the date of the book, we believe our study also provides supporting evidence for the position adopted at the outset, that the book is substantially a product of the exile. We argued that Ezekiel's *nāśî'* owes

---

[62] E.g. most of chapters 1-6.
[63] For an example see Davis, *Swallowing the Scroll*, 163 n.44.

nothing to a post-exilic figure bearing the same title—if indeed there was such a figure.[64] His utopian restructuring of society, involving a new land division, is more likely to have been produced during a time of exile from the land than after the return.[65] What is more, the concern evident for punishing the sins which brought about the departure of the $k^e b\hat{o}d \ yhwh$, and thus the exile—a concern which includes the personal fate of Jehoiachin and Zedekiah[66]—fits most naturally into this period. The lack of impact of Ezekiel's vision on societal structure in the post-exilic situation is best explained in the same way as the lack of impact of his Temple design on the construction of Zerubbabel's Temple:[67] a combination of recognition of the utopian nature of Ezekiel's plan and the innate conservatism of religious and societal structures.[68] Indeed, it was the fate of many prophets, not simply Ezekiel, to see their words largely ignored.[69] As with the question of authorship, definitive conclusions are outside the scope of this study; however, we may point to this study as supporting evidence in favour of an exilic date for the bulk of the book of Ezekiel.

In the course of this study, we have joined Hananiah ben Hezekiah in burning our share of the midnight oil over the book of Ezekiel. We may not have resolved all the *obscuritatibus involuta* noted by Jerome,[70] yet it is to be hoped that some contribution has been made to the field of study. The vision of the return of the glory of the Lord to dwell among his people for ever, a return which will establish justice for the righteous and judgement for the wicked, is worthy of much study. It is a vision which has encouraged and challenged God's people down through the centuries. At the end of the New Testament, another seer records the words of Jesus in terms which owe not a little to the outlook of the prophet Ezekiel:

> Behold, I am coming soon, bringing my recompense, to repay everyone for what he has done. [13]I am the Alpha and the Omega, the first and the last, the beginning and the end. [14]Blessed are those who wash their robes, that they may have the right to the tree of life and that they may enter the city by the gates. [15]Outside are the dogs and sorcerers and fornicators and murderers and idolators, and everyone who loves and practices falsehood.[71]

---

[64] See above, p.16.
[65] Zimmerli comments "Denn auch die ideale Planung der Landverteilung von 48:1-29 verrät noch nichts von einer Störungderselben durch harte Realitäten, denen man begegnet wäre" (*Ezechiel*, 1248). Cf. Hals, *Ezekiel*, 321.
[66] See above p.43f.
[67] On this see Zimmerli, *Ezechiel*, 1249.
[68] Hals, *Ezekiel*, 320.
[69] Lang, *Kein Aufstand*, 186. Note in this context Ezekiel 33:32.
[70] *Ep. ad Paulinam*, 8.
[71] Revelation 22:12-15.

SELECT BIBLIOGRAPHY

Abba, R., "Priests and Levites in Ezekiel", *VT* 28 (1978) 1-9.

Ackerman, S., "A *Marzēah* in Ezekiel 8:7-13?", *HThR* 82 (1989) 245-65.

Ahlström, G.W., *Royal Administration and National Religion in Ancient Palestine* (Leiden 1982).

Allan, N., "The Identity of the Jerusalem Priesthood During the Exile", *Hey J* 23 (1982) 259-69.

Allen, L.C., *Ezekiel 20-48*, WBC (Waco 1990).

Bailey, J., "Usage of Post Restoration Period Terms Descriptive of Priest and High Priest", *JBL* 70 (1951) 217-25.

Baltzer, D., *Ezechiel und Deuterojesaja*, BZAW 121 (1971).

Bartlett, J.R., "The Use of the Word *rō'š* as a Title in the Old Testament", *VT* 19 (1969) 1-10.

Becker, J., "Erwägungen zur ezechielischen Frage", *Künder des Wortes*, L. Ruppert, P. Weimar and E. Zenger, eds. (Würzburg 1982) 137-49.

——, "Ez 8-11 als einheitliche Komposition in einem pseudepigraphischen Ezechielbuch", *Ezekiel and His Book*, J. Lust, ed. (Leuven 1986) 136-50.

Beentjes, P.C., "Inverted Quotations in the Bible: a Neglected Stylistic Pattern", *Biblica* 63 (1982) 506-23.

Begg, C.T., "*bᵉrît* in Ezekiel", *Proceedings of the Ninth World Congress of Jewish Studies* (Jerusalem 1986) 77-84.

——, "The Identity of the Princes in Ezekiel 19; Some Reflections", *EThL* 65 (1989) 358-69.

Begrich, K., "Das Messiasbild des Ezechiel", *ZWTh* 47 (1904) 433-61.

Bernhardt, K.H., *Das Problem der altorientalischen Königsideologie im Alten Testament*, SVT 8 (Leiden 1961).

Berry, G.R., "The Authorship of Ezekiel 40-48", *JBL* 34 (1915) 17-40.

——, "Priests and Levites", *JBL* 42 (1923) 227-38.

Bertholet, A., *Der Verfassungsentwurf des Hesekiel in seiner religionsgeschichtliche Bedeutung* (Freiburg and Leipzig 1896).

——, and Galling, K., *Hesekiel*, HAT (Tübingen 1936).

Bettenzoli, G., *Geist der Heiligkeit. Traditionsgeschichtliche Untersuchung des QDŠ-Begriffes im Buch Ezechiel*, Quaderni di Semitistica 8 (Florence 1979).

——, "Gli 'Anziani' in Giuda", *Biblica* 64 (1983) 211-24.

Biggs, C., "The Role of *nāśî'* in the Programme for Restoration in Ez 40-48", *Colloquium* 16,1 (1983) 46-57.

Blenkinsopp, J., *Ezekiel*, Interpretation (Louisville 1990).

Boadt, L., *Ezekiel's Oracles against Egypt. A Literary and Philological Study of Ezekiel 29-32*, Biblica et Orientalia 37 (Rome 1980).

——, "Rhetorical Strategies in Ezekiel's Oracles of Judgement", *Ezekiel and His Book*, J. Lust, ed. (Leuven 1986) 182-200.

——, "Textual Problems in Ezekiel and Poetic Analysis of Paired Words", *JBL* 97 (1978) 489-99.

Boehmer, J., "*MLK* und *NŚY* bei Ezechiel", *Theologische Studien und Kritiken* 73 (1900) 112-7.

Born, A. van den, *Ezechiël* (Roermond 1954).

——, *Ezechiël - Pseudo-epigraaf?*, Studia Catholica 28 (1953).

Bowman, J., "Ezekiel and the Zadokite Priesthood", *TGUOS* 16 (1955-6) 1-14.

Braun, R.L., *1 Chronicles*, WBC (Waco 1986).

Brettler, M.Z., *God is King: Understanding an Israelite Metaphor*, JSOTS 76 (Sheffield

1989).

Brownlee, W.H., *Ezekiel 1-19*, WBC (Waco 1986).

Brunner, R., *Das Buch Ezechiel*, Zürcher Bibelkommentare (Zürich ²1969).

Burrows, M., *The Literary Relations of Ezekiel* (Philadelphia 1925).

Caquot, A., "Le Messianisme d'Ezechiel", *Semitica* 14 (1964) 5-23.

Carley, K.W., *The Book of the Prophet Ezekiel*, CBC (Cambridge 1974).

——, *Ezekiel among the Prophets*, SBT 31 (London 1975).

Chary, T., *Les Prophètes et le Culte à Partir de l'Exil* (Tournai 1955).

Cody, A., *A History of Old Testament Priesthood*, Analecta Biblica 34 (Rome 1969).

——, *Ezekiel*, Old Testament Message (Wilmington 1984).

Conrad, J., *"zāqēn"*, *Theologische Wörterbuch des Alten Testament*, G. Botterweck, H. Ringgren and H.-J. Fabry, eds (Stuttgart 1977) II, 639-50.

Cooke, G.A., *Ezekiel*, ICC (Edinburgh 1936).

——, "Some Considerations on the Text and Teaching of Ezekiel 40-48", *ZAW* 42 (1924) 108-12.

Coppens, J., "L'esperance Messianique royale a la vielle et au lendemain de l'exil", *Studia Biblica et Semitica T.C. Vriezen dedicata* (Wageningen 1966) 46-61.

Darr, K.P., "Write or True? A Response to Ellen Frances Davis", *Signs and Wonders. Biblical Texts in Literary Focus*, J.C. Exum, ed. (Atlanta 1989).

Davidson, A.B., *The Book of the Prophet Ezekiel*, CBSC (Cambridge 1892).

Davis, E.F., *Swallowing the Scroll. Textuality and the Dynamics of Discourse in Ezekiel's Prophecy*, JSOTS 78 (Sheffield 1989).

De Vries, S., *1 and 2 Chronicles*, FOTL 11 (Grand Rapids 1989).

Douglas, G.C.M., "Ezekiel's Temple", *ET* 9 (1898) 365-7, 420-2, 468-70, 515-8; 14 (1903) 365-8, 424-7.

Driver, G.R., "Abbreviations in the Massoretic Text", *Textus* 1 (1961) 112-31.

——, "Linguistic and Textual Problems: Ezekiel", *Biblica* 19 (1938) 60-9, 175-87.

——, "Ezekiel: Linguistic and Textual Problems", *Biblica* 35 (1954) 145-59, 299-312.

Driver, S.R., *An Introduction to the Literature of the Old Testament* (Edinburgh and New York ⁹1913).

Duke, R.K., "Punishment or Restoration: Another Look at the Levites of Ezekiel 44:6-16", *JSOT* 40 (1988) 61-81.

Dumermuth, F.R., "Zu Ez xiii:18-21", *VT* 13 (1963) 228-9.

Dutcher-Walls, P. "The Social Location of the Deuteronomists: A Sociological Study of Factional Politics in Late Pre-Exilic Judah", *JSOT* 52 (1991) 77-94.

Ebach, J.H., *Kritik und Utopie. Untersuchungen zum Verhaltnis vom Volk und Herrscher im Verfassungsentwurf des Ezechiel (Kap. 40-48)*; Ph.D. diss., University of Hamburg 1972.

——, *"PGR =* (Toten-)Opfer", *UF* 3 (1971) 365-8.

Eichrodt, W., *Der Prophet Hesekiel*, ATD (Göttingen 1970).

Ellison, H.L., *Ezekiel: The Man and His Message* (London 1956).

Fisch, S., *Ezekiel*, Soncino Books of the Bible (London 1950).

Fishbane, M., *Biblical Interpretation in Ancient Israel* (Oxford 1985).

——, "Sin and Judgement in the Prophecies of Ezekiel", *Interp.* 38 (1984) 131-50.

Fohrer, G., *Die Hauptprobleme des Buches Ezechiel* (Berlin 1952).

——, and Galling, K., *Ezechiel*, HAT (Tübingen ²1955).

Foster, R.S., "A Note on Ezekiel xvii:1-10 and 22-24", *VT* 8 (1958) 374-9.

——, *The Restoration of Israel. A Study in Exile and Return* (London 1970).

Fox, M.V., "The Rhetoric of Ezekiel's Vision of the Valley of the Bones", *HUCA* 51 (1980) 1-15.

Freedy, F.S., "The Glosses in Ezekiel i-xxiv", *VT* 20 (1970) 129-52.

Fuhs, H.F., *Ezechiel*, Die Neue Echter Bibel (Würzburg 1984).

Galling, K., "Erwägungen zum Stelenheiligtum von Hazor", *ZDPV* 75 (1959) 1-13.

——, *Die israelitische Staatsverfassung in ihrer vordeorientalische Umwelt*, Der Alte Orient 28 (Leipzig 1929).

——, "Königliche und nichtköniglicher Stifter beim Tempel von Jerusalem", *ZDPV* 68 (1951)

134-42.

Garscha, J., *Studien zum Ezechielbuch* (Berne and Frankfurt 1974).

Gese, H., *Der Verfassungsentwurf des Ezechiel (Kap. 40-48) traditionsgeschichtlich untersucht*, BHTh 25 (Tübingen 1957).

Gottstein, M.H., "*n*^e*śî' "lōhîm*", *VT* 3 (1953) 298-9.

Gosse, B., "La Nouvelle Alliance et les Promesses d'Avenir se Référant à David dans les Livres de Jérémie, Ezéchiel et Isaie", *VT* 41 (1991) 419-28.

Gottlieb, H., "Die Tradition von David als Hirten", *VT* 17 (1967) 190-200.

Graffy, A., *A Prophet Confronts His People: The Disputation Speech in the Prophets*, Analecta Biblica 104 (Rome 1984).

Gray, J., *I and II Kings*, Old Testament Library (London ²1970).

Greenberg, M., "The Citations in the Book of Ezekiel as a Background for the Prophecies", *Beth Mikra* 50 (1973) 273-8. [Hebrew]

——, "The Design and Themes of Ezekiel's Program of Restoration", *Interp.* 38 (1984) 181-208.

——, *Ezekiel 1-20*, AB (Garden City, NY 1983).

——, "Idealism and Practicality in Numbers 33:4-5 and Ezekiel 48", *JAOS* 88 (1968) 59-63.

——, "A New Approach to the History of the Israelite Priesthood", *JAOS* 70 (1950) 41-7.

——, "Prolegomenon", *Pseudo-Ezekiel and the Original Prophecy by C.C. Torrey and Critical Articles*, ——, ed. (New York 1970).

——, "The Use of Ancient Versions for Interpreting the Hebrew Text: a sampling from Ezekiel ii 1-iii 11", *SVT* 29 (Leiden 1978) 131-48.

——, "The Vision of Jerusalem in Ezekiel 8-11: a Holistic Interpretation", *The Divine Helmsman: Studies on God's Control of Human Events, presented to L.H. Silberman*, J.L. Crenshaw and S. Sandmel, eds. (New York 1980) 143-64.

——, "What are Valid Criteria for Determining Inauthentic Matter in Ezekiel?", *Ezekiel and His Book*, J. Lust, ed. (Leuven 1986) 123-35.

Gronkowski, W., *Le Messianisme d'Ezechiel* (Paris 1930).

Gross, W., "Israel's Hope for the Renewal of the State", *JNSL* 14 (1988) 101-33.

Gunneweg, A.H.J., *Leviten und Priester*, FRLANT 89 (Göttingen 1965).

Halpern, B., *The Constitution of the Monarchy in Israel*, HSM 25 (Chico 1981).

Hals, R., *Ezekiel*, FOTL 19 (Grand Rapids 1989).

Hammershaimb, E., "Ezekiel's View of the Monarchy", *Studia Orientalia, Ioanni Pedersen Septuagenario* (Copenhagen 1953) 130-40 = *Some Aspects of Old Testament Prophecy* (Copenhagen 1966) 51-62.

Hanson, P.D., *The Dawn of Apocalyptic* (Philadelphia 1975).

——, "Israelite Religion in the Early Postexilic Period", *Ancient Israelite Religion. Essays in Honor of F.M. Cross*, P.D. Miller, Jr., —— and S.D. McBride, eds. (Philadelphia 1987) 485-508.

Haran, M., "The Law Code of Ezekiel 40-48 and its Relation to the Priestly School", *HUCA* 50 (1979) 45-71.

——, *Temples and Temple Service in Ancient Israel* (Oxford 1978).

Held, M., "The Root *ZBL/SBL* in Akkadian, Ugaritic and Biblical Hebrew", *JAOS* 88 (1968) 90-6.

Hengstenberg, E.W., *Die Weissagung des Propheten Ezechiel, für solche die in der Schrift forschen erläutert* (Berlin 1867/8) = *The Prophecies of the Prophet Ezekiel Elucidated*, tr. A.C. and J.G. Murphy, (Edinburgh 1869).

Herntrich, V., *Ezechielprobleme*, BZAW 61 (Giessen 1933).

Herrmann, J., *Ezechiel, übersetzt und erklärt*, KAT (Leipzig 1924).

——, *Ezechielstudien*, BWAT 2 (Leipzig 1908).

Herrmann, S., *Die Prophetischen Heilserwartungen im Alten Testament*, BWANT 5 (Stuttgart 1965).

Herzog, P., *Die Ethischen Anschauungen des Propheten Ezechiel* (Münster 1923).

Hitzig, F., *Der Prophet Ezechiel*, KeH (Leipzig 1847).

Hölscher, G., *Hesekiel; der Dichter und das Buch*, BZAW 39 (Giessen 1924).

Hoonacker, A. van, "Les Prêtres et Les Lévites dans le livre d'Ezechiel", *RB* 8 (1899) 175-205.

Horbury, W., "Extirpation and Excommunication", *VT* 35 (1985) 13-38.

Horst, F., "Exilsgemeinde und Jerusalem in Ez viii-xi: Eine literarische Untersuchung", *VT* 3 (1953) 337-60.

Hossfeld, F.L., "Die Tempelvision Ez 8-11 im Licht unterschiedlicher methodischer Zugänge" *Ezekiel and His Book*, J. Lust, ed. (Leuven 1986) 151-65.

——, *Untersuchungen zu Komposition und Theologie des Ezechielbuches*, FzB 20 (Würzburg 1977).

——, and Meyer, I., *Prophet gegen Prophet* (Fribourg 1973).

Hurvitz, A., *A Linguistic Study of the Relationship between the Priestly Source and the Book of Ezekiel*, Cahiers de le Revue Biblique 20 (Paris 1982).

Japhet, S., "Sheshbazzar and Zerubabbel against the Background of the Historical and Religious Tendencies of Ezra Nehemiah", *ZAW* 94 (1982) 66-98 and 95 (1983) 218-29.

Jenson, P.P., *Graded Holiness. A Key to the Priestly Conception of the World*, JSOTS 106 (Sheffield 1992).

Jeremias, J., *"nābî'"*, *Theologisches Handwörterbuch zum Alten Testament*, E. Jenni, C. Westermann, eds. (Zürich 1976) II, 7-26.

Johnson, A.R., *The Cultic Prophet in Ancient Israel* (Cardiff ²1962).

Jones, D.R., "The Cessation of Sacrifice after the Destruction of the Temple in 586 B.C.", *JTS* n.s. 14 (1963) 12-31.

Joyce, P., *Divine Initiative and Human Response in Ezekiel*, JSOTS 51 (Sheffield 1989).

Kapelrud, A., "Temple building: a Task for Gods and Kings", *Or* 32 (1963) 56-62.

Kaufmann, Y., *History of the Religion of Israel*, vol. 7 [Hebrew] (Jerusalem 1955).

Keil, C.F., *Biblischer Commentar über den Propheten Ezekiel* (Leipzig ²1882).

Kessler, W., *Die innere Einheitlichkeit des Buches Ezekiel*, Berichte des theologischen Seminars der Brüdergemeine 11 (Herrnhut 1926).

King, E.G., "The Prince in Ezekiel", *Old Testament Student* 5 (1885) 111-6.

Klein, R.W., *Ezekiel: the Prophet and his Message* (Columbia 1988).

König, E., "The Priests and Levites in Ez 44:7-15", *ET* 12 (1901) 300-3.

Kottsieper, I., "'Was ist deine Mutter?' Eine Studie zu Ez 19:2-9", *ZAW* 105 (1993) 456.

Kraetzschmar, R., *Das Buch Ezekiel*, HK (Göttingen 1900).

Krüger, T., *Geschichtskonzepte im Ezechielbuch*, BZAW 180 (Berlin 1989).

Lamparter, H., *Zum Wächter Bestellt: Der Prophet Hesekiel* (Stuttgart 1968).

Lang, B., *Ezechiel. Der Prophet und das Buch* (Darmstadt 1981).

——, *Kein Aufstand in Jerusalem: die Politik des Propheten Ezechiel* (Stuttgart 1978).

Lemke, W.E., "Life in the Present and Hope in the Future", *Interp.* 38 (1984) 165-80.

Levenson, J.D., *Theology of the Program of Restoration of Ezekiel 40-48*, HSM 10 (Missoula 1976).

Lewis, T.J., *Cults of the Dead in Ancient Israel and Ugarit*, HSM 39 (Atlanta 1989).

Lindblom, J., "What is a Temple? A Preliminary Typology", *The Quest for the Kingdom of God. Essays in Honor of George E. Mendenhall*, H.B. Huffmon, F.A. Spina, A.R.W. Green, eds. (Winona Lake 1983).

Long, B.O., "Social Dimensions of Prophetic Conflict", *Semeia* 21 (1982) 31-53.

Lowery, R.H., *The Reforming Kings. Cult and Society in First Temple Judah*, JSOTS 120 (Sheffield 1991).

Lust, J., "Exegesis and Theology in the Septuagint of Ezekiel: The Longer 'pluses' and Ezekiel 43:1-9", *VIth Congress of the International Organization for Septuagint and Cognate Studies*, SCS 23 (Atlanta 1987) 201-32.

——, "Gathering and Return in Jeremiah and Ezekiel", *Le livre de Jérémie. Le prophète et son milieu; les oracles et leur transmission*, P.M. Bogaert, ed. (Leuven 1981) 119-42.

——, "Introduction. Ezekiel and His Book" *Ezekiel and His Book*, ——, ed. (Leuven 1986).

Macholz, G.Ch., "Noch Einmal: Planungen für den Wiederaufbau nach der Katastrophe von 587", *VT* 19 (1969) 322-52.

McConville, J.G., "Priests and Levites in Ezekiel: a Crux in the Interpretation of Israel's History", *TynB* 34 (1983) 3-32.

McGregor, L.J., *The Greek Text of Ezekiel: an Examination of its Homogeneity*, SCS 18 (Atlanta 1985).

McKay, J., *Religion in Judah under the Assyrians*, SBT 26 (London 1973).

McKeating, H, *Ezekiel*, Old Testament Guides (Sheffield 1993).

McKenzie, J.L., "The Elders in the Old Testament", *Biblica* 40 (1959) 522-40.

Matties, G.H., *Ezekiel 18 and the Rhetoric of Moral Discourse*, SBLDS 126 (Atlanta 1990).

Messel, N., *Ezéchielfragen* (Oslo 1945).

Mettinger, T.N.D., *Solomonic State Officials. A Study of the Civil Government Officials of the Israelite Monarchy* (Lund 1971).

Milgrom, J., *Studies in Levitical Terminology, I: The Encroacher and the Levite; The Term 'Aboda* (Berkeley 1970).

——, "Studies in the Temple Scroll", *JBL* 97 (1978) 501-23.

Miller, J.W. *Das Verhältnis Jeremias und Hesekiels sprachlich und theologisch untersucht* (Assen 1955).

Moran, W.L., "Gen 49:10 and its Use in Ez 21:32", *Biblica* 39 (1958) 405-25.

Morgenstern, J., "A Chapter in the History of the High Priesthood", *AJSL* 55 (1938) 1-24, 183-7, 310-31.

Mosis, R., *Das Buch Ezechiel*, Geistliche Schriftlesung 8/1 (Düsseldorf 1978).

——, "Ezechiel 14:1-11 - Ein Ruf für Umkehr", *Biblische Zeitschrift* NForsch 19 (1975) 161-94.

Müller, D.H., "Der Prophet Ezechiel entlehnt eine Stelle des Propheten Zephanja und glossiert sie", *WZKM* 19 (1905) 263-70.

Neiman, D., "*PGR*: A Canaanite Cult Object in the Old Testament", *JBL* 67 (1948) 55-60.

Nicholson, E.W., "The Meaning of the Expression *'am hā'āreṣ* in the Old Testament", *JSS* 10 (1965) 59-66.

——, "The Origin of the Tradition in Exodus xxiv 9-11", *VT* 26 (1976) 148-60.

Niditch, S., "Ezekiel 40-48 in a Visionary Context", *CBQ* 48 (1986) 208-24.

Niehr, H., "*nāśî'*", *Theologische Wörterbuch des Alten Testament*, G.J. Botterweck, H. Ringgren and H.-J. Fabry, eds. (Stuttgart 1986) V, 647-57.

Noth, M., *Das System der Zwölf Stämme Israels*, BWANT 4,1 (Stuttgart 1930).

Orelli, C. von, *Das Buch Ezechiel und die zwölf kleinen Propheten* (Nördlingen 1888).

Overholt, T., *The Threat of Falsehood. A Study in the Theology of the Book of Jeremiah*, SBT 16 (London 1970).

Petersen, D.L., *Haggai and Zechariah 1-8*, Old Testament Library (Philadelphia and London 1984).

——, *Late Israelite Prophecy: Studies in Deutero-Prophetic Literature and in Chronicles*, SBLMS 23 (Missoula 1977).

Phillips, A., *Ancient Israel's Criminal Law* (Oxford 1970).

Pleins, J.D., "From the Stump of Jesse: the Image of King David as a Social Force in the Writings of the Hebrew Prophets", *Proceedings of the Eastern Great Lakes and Midwest Bible Society* 6 (1986) 161-9.

Ploeg, J. van der, "Chefs du Peuple d'Israel et Leurs Titres", *RB* 57 (1950) 40-61.

——, "Les Anciens dans l'A.T.", *Lex Tua Veritas. Festschrift für H. Junker*, H. Gross, ed. (Trier 1961) 175-91.

Pohlmann, K.F., *Ezechielstudien*, BZAW 202 (Berlin 1992).

Price, J.D., "Rosh: An Ancient Land Known to Ezekiel", *Grace Theological Journal* 6 (1985) 67-89.

Procksch, O., "Fürst und Priester bei Hesekiel", *ZAW* (o.s.) 58 (1940/1) 99-133.

Raurell, F., "The Polemical Role of the *ΑΡΧΟΝΤΕΣ* and *ΑΦΗΓΟΥΜΕΝΟΙ* in Ez LXX", *Ezekiel and His Book*, J. Lust, ed. (Leuven 1986) 85-9.

Reventlow, H. G., *Wächter über Israel - Ezechiel und seine Tradition*, BZAW 82 (Berlin 1962).

Reviv, H. *The Elders in Ancient Israel* (Jerusalem 1989).

Rooker, M., *Biblical Hebrew in Transition. The Language of the Book of Ezekiel*, JSOTS 90 (Sheffield 1990).

Rowley, H.H., "The Book of Ezekiel in Modern Study", *BJRL* 36 (1953-54) 146-90 = *Men of God* (London 1963) 169-210.

——, "H. Gese, 'Der Verfassungsentwurf des Ezechiel'" [Review], *JTS* n.s. 9 (1958) 340-2.

Ruppert, L., *"qesem"*, *Theologische Wörterbuch des Alten Testament*, in G.J. Botterweck, H. Ringgren and H.-J. Fabry, eds. (Stuttgart 1990) VII, 78-84.

Rüterswörden, U., *Die Beamten der israelitischen Königszeit. Eine Studie zu śr und vergleichbaren Begriffen*, BWANT 117 (Stuttgart 1985).

Saggs, H.W., "'External Souls' in the Old Testament", *JSS* 19 (1974) 1-12.

Schmidt, M., *Prophet und Tempel* (Zurich 1948).

Schoneveld, J., "Ez 14:1-8", *OTS* 15 (1969) 193-204.

Schulz, H., *Das Todesrecht im Alten Testament*, BZAW 114 (Berlin 1969).

Sedlmeier, F., *Studien zu Komposition und Theologie von Ezechiel 20*, Stuttgarter Biblische Beiträge 21 (Stuttgart 1990).

Seybold, K., *Das davidische Königtum im Zeugnis der Propheten*, FRLANT 107 (Göttingen 1972).

Simian, H., *Die theologische Nachgeschichte der Prophetie Ezechiels. Form und traditions-kritische Untersuchung zu Ez 6; 35; 36*, FzB 14 (Würzburg 1974).

Ska, J-L., "La Sortie d'Egypte (Ex 7-14) dans le Recit Sacerdotal (Pg) et la Tradition Prophetique", *Biblica* 60 (1979) 191-215.

Skinner, J., *The Book of Ezekiel*, Expositor's Bible (New York 1901).

Slotki, I.W., *Chronicles*, Soncino Books of the Bible (London 1952).

Smend, R., *Der Prophet Ezechiel*, KeH (Leipzig ²1880).

Smith, D.L., *Religion of the Landless* (Bloomington 1989).

Smith, J.S., *The Book of the Prophet Ezekiel: a New Interpretation* (London 1931).

Smith, Morton, "The Veracity of Ezekiel, the Sins of Manasseh and Jer. 44:18", *ZAW* 87 (1975) 11-16.

Speiser, E.A., "Background and Function of the Biblical *nāśî'*", *CBQ* 25 (1963) 111-7.

Spiegel, S., "Ezekiel or Pseudo-Ezekiel", *HThR* 24 (1931) 245-321 = *Pseudo-Ezekiel and the Original Prophecy by C.C. Torrey and Critical Articles*, M. Greenberg, ed. (New York 1970) 123-99.

Steinmann, J., *Le prophète Ézéchiel*, Lectio Divina 13 (Paris 1953).

Talmon, S., "The Judean *'am hā'āres* in Historical Perspective" in *Papers of the Fourth World Congress of Jewish Studies* (Jerusalem 1967) 71-6 = *King, Cult and Calendar* (Jerusalem 1986) 68-78.

——, and Fishbane, M., "The Structuring of Biblical Books: Studies in the Book of Ezekiel", *ASTI* 10 (1976) 129-53.

Taylor, J.B., *Ezekiel. An Introduction and Commentary*, TOTC (Leicester 1969).

Torrey, C.C., *Pseudo-Ezekiel and the Original Prophecy* (New Haven 1930 = New York 1970).

Tov, E., "Recensional Differences between the MT and the LXX of Ezekiel", *EThL* 62 (1986) 89-101.

Tsevat, M., "The Neo Assyrian and Neo Babylonian Vassal Oaths and the Prophet Ezekiel", *JBL* 78 (1959) 199-204.

Tuell, S., "The Temple Vision of Ezekiel 40-48: a Program for Restoration?", *Proceedings of the Eastern Great Lakes Biblical Society* 2 (1982) 96-103.

Vaux, R. de, "La thèse de l'amphictyonie israelite", *HThR* 64 (1971) 415-36.

Vawter, B. and Hoppe, L.J., *A New Heart. A Commentary on the Book of Ezekiel*, International Theological Commentary (Grand Rapids 1991).

Vogt, E., *Untersuchungen zur Buch Ezechiel* (Rome 1981).

Warleigh, H.S., *Ezekiel's Temple: its Design Unfolded, its Architecture Displayed, and the Subjects Connected with it Discussed* (London 1856).

Weber, M., *Das Antike Judentum* (Tübingen 1921).

Weinfeld, M., "The Covenant of Grant in the Old Testament and in the Ancient Near East", *JAOS* 90 (1970) 184-205.

Wevers, J.W., *Ezekiel*, NCeB (London 1969).

Williamson, H.G.M., *1 and 2 Chronicles*, NCeB (London 1982).

——, *Ezra-Nehemiah*, WBC (Waco 1985).

Willmes, B., *Die sogenannte Hirtenallegorie Ez 34: studien zum Bild des Hirten im AT*, Beiträge zur biblischen Exegese und Theologie 19 (Frankfurt 1984).

Würthwein, E., *Der 'am ha'arez im Alten Testament* (Stuttgart 1936).

Yates, D.R., *The Eschatological Message Concerning Man in the Book of Ezekiel*; Ph.D. diss., Boston University 1972.

Zeitlin, S., "The Titles High Priest and the *nāśî'* of the Sanhedrin", *JQR* n.s. 48 (1957-8) 1-5.

Zimmerli, W., "Deutero Ezechiel?", *ZAW* 84 (1972) 501-16.

——, "Die Eigenart der prophetischen Rede des Ezechiel", *ZAW* 67 (1955) 1-26 = *Gottes Offenbarung* (Munich 1963) 148-77.

——, *Ezechiel*, BKAT (Neukirchen-Vluyn 1969).

——, "Das Gotteswort des Ezechiel", *ZThK* 48 (1951) 249-62 = *Gottes Offenbarung* (Munich 1963) 133-47 = [ET] *Journal for Theology and Church* 4 (1967) 1-13.

——, "Israel im Buche Ezechiel", *VT* 8 (1958) 74-90.

——, "Le nouvel 'exode' dans le message de des deux grands prophets de l'exil" in *Hommage à Wilhelm Vischer* (Montpellier 1960) 216-27 = "Der 'neue Exodus' in der Verkündigung der beiden grossen Exilspropheten" in *Gottes Offenbarung* (Munich 1963) 192-204.

——, "Das Phänomenon der 'Fortschreibung' im Buche Ezechiel", *Prophecy. Essays Presented to G. Fohrer*, J.A. Emerton, ed. BZAW 150 (Berlin 1980) 174-91.

——, "Planungen für den Wiederaufbau nach der Katastrophe von 587", *VT* 18 (1968) 229-55; = [ET] "Plans for Rebuilding after the Catastrophe of 587" *I am Yahweh*, W. Brueggemann, tr. D.W. Stott, (Atlanta 1982) 111-33.

——, "The Special Form and Traditio-Historical Character of Ezekiel's Prophecy", *VT* 15 (1965) 515-27.

INDEX OF GREEK, HEBREW AND OTHER SEMITIC WORDS

INDEX OF AUTHORS CITED

INDEX OF BIBLICAL TEXTS